The Chase Across the Globe

The Chase Across the Globe

International Accumulation and the Contradictions for Nation States

Dick Bryan

Westview Press

BOULDER • SAN FRANCISCO • OXFORD

Copyright © 1995 by Westview Press, Inc.

Published in 1995 in the United States of America by Westview Press, Inc., 5500 Central Avenue, Boulder, Colorado 80301-2877, and in the United Kingdom by Westview Press, 12 Hid's Copse Road, Cumnor Hill, Oxford OX2 9JJ

Library of Congress Cataloging-in-Publication Data
Bryan, Dick.
    The chase across the Globe : international accumulation and the contradictions for nation states / Dick Bryan.
        p.   cm.
    Includes bibliographical references and index.
    ISBN 0-8133-2356-8 (acid-free paper)
    1. Saving and investment.   2. National state.   3. International economic relations.   I. Title.
HC79.S3B79   1995
337—dc20   95-8137
                                                                                                          CIP

Printed and bound in the United States of America

The paper used in this publication meets the requirements of the American National Standard for Permanence of Paper for Printed Library Materials Z39.48-1984.

10   9   8   7   6   5   4   3   2   1

The need for a constantly expanding market
chases the bourgeoisie over
the whole face of the globe.
—Karl Marx and Friedrich Engels
The Communist Manifesto

Contents

Tables and Figures

Tables

Figures

Acknowledgments

In developing the analysis of this book I am indebted to a number of people with whom I have debated over quite a few years. Scott MacWilliam and Mike Cowan have long had an impact on my ideas, but so also have Neil Ackland (who also gave great assistance in the construction of figures), Geoff Dow, Bob Fagan, Kathie Gibson, Richie Howitt, Geoff Kay, Alfred Oehlers, Michael Rafferty, Stuart Rosewarne, and David Tait. I am deeply appreciative to each of them, even though many of them will disagree with what they find here. Thanks also to Val Jones and Chris Rauchle for assistance with layout. It almost goes without saying that writing a book intrudes on family life. It requires saying that I apologise for the intrusion and greatly appreciate the support provided by Christine in particular, but also Betty and Robbie.

Two chapters which appear here have been published elsewhere, although they have both been significantly rewritten. Chapter 5 has previously appeared in *The Journal of Contemporary Asia* Volume 17, Number 3, 1987; and Chapter 6 is adapted from *Science and Society* Volume 56, Number 3, 1992. The permission granted by the publishers of those journals is appreciated.

Dick Bryan

Introduction

In the *Communist Manifesto*, Marx and Engels wrote, somewhat extravagantly, that precapitalist societies would be forced to adopt the capitalist mode of production 'on pain of extinction'. In the mid-nineteenth century, the style of colonial oppression made the connotations of brutality and militarism quite appropriate. Some will contend that the image of the brutality of conquest continues to depict the extension of capitalist class relations in the post-war, (generally) post-colonial era. And there is no argument that the list of cases of imperialist aggression to support or assert the rule of capital is long, and continues to grow.

But such aggression is not the only means by which the rule of capital is asserted and extended, and reliance on such cases to establish the expansionist nature of capitalism misses the most pervasive and adaptive elements of the process. After all, Marx showed that the exploitation of labor by capital in capitalism is associated with 'free' wage labor — workers are free to sell their labor power where they choose; and they are free to not sell their labor power … but starve. The global expansion of capital and capitalism is similarly conceived in a dual freedom: the freedom of individual capitals to participate in a global market … or liquidate. Competition on a global scale invites capitalists everywhere to shape up to international standards on price and quality, or go out of business. This is what makes international expansion a chase over the whole face of the globe: it is about individual capitalists throughout the world facing the direct discipline of a globally-integrated market.

But it is not simply a chase of individual capitalists or transnational corporations (TNCs) to implant their logos further and further afield. The development of TNCs, significant as this has been in the past quarter of a century, is just one form of the chase. More generally, the chase is about the international movement of commodities and the global integration of capital markets. The underlying nature of the chase is not for individual capitalists to each spread across the globe, but to compete in open battle for a share of profits; for it is a chase in which there is increasingly nowhere to hide. Nation state policies no longer provide sanctuary from the chase.

By the end of the twentieth century, it surely feels that the chase is all but complete. Capitalism may not, as the *Manifesto* rhetorically claims, have knocked down the Great Wall of China, but it has knocked down the Berlin Wall, and it has seen Chinese socialism embracing capitalist calculation as its primary mode of economic allocation. In this process, the last quarter of a century, and particularly the period since the 1980s has been critical.

Capitalism has always been international, but the recent development of a comprehensive integration of capital markets establishes the qualitative difference of the recent period. It means not just that capital has spread across the whole face of the globe, but that our whole notion of space is being challenged. At one level the mobility of capital has made space uniform; yet differentiated space, particularly its national dimension, remains critical to an understanding of the patterns and determinants of mobility.

'Space' has recently become fashionable in scholarly discourse. It is a subject of great interest to our post-modernist colleagues, attempting to explain the unique specificity of the infinite. I must confess that these are debates which do not challenge my understanding of the world; so much so that I acknowledge the possibility that I do not understand their agenda at all. To take an example, Ernesto Laclau contends that "any repetition that is governed by a structural law of successions is space" (Laclau, cited in Massey 1992:68).

This sounds more like a definition of a monarchy than a working conception of space. It certainly does not evoke for me a new way of understanding the perhaps mundane, but vital, issues of exchange rates and trade. Space is something that cars park in, that good footballers run into, and art galleries run out of. In each of these cases, what makes space important is not its physical dimensions, nor how it is produced in the intellect, but that its control is contested; though contested in quite different ways. The chase of capital across the globe involves the contestation of space, and it confronts our standard conception of economic space in terms of national units.

Conventional economic analysis too is rediscovering space; but this conservative discipline is open to new questions to only a limited degree. A concern with production and industry in the context of mobile capital now requires an explanation as to why industries locate where they do. Leading international trade economist Paul Krugman has recently announced his recognition of the importance of the spatial dimension in

Geography and Trade. In criticism of the discipline's neglect of space, he observes:

> [T]he analysis of international trade makes virtually no use of insights from economic geography or location theory. We normally model countries as dimensionless points within which factors of production can be instantly and costlessly moved from one activity to another, and even trade among countries is usually given a sort of spaceless representation in which transport costs are zero for all goods that can be traded (1991:2).

But for Krugman, space is constituted by only 'natural' imperfections (those which cannot be eradicated by 'de-regulation') and historical accidents which cause firms and industries to spatially cluster. This is an advance on the international economics he describes above, but hardly a challenging reconstruction of space.

A concern in conventional economics with exchange and circulation (particularly finance) has seen exactly the opposite argument: that computers, satellites and the lifting of national capital controls are abolishing space. Hence Richard O'Brien (not to be confused with myself) titles his book *Global Financial Integration: the End of Geography* (1992). As with Krugman, space is constituted in terms of distortions within a model of (spaceless) perfection — the demise of distortion in capital markets is then the end of space.

For all its innovation, the economic orthodoxy has remained trapped in the pre-conception that global economic processes must be understood in terms of interacting national units. Nations are, of course, where the most significant policy determinations are made. But the inability of this discipline to theorise the relation between political processes and economic processes sees economists defining economic space in terms of political space, and for no stronger reason than convention.

Alternatively, the development since the 1970s of 'theories of international restructuring', particularly 'world systems theory' has opened up debate, posing the development of a spatial re-ordering of the international economy since the end of the long boom. The international expansion of capital is posed as the process by which restructuring is occurring. Much of this analysis is rich and insightful, though a detailed appreciation of the economic dimensions of restructuring is generally restricted. Moreover, and perhaps as a result of this limitation, this analysis continues to pose the re-ordered world in terms of relations between national units.

The framework of this book attempts to develop a Marxist approach to understanding recent developments in international accumulation.

The analysis is based in the recognition that capital mobility has integrated accumulation globally, but that accumulation is nonetheless ordered primarily through a system of nation states. Nation states play out domestic roles, which now involve more international dimensions than before, for 'domestic' accumulation is now comprehensively integrated into international accumulation. Moreover, the policies which nation states implement are a product of the diverse ways in which individual capitals and industries are integrated into international accumulation. According to the form of integration, so capitals and industries will have different expectations of state policy. Hence nation states are at once domestic in their policy implementation, but also international in the sense that the divided interests they must mediate are constituted in an international framework. There is, in short, a contradiction between the internationality of accumulation and the nationality of the nation state.

The term 'contradiction' is used to indicate that the issues posed here are not just historical or technical 'problems' which await solution. The concept of a contradiction involves a dialectical logic — the recognition that history is unfolding via the opposition between forces. At its underlying level, capitalism expresses the contradiction between labour and capital; and within that general contradiction, there is any number of 'secondary' contradictions through which the history of capitalism, as world system and individual experience, unfolds. Accordingly, this book is not intended to propose policy solutions for national governments attempting to administer national economics in the face of international capital mobility. On the contrary, the concept of a contradiction suggests that the oppositional forces within economic relations (accumulation) are what sustains accumulation and, in the process, these forces ensure that accumulation is constantly changing process. This is certainly not an equilibrium theory, but a theory of what determines change.

The contradictions of international accumulation, which form the subject of this book, are not played out as a 'battle' between the state and accumulation. The contradiction is expressed within accumulation with respect to the role of national spaces, and within the nation state with respect to the different forms in which capital moves internationally. Framed in this way, it becomes possible to see the developments in the international economy which were so unexpected for the orthodox economists — volatile exchange rates, protracted recession, escalating debt and financial fragility, and non-rectifying balance of payments current account positions — as expressions of the contradiction.

Within national policy formation, and largely in reaction to these unexpected outcomes, developments in formal economic theory have become increasingly less important. Policy formation has increasingly pursued *ad hoc* agendas, often informed by the most banal of formal economic propositions — that competition is good, debt is bad, inflation is worse, etc.. Within these foundations, we have found different nation states pursuing differing policy strategies. But increasingly, it can be observed that these national policy paths are being called on to meet the one objective: securing the conditions of domestic production which will enable capital to achieve the internationally competitive rate of profit. National 'autonomy' is more about means to this end, rather than the end itself.

Securing this end is by no means simply a technical exercise of getting the right policy settings. The dilemma for individual states is that so many policy determinations advantage one part of capital, but penalise another. Exchange rates are a conspicuous expression of this reality, and all manner of state policies are scrutinised and judged by the foreign exchange dealers, and so reflect in the exchange rate. But the bias of policy is not restricted to the exchange rate effects. Budgets, interest rates and industry policies all exert differential impacts on different parts of capital. In a world where competition is tight and the stakes so high, state policy-makers have many enemies.

What are nation states to do when they cannot please all parts of capital? The answer which has come with *ad hoc* policy formation is that the domestic burden of internationalised accumulation has fallen on labor. Whether the burden is posed in terms of the need for national belt-tightening because of growing 'national debt' (in fact predominantly private debt which is socialised via policies of domestic austerity), or the requirement of workers to increase productivity to achieve 'international competitiveness', the outcome is consistent. It is also predictable. While capital is internationally mobile, labor remains predominantly immobile, and it is labor which bears the burden of domestic economic adjustment. Domestic state policy cannot contain capital, but it can make labor attractive to capital. Packaged within the rhetoric of national economic development, economic policy has increasingly targeted labor as the one effective area of national policy formation.

The prospect of a high-productivity, high wage economy is held out to labor as the rationale for short-run sacrifice — working harder, and longer, and for less remuneration — to generate long-run national success. 'World's best practice' is the organising theme. But these require relative, not absolute national productivity gains. Increased productivity will not be sufficient in itself to achieve best practice and competitive industries. The increase must be higher than in other countries. Thus the whole global ethic of competitiveness in the context of global accumulation is appearing as an alarming competition between nationally-administered working classes. As in all competitions, only some can be winners, but the culture of competition has become pervasive, and throughout the world, labor has taken up the challenge to win the World Productivity Cup. Workers on the lowest wages in the poorest countries have nothing to lose; those in the higher wage, richer countries can't afford to give ground.

Surely capital is the winner. After the furore of international volatility and realignments of the last third of the twentieth century dies down, capital will see a more trained, passive and productive labor force than it could have ever consciously planned for. Concomitantly, the increasing expulsion of labor from production associated with the development of the forces of production appears to be developing a wasteland of surplus population, living at ever lower absolute standards of impoverishment, and possibly no longer even a credible part of the labor force.

Where the chase of capital is taking us is a question that is insufficiently reflected upon. When it is, the answer is invariably alarming, whether from a social, political, environmental or psychological standpoint. This book is not so much concerned to expand upon these alarming consequences; indeed, they are rather an assumed starting point. Instead, the object is to explore the historical logic of the chase, and in particular to address the wishful view that nation states can confront the chase, and avert its damning consequences. The analysis is by no means dismissive of the role of nation states, but confronting the consequences of the chase of capital requires a broader politics than can be achieved by the re-direction of national policy.

In developing this analysis, the book is effectively divided into two sections. The first develops a conceptual framework, and the second applies this framework to an understanding of national policy formation. In the first section, Chapters 1, 2 and 3, establish the contradictions which are particular to the period of 'recent' internationalisation. Chapter 1 identifies the characteristics of 'recent' internationalisation of capital, focusing on the distinctive role played by the mobility of money in the last twenty five years, and particularly since the 1980s. Chapter 2 draws out the analytical difficulties for economic theory associated with the dominance of money. All economic theory has difficulty in understanding money, and its relation to so-called 'real' economic activity of investment and production. Hence when money is the dominant face of international mobility, and it is expressed not as a stable process, reflecting 'real' processes, but as volatile exchange rates, stock market instability and general unpredictability, there is a potential problem for economic analysis. This chapter contrasts the neo-classical and Marxist ways of coming to grips with this dimension. Chapter 3 then looks at 'recent internationalisation' in the context of contemporary theories of restructuring.

Chapters 4 and 5 develop an alternative theory of internationalisation of capital and nation states, based in Marx's theory of value, and particularly the circuits of capital. Chapter 4 looks at value formation on an international scale, identifying the essential roles which nation states must perform in securing the process of (global) accumulation. There are three basic roles: securing the supply of labor power, securing the money system, and mediating contradictory interests of capital in accumulation. This chapter establishes that there is no incompatibility between nation states and international accumulation, but that there are contradictions in accumulation which nation states cannot 'resolve'. Systematically, the onus falls on labor to provide profitability and stability to accumulation. Chapter 5 develops an analysis of how those contradictions can be understood within national spaces. It formulates a method for identifying the contradictory interests of different parts of capital, with respect to the way in which they are integrated into international accumulation.

These national expressions of the contradictions of international accumulation which have so far been considered conceptually, are applied in the second section to the formation of national economic policy. This section shows how national policy formation in an era of international capital mobility has systematically led to the direct targeting of labor as the object of policy formation.

The development of comprehensively internationalised capital markets has created new potential for accumulation; it has also generated a changing role for national economic policy. Contemporary debates about monetary, fiscal and industry policy are significantly different from what they were twenty years ago, not because the current generation of economists has discovered a truth beyond the comprehension of the previous generation, but because historical circumstances have created different forces to which policy must respond and different interests which influence policy direction. Yet within the shift, the focus on the national unit as both the subject of policy formation and the object of policy implementation has been inherited largely uncritically.

This must be challenged. The degree of national discretion in national economic policy and the effectiveness of nationally-directed policies have both been transformed by history, but this has been recognised in a very limited way only by economic analysis and policy. What is consistently missing is an explanation of why internationalised accumulation will (or should) be compatible with mechanisms which equilibrate accumulation for individual national units and why nationally-focused state policy can ever be successful in achieving policy objectives. Put simply, it must be asked whether the popular range of policy 'tools' to improve national economic performance can solve (even in a limited sense) national economic problems in reality, or is the pursuit of national solutions predominantly just a construct of economic theory itself?

There is no suggestion here that the dominant theory and policy makers are unaware of the impact of international momentum: the pre-eminence of policies for 'international competitiveness', and the importance of international financial flows to monetary policy are clear recognition of national policies focusing on international capital mobility. The issue is not whether a change has been recognised and addressed, but how it has been understood in theory and applied to policy.

Chapter 6 addresses the contradictions of national monetary policy. These arise from the inability of economic theory, and much policy formation which flows from it, to reconcile the desire for national regulation when the phenomenon being regulated (money) is itself part of an internationally-integrated capital market.

The same theme is developed in Chapters 7, 8, and 9 in relation to the balance of payments. Chapter 7 identifies the accounting structure of the balance of payments as misrepresenting the nature of international capital movement, by imposing a national taxonomy onto inherently global processes. A case study of the United States balance of payments in the mid 1980s is developed in Chapter 8 to illustrate the contradictions of nationalist balance of payments categories. This is more than a randomly chosen period. It is critical to what has been called the end of United States hegemony, and it was the period in which national balance of payments instability became an entrenched global phenomenon. Chapter 9 then looks at the implications of national policy makers placing reliance on national balance of payments data.

The outcome in relation to balance of payments policy, as with monetary policy, is that the nation state's inability to manage these aggregates directly is seeing recourse to a class politics in which the rate of exploitation of labor is the explicit agenda. The exploitation of labor is inherently the economic core of capitalism, but with international developments in the last twenty years, the underlying logic has been played out as explicit nation state policy. National policies increasingly see labor, its income and productivity, as the key to an 'internationally competitive economy'. National policy is seen to reinforce the international nature of capitalist class relations.

The final chapter provides a brief summary of the argument, and develops the case that the contradiction between the internationality of capital accumulation and the nationality of the state cannot be resolved because the contradiction between labour and capital is not resolvable within capitalism.

1

What Is the Internationalisation of Capital?

Internationalisation is an unfortunate term, for its etymology suggests the primacy of nationality in the study of changes in global accumulation. Internationalisation suggests the extension beyond national units, but not in any sense the transcendence of national categories, for it expresses the development of relations between nations.

In its political-economic dimension, it suggests that accumulation was once national and then undertook a process of 'internationalisation' — a 'spilling over' of national accumulation. This, of course, is a false depiction of the history of accumulation. Accumulation has never adhered strictly to national boundaries. Indeed, trade in particular, but also investment were to some degree 'international' before there were 'nations'. This signals to us that accumulation has only a partial relation to the national unit and to the nation state — it is not reducible to the economic relations between nations. Yet most analyses, certainly those pertaining to economic processes, start with the primacy of national units, so that the spatial extension of accumulation is posed as the increasing interaction between national units, and, by some, as the decline in the economic autonomy of national units.

The processes which are characterised as 'internationalisation' can be posed as other than relations between nations. These may be spatially-extended relations between companies or other institutions, between individuals, or between classes; or the extension of relations within any of these categories. An understanding of these relations may be impeded if the categories are uncritically attributed national characteristics.

With this in mind, it must be recognised that any definition of internationalisation in terms of capital outgrowing the nation has already imputed a whole conceptual agenda onto the role of the nation and the nation state in accumulation, and one which, it will be argued, has constrained a whole generation of analysis, both Marxist and non-

Marxist. Here the fundamental theme of this analysis is immediately confronted: what does it mean to understand accumulation in terms of national units, and thus the extension beyond national units, and what does this imply for the role of the nation state in accumulation? More importantly, how is accumulation changing as it 'internationalises', and how are the roles of nation states changing in association with this process?

Yet the term 'internationalisation' shall be retained because it signals that the expansion of the space of the process of accumulation is not devoid of a national dimension. There may exist cultural and social factors which make economic relations beyond the nation qualitatively different from domestic relations. But beyond such possible particularities, it is the role of nation states which signals an inherent qualitative difference to the conditions of domestic and international accumulation. This, it must be emphasised, is not based on some notion that the nation state 'intervenes' to 'distort' accumulation, affecting a differentiation of domestic and international conditions. Such a proposition rests on an idealised and trivial notion of (potentially) stateless accumulation.[1] Rather, a national dimension rests on the recognition that the state plays some intrinsic roles in capitalist accumulation, not least of which are securing social stability and the supply of a stable money system. There cannot be capitalism without states and, in the current world, this means predominantly *nation* states.[2]

There is, therefore, a distinct role for nation states in international accumulation. Accumulation does not spread like an oil slick across the globe, because the movement of capital, while having a general character, is also to be understood as the aggregation of discrete and differentiated individual processes. Capital moves at different rates in different forms and in different directions at different times, and an analysis of internationalisation must explain this. Moreover, as part of this movement, the role of national states is decisive, both in facilitating some movements, at some times and in some directions, and retarding other movements, at other times, in other directions.

So while one side of the fundamental theme of this analysis relates to national conceptions of international accumulation, the other side relates to a conception of the international role of nation states. Without entering the minefield of specifying the general 'role of the state', a simple point can be proffered. Whether it is contended that the state 'represents' the so-called 'national interest'; or 'national' capital; or even the logic of co-ordination of capital, these have all been understood as nationally centred agendas. Debates about the state, both theoretical and 'applied' have centred on which of these agendas is 'true', and how it is pursued. But as capital internationalises, it has to be asked: whose interests are the national interest; what part of capital is to be ascribed the label of 'national'; and what is the space within which co-ordination is required?

Central to an alternative analysis, is the contradiction between the internationality of accumulation and the nationality of state regulation of accumulation, and the way this contradiction has been played out since the end of the long, post-war boom in the international economy in the late 1960s, and particularly since the mid 1970s. This contradiction is neither novel nor temporary, but during the post-war boom in the international economy, it could be said to have been 'hidden' in the buoyancy of the international economy.

Internationalisation of capital and the nation state therefore are inseparable as aspects of accumulation. While this relationship is always played out historically in particular circumstances, the general tendency towards the international mobility of capital suggests that the relationship between the state and accumulation is changing.

Since the end of that long boom, there has been two decades of protracted recession, punctuated by brief, and therefore rather superficial 'booms'. It is in this context that the contradiction has been pronounced, for it has been associated with the rapid escalation of the international movement of capital on the one hand, and the imposition of predominantly national strategies to resolve recession on the other. Hence 'the internationalisation of capital' is a term which must be further clarified, particularly as a prevalent dimension of contemporary global changes in accumulation. In this chapter, the changing character of accumulation on an international scale will be explored. The playing out of the contradiction involved in this change is addressed in Chapter 2.

Internationalisation as a Recent Phenomenon

Capital has always been international to some degree. International movement of capital, in the form of commodity trade and usury or credit, pre-dated and indeed was the precondition of the development of capitalism (Polanyi 1957; Dobb 1946; Kay 1975). Moreover, capitalist class relations have been internationalising at least since the beginnings of European colonialism.

Hence when internationalisation is depicted as a distinct, recent development of capitalism, particularly of the period since the 1970s, there is need for clarification, for any perceived transformation should not be overstated. We must be aware that changes which may seem monumental at the time can appear much less decisive in retrospect. Moreover, there is the danger that the proclamation of internationalisation as a 'new era' for capitalism can use newness (the image of a 'clean slate') as a means to avoid analysing and explaining developments within the 'old'. Indeed, the orientation to put a label on this recent period (for example, the transition from 'early' to 'late monopoly capitalist imperialism' (Szymanski 1981); or from 'national' to 'metanational capitalist accumulation' (Borrego 1982); or from 'monopoly' to 'global capitalism' (Gibson and Horvath 1983; Ross and Trachte 1992); or from an 'old' to a 'new international division of labor (Froebel, *et al.* 1980)[3] creates the impression that the 'new' period is distinct and, in its own terms, stable, thereby warranting its 'own' period classification. The labelling exercise seems both to foreclose debate about the nature of change, and to impose the interpretation that change occurs by quantum leaps.

Thus the 'recent phenomenon' of internationalisation should be read as current transformation in accumulation of modest, though significant, proportions. The significance of recent changes therefore stands as a theoretical issue, which will be identified in Chapters 2 and 3. First, it is necessary to identify the forces which led to what will be hereafter referred to as 'recent internationalisation', being the forms of international mobility of capital which have developed since the end of the long boom in the international economy.

Recent internationalisation involves a process of global integration of accumulation. Economic calculation of all kinds — by governments, corporations, workers, and consumers — are integrated globally due to the global extension of the process of competition. While competition is not always experienced by participants as a global process, developments since the 1970s have been increasing the extent to which competitive processes in any location adhere to international determinants.

The change in the 1970s can be identified with the growing size and importance of transnational corporations; advances in transport and communications which facilitate commodity trade; and developments in computer and telecommunications technology which permit the operation of internationally-integrated capital markets, not to mention the political hegemony of the economic theories of 'international competitiveness'. All these developments have made the scale of recent internationalisation technically possible.

While these developments have been critical, they do not explain why recent internationalisation arose when it did. Each of the above-mentioned technological developments has its own long history: they did not suddenly emerge or suddenly and spontaneously combine together to form 'internationalisation' at the beginning of the 1970s. Just as important was the changing nature of production in the advanced capitalist countries during the 1950s and particularly 1960s.

It is therefore important to look briefly at the evidence of a phenomenon of 'recent internationalisation', in terms of the historical developments from which they derive. Unfortunately, the phenomenon is difficult to measure in its full dimensions. Some evidence is provided in the rapid growth of cross-national trade, credit, and investment. These processes increased significantly in all countries in the 1970s and accelerated in the 1980s, as will be seen shortly. But these increases in themselves are insufficient to substantiate the impact of recent internationalisation, for while cross-border flows of trade, credit and investment have grown rapidly, they remain far less than the total of all domestic flows.

What makes the current period distinctive, is that the impact of 'internationalisation' is more pervasive than cross-border flows. There is a breaking down of the difference between cross-border and domestic flows, for they are all becoming subject to the same calculation. So in addition to cross-national resource flows, and more importantly, recent internationalisation is reflected in the impact of international forces on domestic resource uses. This impact is somewhat more nebulous than resource flows, for it involves an interpretation of the extent to which domestic resource uses are influenced by and subject to international movement of capital.

The global integration of accumulation means that economic calculations of all kinds — from purchases in the supermarket to the determination of the prime interest rate — are subject, quite explicitly, to international calculation. In the supermarket, the increasing availability of imported goods and their price is a reflection of the increasing international mobility of commodities and the international determination of relative currency values. The level of wages with which to purchase these commodities is increasingly being determined with reference to the international cost competitiveness of local industry.

In the money market, the local rate of interest is increasingly driven by the exchange rate of the local currency in international markets, combined with the relative profitability of borrowing locally compared with internationally, and of lending locally compared with internationally. Not only are these international determinants now manifesting in local money markets more quickly then before, but there is now no significant notion of a distinct 'local' money market.

Nonetheless, in identifying evidence of recent internationalisation, it is necessary to start with cross-border resource flows. The less obvious, but more significant, aspects of global integration of calculation are developed throughout the book.

Trade

Table 1.1 shows world average annual rate of growth of exports and imports from 1950 to 1990. As broad figures, not too much reliance should be placed to support detailed stories, even if these figures are broken down into groups of nations, or even specific national data. But the broad pattern is clear. The period after the long boom saw the rate of growth of trade more than double. The annual rate of growth of exports and imports increased from 9% in the 1960s (itself a significant increase over the 1950s) to 20% in the 1970s,[4] but then fell back to 5% in the 1980s, although the rate of growth on the second half of the 1980s was 12%. Notice, however, that because Table 1.1 shows rates of growth, not absolute levels, the performance of the 1980s is not to be seen as a falling away of commodity flows, but a consolidation of the growth of the 1970s, retaining and indeed increasing the level of international commodity flows achieved in the 1970s.

The explanation for the accelerated increase in trade at a time of international down-turn is a difficult matter; indeed one not widely considered. Some, particularly those advancing the 'profit squeeze' theory of the end of the long boom (for example, Armstrong, Glyn and Harrison 1991) have sought explanation in terms of a fall in domestic demand in the industrialised countries leading to the pursuit of external markets in the 'socialist' and 'less industrialised' countries. But trade expanded predominantly within the industrialised countries. Other observers, such as Mandel (1978), associated these changes with the development of over-production, portending the on-set of a period of crisis for capitalism. This was certainly consistent with historical processes for there did follow a period of sustained crisis of accumulation, beginning in the mid to late 1960s as the rate of profit started to fall in the industrialised countries, and clearly manifesting as global recession by the mid 1970s.

But the explanation of the end of the long boom is not the immediate

TABLE 1.1   Annual Average Rates of Growth of Global Trade[a], 1950-1990
(in percentages)

1950-1960	1960-1970	1970-1980	1980-1990
6.5	9.2	20.3	5.2

[a] Figures are for exports. Due to statistical error, figures for imports and exports are not equal. For 1960-70 and 1970-80 import growth was 0.1% lower than export growth.

Source: United Nations, 1991.

concern of the current analysis. Indeed, it is important in this context to recognise that the tendency towards internationalisation was not as a response to recession, but the product of boom. The growth of international trade was the expression of growing production, not over-production. Growing production associated with increasing scale becomes over-production only in the context of other processes within accumulation. The fact that increased production for export was experienced eventually as an international crisis of over-production is the expression of the inability of international trade to provide a 'solution' to a crisis whose origins lie in the sphere of production; but it does not follow that internationalisation arose as a 'solution'.

Thus the growth of trade has to be explained, in the first instance, outside the onset of recession, as an underlying momentum of accumulation. Several broad factors are relevant here:

- For industrialised countries throughout the 1950s and 1960s, trade had increased faster than production, and the gap was widening. Between 1953 and 1963, the volume of industrial production in capitalist countries rose 62%, while exports rose 82%. Between 1963 and 1972, production rose 65% and exports 111% (Mandel 1978:19). Thus the experience of trade increasing more quickly than production was not distinct to the 1970s.
- During the 1960s the composition of exports changed, with agricultural product trade declining and trade in manufactures increasing. Manufactured goods made up less than half of world trade at the beginning of the 1950s, but almost two thirds by the end of the 1960s (Harris 1983:44-5). Within manufactures trade, the main increases were in chemicals, machinery and transport equipment (Cornwall 1977:86). Unlike agricultural production at this time, manufacturing expansion was based on large-capacity production units which required increasing levels of output in order to produce at lower unit cost. Exporting thereby became a conspicuous technical necessity in manufacturing (Batchelor, Major and Morgan 1980) and its expansion was consistent with sustained boom conditions (Mazier 1982). But this necessity did not change with the end of the boom.
- The growth of manufactures trade during the 1950s and 1960s became less dependent on the growth of the market size, and more on imported goods increasing their share of domestic markets. Between 1950 and 1963, around half the imported manufactures were due to penetration of the domestic market; the other half to the growing size of the market. Between 1963 and 1971, two thirds of the increase in manufactures trade was due to market penetration

(Armstrong, Glyn and Harrison 1991:216). This development was accentuated by the rise of Japan and Germany as industrial powers and manufacturing exporters.[5] Japan's exports grew 75% faster than other industrialised countries' in the 1960s (United Nations 1991:17), though manufacturing import penetration hardly increased. Similarly, Germany's manufacturing export growth in the 1950s outstripped both domestic production and imports (Llewellyn and Potter 1982). Thus the expansion of manufactures trade was reducing its reliance on expanding demand, which was consistent with continued expansion during recession.

These factors combined suggest that trade was likely to grow in the 1970s irrespective of recession, for the tendency towards increased trade had already been established in technology and patterns of demand.

Credit

The case of the internationalisation of money is slightly different from trade. There was the same historical momentum to internationalisation of money as there was for trade, expressed particularly as long-term growing levels of international equity investment and the emergence of large international markets for credit. But as well as this trend, the onset of international down-turn directly precipitated a crisis in the international money system dating from the late 1960s, and a conspicuous response to this crisis was to further the momentum towards the international movement of money. Thus the internationalisation of money is both the product of boom and, in a later phase, a response to crisis. The relation between boom and crisis in the international movement of money will be examined in more detail after observing the evidence.

The data on international money flows are less reliable than for trade, both conceptually and in accuracy. The expansion of money markets internationally and the removal of official reporting requirements due to so-called 'deregulation' makes accurate data difficult to acquire. It also makes the origin of money difficult to verify. The additional factor is that the form of international funds changed in the 1980s, with the shift from international bank lending to the so-called 'securitisation' of capital flows, associated particularly with the development of international bond markets.

It is therefore useful to first compare the growth of trade with funds raised internationally up to 1985, and then look at international capital market development more broadly. It has already been seen that commodity flows increased rapidly in the 1970s, steadying in the 1980s, but this increase was modest compared with the growth of international credit. Between 1972 and 1985, funds raised in international financial markets increased at an annual rate of 23% over the period, while trade increased at 'only' 13% per annum (United Nations 1989:64). Yet the major developments in international credit occurred since the mid 1980s, as the international bond market took off.

Figure 1.1 shows that funds raised in international capital markets increased from just over $US 100 billion in 1980 to over $US 600 billion in 1993. These funds comprise both international bank credit and internationally-issued bonds. While bank credit was dominant throughout the 1970s and early 1980s, the rate of issue was not increasing significantly. Conversely, while international bond issues were less than $US 50 billion per year in the early 1980s, by 1993, they were almost $US 500 billion per year.

The international bond market — the market for securities issued outside the country of their currency — arose particularly within Eurofinance markets. Eurofinance markets themselves first emerged in the 1950s, particularly associated with holdings of United States dollars and the need of Eastern European countries to trade in hard currencies.

FIGURE 1.1 Funds Raised in International Capital Markets, 1979-1993

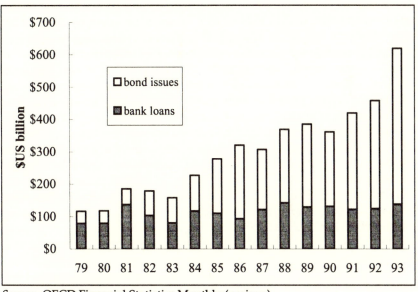

Source: OECD Financial Statistics Monthly (various).

They developed in the 1960s as holdings of United States dollars expanded associated with increasing United States budget deficits. Further growth from the late 1960s was associated with a loss of international confidence in the United States dollar as the international trading and wealth-holding currency, and accelerated from the mid 1970s as OPEC oil money sought outlets via international credits. In the 1980s, these markets became increasingly oriented to bond issues. The expansion in the first half of the 1980s was associated with national financial liberalisation (especially in Japan and the United Kingdom); falling real interest rates, and the development of a market for currency swaps (Benzie 1992:14-24). Borrowing was predominantly by public sectors, attracted by low interest rates to fund budget deficits. Increasingly over the 1980s, the market was for privately issued bonds, with 'junk bonds' signaling the largely speculative component of the growth.

Investment

Funds raised in international capital markets are one aspect of the growth of international money movement. A further aspect is the growth of foreign direct investment — that is, investment by transnational corporations (TNCs) outside their 'home' country. Figure 1.2 compares the growth of foreign direct investment and domestic investment for all countries over the period 1970 to 1990. As with the data on commodity trade, there should be no attempt, at this level of aggregation, to make anything but the most general observations. Nonetheless, there is a clear trend, closely parallel to the trend for funds raised in international financial markets. Global direct foreign investment grew steadily over most of the 1970s, as it had throughout the post-war period. This was significant, but not unexceptional, for even up to the mid 1980s, the rate of growth of direct foreign investment was roughly comparable with the rate of growth of domestic investment. But from the mid 1980s, these growth paths diverge. While domestic investment increased by 50 percent from 1985 to 1990, direct foreign investment increased by 400 percent. By 1990 there were 35 thousand TNCs with 150 thousand foreign affiliates, and a foreign-held stock of $US 1.7 trillion (United Nations 1991:17).

The quantum leap in cross-country trade, finance and investment is clear, and provides some signal of a development which warrants particular attention. But, it has already been noted, internationalisation means more than the increased resource flows between countries. More than a growing interaction between national economies, as the data have shown, internationalisation involves an increasingly explicit global

FIGURE 1.2 Global Foreign Direct Investment Outflows and Domestic Investment, 1970-1989

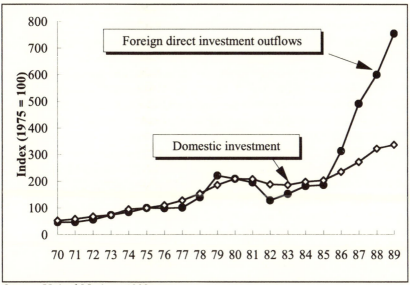

Source: United Nations 1992

integration of economic processes. It is the growing integration which characterises the qualitative difference in accumulation in the past twenty five years, and particularly since the early 1980s.

Thus the conventionally-defined measurement of economic internationalisation has changed from the measure of resource flows between countries, which is eminently measurable in balance of payments data, to the integration of markets — markets for goods and services, capital, and foreign exchange. It will be seen in Chapter 2 that there is a distinct neo-classical agenda in the calculation of integration by reference to markets, but the general nature of internationalisation as something beyond resource flows is critical to the characterisation of the recent period.

Money and Recent Internationalisation

Of the multiple forms of global integration, it is currently money and near money in which the tendency towards integration is most pronounced. It is the mobility of money which gives the period since the long boom, and since the 1980s in particular, its distinctive quality. The conspicuous characteristic of money is that its portability and convertibility have integrated global capital markets. Moreover, money's centrality at every stage in the accumulation process means that the effect of international mobility is pervasive. With 'national' capital markets integrated, it would be difficult to argue that other markets can be disentangled from the same process.

There are conspicuous technical reasons why money has 'led' internationalisation. Money has always been fluid — both portable and convertible. But more recent developments in technology have made these financial flows close to instantaneous and costless. Advances in telecommunications have permitted both twenty-four-hour-a-day screen-based international dealing in assets, and rapid innovation in financial markets. The development of a range of financial instruments including currency swaps, interest rate swaps, and financial futures and options has permitted forms of portfolio diversification directly dependent on internationalised financial markets.

But the pronounced role of money in internationalisation cannot be reduced to technical explanations. Moreover, its leadership has potential implications for accumulation, both domestic and international, which must be canvassed. Historically prior to these technical innovations was a severing of the close link of the national money system to national accumulation, and a growing international market for money. These changes can be associated with two general developments within the sphere of money, both of which have been widely documented, and need not be elaborated here in any detail. The first is representative of the general tendency towards international movement of money, associated with what might loosely be called capitalist development. The second is representative of the acceleration of international movement associated with crisis in the international money system.

The first was the sustained post-World War Two growth of debt financing of capital accumulation, of production in particular, but also of consumption.[6] The explanation for this change strangely remains largely impressionistic, though generally associated with 'artificially' low levels of debt at the end of the war, with debt exposure increasing as a reflection of corporate confidence in fixed capital investment during the 'long' boom and, by the mid 1960s, with a loss of internally-generated funds due to falling profit rates (BIS *Annual Reports*, esp 1964:32-6).

While debt was initially largely domestically funded, it also tied in directly to the availability of (generally) cheap credit available in Eurofinance markets. The expansion of internationally-mobile credit from the 1950s was, therefore, associated with the growth of debt-financing of accumulation generally which was itself the expression of conditions pertaining to production by industrial capital.

The second general development which advanced the internationalisation of money was associated with the end of the Bretton Woods Agreement on international currencies. From the late 1960s, but formally in 1971, the United States dollar ceased to be recognised as a stable currency for international trade and asset-holding. The system of fixed exchange rates which ruled the post-war period came to a gradual end with the inability of the United States to provide the world with currency of stable convertibility.

Key to the demise of the dominance of the United States dollar was that the United States lost its global industrial pre-eminence, particularly as international trade in manufactures expanded in the 1960s. Most significant was the low post-World War Two productivity growth of United States industry. According to calculations by Maddison (1982:96-124) productivity growth increased rapidly in the OECD countries from 1950 to 1973,[7] except in the leading country, the United States, where productivity growth was no greater than in the period 1913 to 1950. So in the post-war period, Europe and Japan lost their technological and productivity lag: the United States lost its industrial pre-eminence.[8]

The loss of industrial pre-eminence reflected in the United States balance of trade with the rest of the world, as the United States lost export growth, and imports increased. It would have been 'appropriate' in this context for the United States dollar to depreciate (Branson 1980:186). But the Bretton Woods Agreement, based on the convertibility of the United States dollar for gold at a fixed rate of thirty five dollars per ounce, precluded dollar depreciation. So when the devaluation of the United States dollar occurred, it signaled the end dollar convertibility and so the end of the post-war monetary system. The added factor of high United States inflation in the 1960s, associated with fiscal expansion, served to accentuate the loss of international confidence in the convertibility of the United States dollar.[9]

The result was that gradually, and in retrospect rather chaotically, national governments sought to disentangle their currency from direct attachment to the United States dollar. Progressively, national currencies (exchange rates) were floated[10], and this led quite predictable to the growth of international currency markets, and the increased movement of money between currencies.

What became most remarkable about international money movements in the 1970s, and particularly the 1980s, was not just that the conditions of mobility were so transformed and the volume of flows increased so rapidly, but that these conditions were associated with widespread volatility in interest rates and exchange rates. The volatility was in stark contrast with the predictions of the economic policy makers around the world, who were expecting deregulated, integrated markets to gravitate towards stable equilibrium. Why the expected outcome has not been realised, and the implications for the regulation of acumulation on a national scale, are issues to be addressed in detail in later Chapters. At this point, it is important to note simply that the 'leadership' of money in recent internationalisation has been associated with instability and uncertainty.

For some observers, the volume and volatility of international financial flows is attributed to the decisions by national governments to deregulate their exchange rates and capital flows. But to explain the recent internationalisation of money in terms of a 'relinquishement' of national controls would involve placing undue emphasis on legal changes in financial regulation, to the neglect of the broader historical forces which generated global money movement and volatility. The reality in almost all countries at the time of deregulation is that the defense of the 'fixed' rate in international markets was requiring unsustainable levels of central bank buying and selling. Acceding to the size of the international market became an inevitable outcome. Invariably, floating was the only alternative.

Nonetheless, the fact that mobility was facilitated by laissez-faire-informed national policy interventions has proved critical. Because that ideology attributes no special significance to the role of money, and 'efficient' outcomes to the market process, money was usually deregulated just as any other market would be deregulated — with the regulation of competition supplanting direct state supervision. There was recognised only a minimal role for the state in supervising the money system nationally, and no role at all on an international scale, until it was to some degree clawed back in the late 1970s in Europe for other countries in the mid 1980s. In the meantime, the internationalisation which was transmitted by 'free' international capital markets generated large swings in exchange rates and interest rates.[11] Recent internationalisation was manifesting as anything but the a smooth expansion in markets and global efficiency in resource allocation.

The issues surrounding international financial markets are many and complex. The analysis at this stage rests on a single point of underlying significance. Both the rise of international currency and other financial asset markets and the decline of the Bretton Woods system signal a fundamental change in the relationship between national processes of accumulation and the national monetary system: in the former because of the development of an extra-national credit system; in the latter because expanding accumulation has required direct engagement in international money markets.

Conclusion

The expansion of international trade, investment and finance has been a continuing feature of world history. In this respect, capitalism has always developed as a global system, and the period since the 1970s has been an accentuated period in that history, with the development of a globally-integrated capital market, and the diversification of that market, being its outstanding feature. Particularly in contrast with the post-war boom, the notion of a discrete national pattern of accumulation has been diminishing.

But what makes the period since the 1970s so distinctive is that monetary integration has been associated with volatility in the international monetary system. While cross-national currency and investment was as significant to the pre-World-War-One economy as it is now, it is important to recall that the earlier period was characterised by the gold standard — a system of guarantied global financial stability. International capital movement reflected confidence in the global money system. This can in no way describe the rationale for, or the effect of, the mobility for capital since the 1970s.

An effect of portfolio diversification under advanced technology is that the movement of money internationally has lost any systematic relationship with the movement of commodities, and thereby with the production of commodities. The loss of this relationship has had some profound implications. By the mid 1980s, around 3 percent of cross-national money flows were associated with payments for internationally-traded commodities, the other 97 percent being 'purely' financial transactions of the kinds identified above. The pool of mobile speculative funds proved critical to the exchange rate volatility which was prevalent in the 1980s, and contributed greatly to the growing national balance of payments current account imbalances (both surpluses and deficits) in the advanced capitalist countries.

Volatile exchange rates and large current account imbalances signal the difficulties for individual nation states in managing or regulating accumulation. No matter what agendas and processes are attached to the terms 'management' and 'regulation' (except for the most fanciful idealisation of laissez faire), all nation states must face the reality that global extension of accumulation has had profound effects on the formation of national policy. For national policy, the leadership of money in recent internationalisation points to a series of issues which must be explored in later Chapters. One issue, addressed in Chapter 2, is how economic theory explains the volatility in financial markets which has been experienced since the 1970s, and the implications of this explanation for understanding the relation between money and production, and the relation between national and global space. A further, associated issue, addressed in Chapter 3, is the relation of recent internationalisation to the so-called international restructuring of capital: the process by which industry has reformed on an international scale in response to the crisis of profitability which began in the 1970s, and continues into the 1990s.

Notes

1. This will be recognised as the neo-classical economists' conception of the state. Of course, there are recognised functions of the state associated with property rights and so-called 'market failure', but accumulation is, in general, deemed to work best when the state performs these minimalist functions.

2. There are, of course, some supra-national state functions performed by institutions such as the United Nations, the International Monetary Fund and the World Bank. There is also some tendency in the world to form functions of a supra-national state via the amalgamating of nation state functions, such as is unfolding in Europe. Important as these are, they do not supplant the primacy of the nation state in regulating accumulation. Supra-national state functions are considered further in Chapter 10.

3. Some of these are identified in Chase-Dunn (1989:70).

4. There may be some basis for dividing the 1970s. The first half included the OPEC oil price increases, and the associated international stockpiling of resources (the 'speculative boom' of 1972-73) expressed as a dramatic increase in raw materials trade, in price and volume (Mandel 1978:183-84; IMF *Annual Report* 1975:6-7). Conversely, the second half of the 1970s shows the effects of the slump of 1975, perhaps leading to the expectation of reduced trade levels. Indeed, trade levels were lower in the second half of the 1970s than in the first (25.9% in the first half; 18.0% in the second half) and this general pattern is consistent across all industrialised countries (United Nations 1991). But the evidence cannot support a conclusion that trade fell due to recession: the rate of growth in the post 1975 period was twice that of the 1960s.

5. In the United States between 1960 and 1985, imported manufactures as a proportion of manufactured value added increased 7 fold — from 5% to 35%. For Germany, the comparable increase was from 27% to 43%, and for Japan, the increase was from 7% to less than 10% (BIS *Annual Report* 1988:29).

6. For Europe, see BIS *Annual Reports* (esp. 1963:41). For the United States, see Friedman (1980:16-26). In both the United States and Europe, the growth of 'private' indebtedness in the 1950s , 1960s and even the 1970s offset the fall in 'public' indebtedness in the post-war period.

7. Fastest growth was in Austria, Germany, Japan and Italy. This is hardly surprising, given their low post-war industrial base. What is more surprising is

that they had all but 'caught up' to the United States by the beginning of the 1970s.

8. The possibility that the United States' fall from supremacy as a trading nation was in part due to production outside the United States by companies of United States origin is an irony which itself reflects the anachronism of associating national currencies with national economic 'performance'. This issue is discussed in Chapter 8.

9. It has often been argued that fiscal expansion, particularly associated with the funding of the Vietnam War, generated inflation in the United States and that this expansion was serving to reduce the 'real' worth of United States dollar holdings. It is unlikely that inflation alone, or even primarily, could have undermined the convertibility of the United States dollar if that country's industrial pre-eminence had remained as it was at the end of the 1940s.

10. This began with the removal of capital controls in Germany, the United States, Canada, Switzerland and the Netherlands after 1973, leading to a more generalised and widespread financial sector deregulation in the late 1970s and early 1980s.

11. This is the subject of Chapter 6 and, in relation to the United States, Chapter 8.

2

National Economies and International Capital: The Economists' Bind

The evidence of cross-national trade and investment and the rapid growth of international financial markets creates an impression that something about how the world's economy operates is different now from what it was at the beginning of the 1970s. But what is that difference? Trade, and even direct investment have been posed in Chapter 1 as the products of boom — the predictable consequences of an expanding market. Hence they are, in important ways, an expression of continuum, not of difference. But money, and integrated capital markets, have involved a qualitative change in the nature of accumulation, and one more difficult to comprehend. In part, this is because money has always been a difficult subjects for economists. Money's status as a collectively recognised symbol has sat uneasily in a discipline which embraces neither collectivism nor symbolism. Money's relation to so-called 'real' economic processes has been contentious and therefore at the centre of paradigmatic shifts in the discipline.

In part also the difficulty of comprehending integrated capital markets arises in the relationship between the role of the nation state in managing the national money system, and the prevalence of the international mobility of money. Lying behind this difficulty is the way in which national space is constituted in economic analysis, and the fact that international integration has exposed the paucity of understanding of the national political form within economic analysis. We find international economists going back to rediscover the dimension of space and of nations once these can no longer be defined simply in terms of immobility and barriers.

The analysis in this book draws directly on the economic analysis of Marxism, but this provides no ready-made solution to these difficulties. Marxism, as well as mainstream economics, has difficulties comprehending the dominance of money in international accumulation, and the constitution of national space and the associated role of the nation state. These will be addressed shortly in an abbreviated form before they are developed in detail through the book. But first, it is useful to see how the mainstream of economics has constituted these issues, both as a contrast with Marxism, and as a guide to the construction of a Marxist analysis.

The Economic Orthodoxy

The fact of internationalisation has become integral to mainstream economics, but how it is to be inserted into economic theory remains a point of ambiguity. The discourse of mainstream economics has been pervaded by the disjuncture between its 'microeconomic' and 'macroeconomic' components, and this disjuncture proves critical in the different ways internationalisation has been absorbed into economic theory. This theoretical disjuncture seemed to be disappearing during the 1980s, associated with the ascendency of 'deregulation' and 'small government'. This development privileged the micro-economic agenda of efficiency as a macroeconomic objective, and so removed the legitimacy of many of the distinctly 'macroeconomic', 'interventionist' policy agendas. In national economic policy, the primacy of efficiency was expressed in the ideal of laissez faire; politically, in the ideal of individualism, captured in the proposition, attributed to Margaret Thatcher, that there is no such thing as '*society*'.

The disjuncture between the macro and micro agendas has re-appeared starkly in dealing with international capital mobility and the integration of global markets. For the micro analysis, globalisation is posed in terms of globally competitive markets, with portfolio analysis establishing the conditions under which optimising individuals manage their financial assets. In this framework, national controls are constituted as distortions to the competitive market.

Conversely, the macroeconomic agenda remains bound by the assertion of the ontological primacy of national units. Internationalisation is posed in terms of the growing impact of the 'external sector' on the national economy. The understanding of internationalisation, therefore, is not in terms of global integration, but (increasingly intrusive) cross-national interaction. So-called 'open-economy macroeconomics', which inserts the centrality of floating exchange rates and 'free' capital mobility into national aggregate analysis, is a clear reflection of this style of construction.[1]

The persistence of the assumption of the ontological primacy of nations, and how the assumption has constructed economic analysis, is a central theme of the second half of this book, and will not be explored here in detail. Suffice it to signal at this point that, by assuming national economic coherence, economic theory, and the national policies it recommends, have not had to constitute theoretically the basis of national coherence. The national taxonomy of capital (in the senses of commodities, money and companies, too), which is pervasive in economic discourse, consistently constructs theoretically the differentiation of national space. The possibility of a loss of national coherence (or the way in which national coherence is being reconstructed) associated with recent internationalisation cannot be posed. Hence the process of global integration is leaving the mainstream of economics with processes it can explain only as distortions — exchange rate volatility; sustained balance of payments current account imbalances, and the relative 'unresponsiveness' of national economic performance to the national policies it advocates.

Over time, the effect has been that policy formation has become increasingly divorced from the insights of economic theory.[2] When the movements in the 'real' economy are unpredictable, and the outcomes of policy initiatives uncertain, policy itself comes to turn on the subjectivity of estimates and impressions. It is little surprise that it is increasingly the bankers and policy consultants, not the theoretical economists, who are looked to by the media to comment on economic affairs.

For the microeconomic angle, the opposite is true: to comprehend globalisation, the theory has divorced itself from the agenda of national economic management. From the micro-perspective, the principal concern is to calculate the extent to which particular markets, especially financial markets, are fully (or less-than-fully) internationally integrated. The degree of integration then represents a measure of global efficiency in resource allocation, with completely integrated markets associated with 'perfect' capital mobility. Within this definition of integration, there need be no international resource movements: integration could be expressed entirely via domestic price adjustments responding to international market signals.[3]

Here, integration is measured by reference to spatial differences in the outcomes of market processes. For example,

> To the extent that ... developments have led to greater financial integration, arbitrage should drive the risk-adjusted nominal rate of return on financial assets denominated in different currencies and/or issued in different countries into uniformity. This proposition is directly testable by examining interest rate parity concepts, adjusted where appropriate for

expected exchange rate depreciation (Blundell-Wignall and Browne 1991:5).

The central characteristic of this approach is that the benchmark for the measurement of integration is global perfect competition (perfect capital mobility): globally uniform rates of return signal complete integration. Models of perfectly competitive markets have a time-honored role in the orthodoxy, and it is not intended here to challenge that construction. But a few important points should be noted.

The neo-classical analysis of capital mobility focuses on market outcomes, not processes: its concern is the equilibrating role of arbitrage, not the active role of money in internationalising accumulation. The latter, which is characteristic of the Marxist approach, is by no means driven by an equilibrating function, for money is not to be understood as the activity of an isolated market. The focus on outcomes has raised a basic difficulty for the neo-classicals. While computer and satellite technology, combined with progressive developments in national deregulation of capital flows, have secured technical conditions approximating perfect capital mobility,[4] actual market outcomes have been found to not reflect the predicted outcomes of the perfect market. In particular, exchange rates have not behaved as the theory expected, with the result that there has not been a convergence internationally of real interest rates in different countries,[5] and it has been argued that there continues a strong relation between national savings and national investment, indicating that money does not flow systematically internationally from savings surplus to savings deficit countries (Feldstein and Horioka 1980).

Within the debates on this analytical dilemma,[6] a fundamental conceptual problem of the paradigm comes through: the relationship between money and the 'real' economy. The market for money is treated as is any other market: an organic whole, reaching an internally-generated equilibrium. In applying this conception to international capital markets the problem is that these markets engage with the 'real' economy at two points: interest rate determination and exchange rate determination. Thus there is not a single logic to equilibration in these markets, but a dual one. Observed market outcomes are a reflection of the 'balance' between the interest rate and the exchange rate components, and they therefore do not secure the expected global continuity in the international money system.

Two (not incompatible) options are therefore followed. One is to take exchange rates conceptually out of the sphere of money *per se*, and view them as relative asset prices (money as store of value, rather than money as medium of exchange). This permits expectations and uncertainty to be structured into the theory of exchange rates, and for the volatility of exchange rates to be posed as a reflection of this inclusion. But the agenda is restricted to an explanation of optimising individuals managing their portfolios. It is not a perspective which contributes to an understanding of the broader, macroeconomic (including global economic) dimensions of recent internationalisation, for it loses the role of money in accumulation, and the role of exchange rates in securing an international money system.

The other option is to identify the relation between domestic determinants of exchange rates within the sphere of monetary theory. For real interest parity to occur, exchange rates must be a direct reflection of resource values in different countries (the purchasing power parity notion of exchange rates[7]). But purchasing power parity exchange rates do not hold in the short or medium term — they are now understood by the neo-classicals to be at best a very long run tendency — 30 years or more (Dornbusch 1988; Mussa 1990). Thus exchange rates are themselves determined in part by forces within the capital market, by processes which are still not well understood, and exchange rate volatility is a direct result (McDonald and Taylor 1990).

As a consequence, there is a risk premium associated with holding particular currencies. The currency risk overrides international interest rate parity. It also creates the appearance of national weightings in money movements, and so the appearance of correlation between national savings and investment (Frankel 1992). The result is 'imperfect' international capital market outcomes within the technical conditions of a (approximately) perfect international capital market.

The neo-classical conception of integration through the model of prefect capital mobility understands any lack of perfect market outcome as a distortion, just as any deviation from perfect competition is constituted as a distortion. This has led the orthodoxy to two related explanations of distortion.

First, because of the technical completeness of international capital markets, distortions (incomplete integration) are understood in terms of individual market dealers operating with incomplete information, particularly in relation to exchange rates. Information is 'incomplete' not just in the sense of extant factual data, but also related to inappropriate expectations of future market movements, which are no less important in determining current decisions.

In response to this problem, theoretical solutions are thought to lie in imputing certain strategic behaviour onto individual market dealers (hence 'rational expectations'). Policy solutions are thought to lie in improving information. Thus more fundamental questions about the changing nature of internationalised accumulation are converted into an individualised impediment to perfection.

Second, the association of integration with globalised perfect competition has reduced the role of nation states to passive responder; the facilitator of market outcomes. Where the state initiates intervention in the conditions of international capital movement, it creates distortions. Conversely, 'misalignments' in (internationalised) financial market prices creates the terrain for state macroeconomic policy. Here, too, there is debate within the orthodoxy about 'correct' macroeconomic policy. Nonetheless, the shared position is that active state intervention retards integration.

In summarising this brief review of the mainstream economic analysis, the history of the past twenty years can bee seen to play out its ambiguities. Trade, investment and finance now flow across national borders, and markets are integrated, in a way completely unexpected twenty five years ago; but it has not involved the emergence of a 'seamless globe'. Exchange rates have been floated but they remain volatile. They have not secured a stable international money system. Trade barriers are lifting, but balance of payments current accounts are not gravitating towards balance. There is even a momentum for the formalisation of various types of multi-national integration: European free trade and currency union and the North American Free Trade Agreement (NAFTA) stand out. Yet such developments have not been without their contradictions. European currency union has run aground on the rocks of Danish and British nationalism. The 'microeconomic' efficiencies of integration are not being reconciled with the macroeconomic pursuit of national state management. NAFTA has created North American integration, but at some cost of an increase in (collective) isolation from the rest of the world.

What marks the mainstream approach to recent internationalisation is its inability to constitute these various developments as contradictions — that the national form and global economic processes are bound together, but in unpredictable and unresolvable ways. It is the tensions between the national and the global which create historical developments. So the best data sets and the most elaborate resource flow models cannot explain the constitution of the national dimension of accumulation in a world of globally integrated, yet discontinuous, capital movements.

A Marxist Agenda of Analysis

For much radical analysis, recent internationalisation has been about the decline of national autonomy, and the reduced power of the nation state to regulate accumulation. This interpretation, which will be addressed in Chapter 3, should not be confused with Marxism. For Marxism, recent internationalisation calls forth no such judgments. Internationalisation is more a matter of 'situating' the conspicuous trend to cross-national movement of capital and integrated markets within the process of accumulation and class relations, mediated by a system of nation states, and then posing the way in which this trend has transformed the contradictions of capitalist accumulation. It is appropriate to first characterise the process of international movement of capital within a Marxist framework, and then see how the national form is constituted, and being reconstituted, within that process.

Internationalisation of Capital, Not Just TNCs

Marxist analysis of internationalisation focuses on the spatial extension of capital. The term 'capital' has multiple uses within Marxism, reflecting the multiple aspects of capital, but also adding some linguistic confusion. It is important to avoid the confusion, and also to identify the relation between the different aspects of capital. There are two forms of capital, and two units of aggregation of capital. One form of capital is the class relations which define capitalism — Marx's proposition that capital is not a thing but a social relation between the class of capital and the class of labor. The other form is capital as value, where internationalisation involves the spatial movement of value — Marx's conception of capital as the social relation of value in movement. The processes which determine value accumulation involve the interactive relation of money, production and commodities to which the class relations of capitalism give rise — their interdependence and their contradictory relations.[8]

Capital as money, value and commodities, and as a class relation, can be understood within two units of aggregation: individual capitals and total capital. Individual capital can be equated with a firm or company, although because companies are legal entities, not defined with reference to the movement of money, production and commodities, the equation is only approximate. So individual capitals are the units within which capital circulates, and the units within which class relations are 'played out' as a labor process. Total capital is the aggregation of individual capital, and thus the aggregate movement of value. It is also the unit in which class relations are understood as broader economic relations between all capital and all labor.

Capital as value moves between the forms of money, production and commodities in a process of competition. This is not just competition in the neo-classical sense of market structures, but the process in which capitals seek a maximum share of total surplus value (Bryan 1985). In this conception, competition is the process by which capital circulates, and 'resources' are allocated to different uses. Thus the process of competition is not restricted to inter-corporate relations of exchange — competition occurs also within corporations, in the way investment funds are allocated between alternative uses. Indeed, it can be argued that the largest corporations are those which are most responsive to investment options, because they face more choices than do smaller and specialised firms as to how to reinvest their surplus (Clifton 1977). In this sense, there is no incompatibility between corporate size and the process of competition (Jenkins 1987:Ch.3).

For Marxism, wherever there is movement of capital, there is a process of competition which determines the 'terms' of its movement.[9] Total capital, as the aggregate of the movement of capital between the forms of money, production and commodities, therefore cannot be conceived outside of competition. As competition is global, so also is total capital. By a combination of exchange between individual capitals, and resource movements within individual capitals, value is created and moved (circulated) around the world. But individual capitals, which are but components of total capital, have all manner of different forms and degrees of cross-national movement. They may be transnational corporations, or they may simply use imported components, or even purchase components from a firm which borrowed internationally, and will pay interest internationally. These are all the individually 'small' international links which add up to globally integrated total capital.

Recent internationalisation is involving the growing global integration of individual capitals, in addition to the inherently global nature of capital overall (total capital), and this is the critical, distinctive aspect of 'recent internationalisation'. It means that individual capitals have increased their direct, perhaps even 'conscious', integration into international economic calculation; they are actively international in orientation, rather than localised recipients of destinies determined 'out there' in the international 'system'. This does not mean that individual capitals have all become transnational corporations, but that individual decisions with respect to accumulation are now made explicitly on the basis of international options and international constraints. The dominance of money within recent internationalisation has served to internationalise most all individual capitals through their call on (internationally-mobile) money capital to fund investment.[10]

Nonetheless, there is a widespread conception held within Marxism, and the 'left' generally, that TNCs are the centre-piece of the internationalisation of capital. Some broad empirical evidence identifying the growth of TNCs since the 1970s has already been observed in Chapter 1. Concern here is with how the focus on TNCs as the bearers of internationalisation serves to limit, and to foreclose debate on, the range of issues to be addressed in a Marxist conception of internationalisation.

The identification of contemporary international capitalism with the pervasive power of TNCs has a long tradition within 'Marxism'. Indeed, the characterisation of a discrete branch of 'neo-Marxism' depends centrally on the capacities attributed to TNCs.[11] Many analyses, theoretical and empirical, address internationalisation in terms of the pattern of international industry relocation. Here, pre-eminence is attributed to the centralised power of TNCs, either in initiating this process of industrial change, or in being the principal beneficiaries of the change.

From those who see TNCs as initiating change, it is widely suggested, for example, that TNCs have 'constructed' a New International Division of Labor. TNCs are relocating investment in certain industries from the advanced capitalist countries to the 'peripheral' countries in order to reduce costs of production by means of the 'periphery's' supply of low wages and surplus labor (for example Froebel *et al.* 1980; Frank 1980). The New International Division of Labor thesis will be looked at in Chapter 3, as a theory of restructuring.

Those who see TNCs as the principal beneficiaries of internationalisation, whether or not they are the initiators, focus on the gains of internalised spatial specialisation for TNCs. A global horizon to accumulation creates flexibility for TNCs, for internal units of the firm can shift on a global scale to gain maximum advantage: they can globally integrate their productive capacities by producing components and assembling where it is cheapest; they can shift their financial assets in the way which is most profitable (Harrison 1987; Scott and Storper 1986).

There is no doubt that TNCs are a powerful agency in the internationalisation of capital, and they must be part of any theory of internationalisation. But to make them the centre-piece leads to two misconceptions.

First, a focus on TNCs limits the range of processes within the circuit of social capital which come under the rubric of internationalisation. This follows directly from the Marxist concept of capital, discussed above. The internationalisation of capital involves the international movement of money (M) and commodities (C) as well as the international relocation of productive capital (P). The focus on TNCs addresses directly just the third of these; that is, companies which undertake production (P) in more than one country. Of course, TNCs do engage extensively in the international movement of money and commodities, but these movements are taken to be germane only insofar as they are attached to the operation of TNCs: they are not forms of internationalisation in themselves which warrant their own specific analysis. To restrict internationalisation to the former, even to pose them as the primary determinant of internationalisation, leaves aside a large proportion (quantitatively) of internationalised capital, and makes the pattern of internationalisation appear much more simple than it must indeed be.

Second, and following the point above, the focus on TNCs gives to internationalisation a 'premature' institutional perspective (TNCs as companies rather than organisational forms taken by capital). It is premature because, while an explanation of internationalisation should be able to comprehend the institutional forms of its occurrence, our understanding must also comprehend the underlying processes of which institutional forms are an expression (Marx 1939:100-01). The focus on TNCs has created the impression that internationalisation and the monopoly power of large corporations are one and the same force. The most conspicuous effect of this institutionalised conception of internationalisation is that it has led to the identification of the contradictions of internationalisation in terms of contradictory institutional relations, again limiting the range of contradictions thrown up by the process of internationalisation. In particular, the contradiction which has structured much of this analysis is whether internationalisation (meaning the extension of TNCs) has increased or decreased the regulatory power of nation state institutions and, as a corollary, the extent to which TNCs have eradicated national autonomy.

The celebrated debate between Robin Murray and Bill Warren (Murray 1971; Warren 1971, reprinted in Radice 1975) is the first round of this polemic,[12] but it remains on-going, with authors demanding their readers choose between the proposition that TNCs are all-powerful or that the nation state remains sovereign (for example Lipietz 1987; Gordon 1988). This formulation has served to drive Marxism into the same limitation which has constrained the mainstream analysis. Instead of the microeconomics of integrated markets, we have the integrating power of TNCs; and instead of the macroeconomics of national policy, we have the macro politics of (eradicated) national sovereignty.

The alternative formulation of the question contends that recent internationalisation has not made the general nature of capitalism more international: (total) capital has always moved internationally and classes have always been international in nature. But total capital, though in its expression as so many individual capitals, has been mediated by political boundaries. Class relations, too, take a predominantly national form. The neo-classical bind of explaining the national form within internationally-integrated markets becomes the centre-piece of the Marxist analysis. Hence the on-going debate about TNCs and national sovereignty does signal an important issue which the neo-classicals have been unable to capture, but which must be central to a Marxist analysis: the way in which the role of national policy, and of the nation state itself, has been transformed in recent history.

The critical development required of Marxism, therefore, is to pose the relation of the national form to global accumulation in a way not reliant on market imperfections to signal national difference, and constrained by an assessment of the relative strengths of state and corporate institutions.

Internationalisation and the National Question

For economic analysis, the relation of the national form to global accumulation pivots directly on the role of the state in accumulation: that there can be no capitalist accumulation without a capitalist state. This does not, *ipso facto*, imply a nation state. There are also supra-national state functions. The agenda for European economic union and some of the operations of institutions such as the World Bank and International Monetary Fund are state functions not performed by nation states.[13] There is also an aspiration, expressed by some Keynesians, for a global state to manage the global financial system and counter-cyclical policy. Nonetheless, in the past and foreseeable future, it is nation states which secure the conditions of accumulation.

The 'national question' has a long history in Marxist debate. Much of the debate about the nation in the context of internationalisation is not applied to the current issues of recent internationalisation. The debates have focused on nationalism, and the question of imperialism and nationalist opposition. Thus they have been informed by a directly politicised agenda, posed in the issue of whether nationalist movements are, or can be, progressive from the perspective of socialism.

It is not within the objective of the current analysis to consider these political/strategic issues. With recent internationalisation, and the growing integration of national economic processes into a global process, there remains the underlying question of national differences, and how these relate to a thesis of the internationalisation of capital.

Here, there are two related issues. The first is whether the national economy remains an 'economic reality' in the sense of expressing a significant degree of internal coherence and interdependence in production and circulation ('autochthonic accumulation'). The second issue is the survival or indeed development of a nationalist conception of accumulation which occurs within the nation. Though related, these issues are distinct because even though the latter is premised on the reality of the first, it can remain a powerful force even if the first can be shown to be anachronistic.

The answer to the first question is relatively clear (although it is generally clouded by the conflation of these two issues): there is decisive evidence of the continuing demise of national economies as distinct entities. Its most conspicuous expression is found in increasingly rapid international transmission of economic cycles: that booms, recessions, inflation and unemployment are now shared international experiences from which national economic policy can provide little long-term insularity. This can be verified by evidence of increased capital mobility and increasing ratios of traded goods and services to national output, the almost-universally-accepted notion that national markets and processes are being integrated into international markets and processes — in short, what has here been termed recent internationalisation. Of course, this is occurring in different ways and at different paces for different regions (nations). It manifests as reduced domestic linkages between industries and reduced association between local industry and local ownership of capital. It eradicates the notion of nationals having a 'shared' experience of the international economy; except for the fact that the second issue inserts itself to transform the perception of experience.

This second issue relates to the role of state policies to socialise those individual experiences of the international economy. This issue of explaining nationality becomes an aspect of the wider issue of nationalism *qua* patriotism: the construction of national culture and identity (including economic identity), or what Benedict Anderson (1983) characterises as "imagined communities". It involves the recognition that the concept of a national economy is itself a part of the construction of national identity, and that, in important respects, the national economy is an 'imagined economy'. It is the image of the national economy that makes it 'real'.

Anderson (and indeed all analyses of nationalism) poses roughly the same question of why individuals who have no direct personal relation and indeed may exist in a social relation of inequality and exploitation still conceive of a community of "deep, horizontal comradeship". An equivalent question is why individual capitals (or firms) and people in their capacity as economic agents are perceived to have a common experience of, and goals with respect to, accumulation. It should be noted, however, that the questions are different in an important respect. There is a difference between society's perception of capital (firms, products) as belonging to it, and capital's 'perception' of its own belonging. Capitals (strictly, the agents of capital), as will be seen in Chapter 5, can be entirely self-conscious as to whether they project a national identity — it is a strategic calculation. Nonetheless, the image of the national economy requires at some level that industry is identified with nation.

But what Anderson goes on to argue is that while nationalism may have had its origins in the rise of the 'modern' state, particularly as a European experience, it was transported by imperialism to the rest of the world, but thereby becoming a series of 'modular' experiences which could be copied and contrived. Nationalism in its modern form became a conscious construction. As Anderson observes, "the one persistent feature of this style of nationalism was, and is, that it is *official* i.e. something emanating from the state" (1983:145). Similarly, Balibar emphasises the importance of the state in the construction of *homo nationalis* (1991).

Economic processes are similarly being constructed along nationalist lines. In this context, Radice has posed the image of the national economy as a 'Keynesian myth' (1984). The argument here is that the Keynesian (post-war nationally-oriented policy going under the label of Keynesianism) conception of national accounting and its associated program of national economic management have imposed the conception of national coherence and cohesiveness which is incompatible with the wide-spread international mobility of capital. In this post 'Keynesian' world, the image of the national economy is, at best, an anachronism.

But while the image of the national economy must be understood as a construct, perhaps consistent for a time with 'Keynesianism', nor was it a 'myth' in the sense of being 'false'. Rather, the post-war economic nationalism of 'Keynesianism', which focused on independence and sovereignty, went into decline as the recent internationalisation of capital undermined the material basis of a theory of domestically-centred accumulation. In its place, we found the ascendancy in the 1980s and 1990s of a 'new', internationally-oriented economic nationalism.[14]

The new nationalism is associated with the agenda of international competitiveness: the pursuit of national industries' performance in international markets. This is in direct contrast with the 'old' nationalist focus on the domestic aggregates of demand, investment, employment, etc., and the application of state policy to regulate those aggregates. The new nationalism of state policy focuses directly on the nation's international standing. The balance of payments, particularly export performance and the level of foreign debt, even the level of the exchange rate, are understood as international judgments of shared national performance. Improving the balance of payments has become, throughout the world, an issue of national pride. The role of balance of payments accounting in internationalised accumulation, and in the construction of economic nationhood, is addressed in detail in Chapter 7.

What makes this a new nationalism is not that the balance of payments is a recently-discovered monitor of the national economy, but that the increased international mobility of capital has made all the aggregates which make up the balance of payments and determine exchange rates much less subject to direct national state control. 'Free' international movement of money means that exchange rates are difficult for nation states to regulate, and flows of credit, and thus income remittances shown in the current account, are largely beyond national-state control. Indirectly, international integration has left commodity markets, and thus cross-national commodity flows less subject to national restrictions. With reduced use of direct controls over cross-national flows of money and commodities, state policy becomes posed in terms of creating the 'right environment' for capital itself to deliver the desired outcome for the nation.

In this context, state policy for national management increasingly takes the form of exhortation for the nation to become more productive and, in the case of 'the nation's debt', more contrite. Accumulation has increasingly assumed the metaphor of an international sporting contest, with 'national' industry as the players[15] and the state as manager. Allusions to 'level playing fields', the international arena, and various notions of sacrifice for the collective long term good, not to mention the whole vocabulary of competition, are expressions of the metaphor. It is by this means that 'economic' and 'political' analysis become re-integrated by their shared national objectives, with class reduced to, at most, a secondary issue of distributional equity.

So while capital is increasingly internationally mobile, making the national economy in the Keynesian sense increasingly false (domestic linkages, exclusive of international determinants, are not dominant), the national economy remains a pre-eminent ideological construction. The fact that it is no longer based in nationally autochthonic accumulation means that the ideology of economic nationalism is being constructed differently, but it plays no less a role in organising accumulation and class processes. And, recalling Anderson's emphasis, the critical feature of both the 'old' and 'new' nationalisms is that they emanate from the state. For this reason, if no other, the nation state must be central to an understanding of the internationalisation of capital.

Internationalisation, but Not Uniformity

Some observers, particularly within the tradition of 'world systems theory', have postulated that common determinants are creating cross-national uniformity of economic experience; if not global uniformity, then at least bipolar uniformity within the 'core' and 'periphery' countries. More often, the uniformity of experience thesis is put by those who wish to caricature a focus on internationalisation in order to assert its antithesis: the primacy of national sovereignty and discrete national experiences (Aglietta 1982; Gordon 1988; Lipietz 1984). But the polemic is unhelpful, and ultimately based on a simplistic conception of the relation between capital and the state as having 'competing' powers.

Common determinants should not be interpreted to mean 'gravitation to a norm', as if capitalism everywhere is becoming indistinguishable. While there are elements of this tendency, particularly seen in the global standardisation of commodities and the international integration of production systems, it does not provide a working principle for explaining observable change in the world. But it does offer, to some degree, a general measure of what observable regional (national) change is a reaction to.

In part, this is a national question; that different societies with different histories, different class compositions and different forms of integration into international accumulation display different expressions of internationalising capital. Hence, a theory of internationalisation is at once a theory of the nation — the way in which internationalisation is associated with the reproduction of nationalism, and hence national difference.

More fundamentally, the idea must be rejected that internationalisation is causing capitalism everywhere to gravitate to a norm because there is no 'norm' of capitalism. There is no single strategy to secure profitability; no decreed priorities of state economic management; and no linear path of development. Indeed, the adaptability of capitalist accumulation to different forms of class relations, different industrial processes, and different forms of state power is a characteristic of its historical flexibility and resilience.[16] Developments in the application of casual and self-employed labor, which is the focus of theories of 'post-Fordism', discussed in more detail in Chapter 3, illustrate the adaptability of capitalist class relations in the late twentieth century, while still being driven by the same goal of the appropriation of surplus value from labor.

Nonetheless, with the internationalisation of capital, the various forms of class relations — from the peasant household to the worker-managed factory — become increasingly subject to the ubiquitous rule of a unified capitalist calculation. By capitalist calculation is meant the requirement of capital to expand its value, and the requirement of those who administer capital to organise the process of investment, production and exchange to facilitate the pursuit of this requirement.

While the analysis here will be focusing on internationalisation and the 'advanced industrial' nations, it is worth considering briefly the pervasive impact of capitalist calculation in other social formations. Peasant farmers, for example, may appear to be isolated from the 'global market' (except in the case of production of exportables), but they are not isolated from the dictates of capitalist calculation. As the market for money capital is an internationalised market, peasant access to credit establishes an international link, with credit advanced on the basis of its expected rate of return, and interest on loans becoming internationalised surplus value. Indeed, with credit to peasants coming from supra-national institutions like the World Bank, the link between peasant production and the most internationalised form of finance can be quite direct. Moreover, access to international credit, providing peasants with means to increase their productivity (rate of surplus value), may even dictate requirements of technological development in household production in order to ensure that costs remain competitive with other quarters of the market. In short, credit brings both competition and international market determination to the peasant household: the two elements of capitalist calculation.[17]

It is by means of the imposition of capitalist calculation that the 'leadership' of money in recent internationalisation is critical, for the money form of capital most readily converts distinct and spatially diverse activities into a common unit of measurement (calculation). Put simply, this dominance of money has asserted the primacy of an internationally-determined rate of return on economic activity, though without determining how that rate of return must be achieved. This calculation therefore operates as a limiting factor — dictating what class relations and what industrial organisation are not sustainable, and specifying the criterion to which they must adapt. But there is no specification of what they must be or become.

So the international mobility dominates, but does not determine in any precise sense transformations in accumulation. The task for analysis is therefore to identify the various ways in which the tendency towards unified calculation is expresses, and to identify the multiple points of resistance to that process which secure or retain differences within that unity. This is the general level at which the internationalisation of capital expresses a contradictory process, with indeterminate outcomes. 'Beneath' it is a series of contradictory relations, expresses as relations between classes, relations between different parts of capital, and, derived from the latter, relations between nation states, which determine the observable differential impact of internationalisation in different sites.

Conclusion

While there has been a dramatic international integration of individual capitals in the past twenty years, society is ordered internationally through a system of nations, in which nation states are both defining and central. For the neo-classical orthodoxy, this reality represents a theoretical bind. The reliance on ahistorical categories and the preoccupation with market outcomes means that nations exist conceptually as discrete entities and by assumption, and appear in the analysis as the source of distortions in global markets.

For Marxism, the relation of the nation to internationalisation presents (or need present) no such bind. National processes cannot be disentangled from international processes, and any attempt to do so immediately denies the profound impact of recent internationalisation. National processes may not be domestically centred. The nation state is not inherently nationalistic. What the recent internationalisation of capital shows is that the role of the nation state in securing the conditions of accumulation is not an exclusively national function: as part of its domestic role, the nation state must mediate the conditions under which different parts of capital engage with the circulation of capital internationally.

The relation between the internationalisation of capital and national forms therefore has two dimensions. One is the relation between internationalised accumulation and national economies, where the latter are understood as socially constructed. The second is the relation between international accumulation and the nation state, where the state plays an indispensable role in securing the reproduction of (international) accumulation. If we further proffer that the image of the national economy is itself a construction of the state — for reasons of 'national political harmony' — then the contradictions of internationalisation become expressed inherently within the nation state, in the dual requirements of nationalism and internationalism.

Since states (understood historically as nation states) are indispensable to (internationalised) accumulation, the principal contradiction is not that between the nation state on the one hand, and internationalised capital on the other, as much Marxist analysis and 'world systems theory' would postulate. It is the contradiction of the inability of nation states to successfully secure the conditions of reproduction of internationalised accumulation. This inability then manifests as a contradiction both within internationalised accumulation (that the necessary functions of the state performed on behalf of capital cannot be performed with international coherence) and within nation states themselves (as the inability to reconcile the duality of nationalism and internationalism).

This latter dimension of the contradiction has been manifesting since the 1980s as the inability of state economic policy to reconcile the conditions required for cross-national movement of capital with 'domestic' economic management. Strategies for international competitiveness conflict with strategies for employment generation. Interest rate strategies face the contradiction of the 'needs' of the balance of payments for capital inflow, and the 'needs' of the national economy for investment management. The sectional pressure for protectionism, most conspicuously in the United States and France, are in conflict with national commitments to free trade, as found in NAFTA and the Uruguay Round of GATT. Similarly, the 'sterling crisis' of September 1992 has raised for the British state, and by implication for all European currency states, the contradictions involved in reconciling the facilitation of international (European) accumulation with the perceived necessity of domestic 'management' in the face of recession.

These policy 'crises' are all being played out within each country as specific and national policy dilemmas and debates. But the universal nature of the underlying contradiction is clear. Moreover, as a general tendency, it is apparent that each state, while unable to reconcile the opposed needs of capital, is responding to the aggregate agenda of capital, compared with labor. The corollary is that the domestic role of the state, in reproducing class relations consistent with this international agenda, is oriented towards the reproduction of a specific image of the national community: the 'internationally competitive' economy, in which increased rates of surplus value, by lower wages or higher productivity (generally both) are paramount.

Notes

1.   The agenda of open-economy macroeconomics is developed in Chapter 6.
2.   This is considered in Chapter 6 in relation to monetary policy; and Chapters 8 and 9 in relation to balance of payments policy.
3.   Here is the neo-classical support for the proposition in Chapter 1 that international resource flows alone are an inadequate indicator of internationalisation.

4. The model of perfect competition is only an allegory for understanding the neo-classical conception of economic processes, so the finding that 'reality' does not exactly fit the model is not to be taken as a critique of the model, nor of its usefulness in understanding reality.

5. The difference between covered- and uncovered-interest parity is central here, for uncovered interest rate parity by and large reflects exchange rate movements. This gives covered interest rate parity (comparative national interest rates with 'allowance' for exchange rates) the appearance of much greater equality.

6. See Frankel (1992) for a review.

7. Purchasing power parity is considered in more detail in Chapter 6. In the current context, it is sufficient to equate purchasing power parity with exchange rates which serve to equalise prices internationally.

8. This approach is further developed in Chapter 4.

9. A more technical version of this proposition is that competition determines the commensurability of capital value as it moves between the forms of money production and commodities. See Bryan (1985).

10. The close parallels between this and the neo-classical conception of global integration should be acknowledged.

11. See Jenkins (1987) for an considered discussion.

12. In a non-Marxist framework, Raymond Vernon (1971) was an original contribution to the proposition that TNCs were undermining the power of nation states.

13. There is a literature which contends that 'international' institutions like the International Monetary Fund and the World Bank are only supra-national in appearance, for they in fact express the international interests of the United States (for example, George 1992). It is not the purpose of the current study to determine whose interests are being served by these institutions, but it must be recognised that they are performing state functions, and at a 'level above' the nation state.

14. For a discussion in the Australian context, see Bryan (1991).

15. Whether 'foreign' firms are seen to be playing for their country-of-residence or country-of-origin is often a point of domestic political debate.

16. It is the appropriation of a surplus from labor in the value form which is the critical defining characteristic of capitalism. Debates over which societies and which production activities are to be classified as 'capitalist', a debate which is generally recognised to reach its height with the contribution of Brenner (1977), appear overly centred on the immediate relations of production, to the neglect of the broader issues of capitalist accumulation.

17. This form of analysis of household production has been developed particularly by M.P. Cowan (for example 1986).

3

Internationalisation, Crisis and Restructuring

In Chapter 1, a process of 'recent internationalisation' of capital was identified with developments in capitalism since the end of the 'long boom' in the international economy, and particularly with international money market integration which accelerated in the 1980s. The question remains, however, as to the relationship of internationalisation to the end of the long boom or, for shorthand, the relationship of internationalisation to a period of sustained international 'crisis'.

This chapter explores this relationship in the context of analyses of the international 'restructuring' of capital. Capital is, of course, in a continual process of change: it is always, in some sense, 'restructuring', including in an international-spatial dimension. But the term 'restructuring' means more than change *per se*. It refers to something systematic about change; in its global-spatial dimension, something systematic about the international mobility of capital (the movement of money and commodities, and the changing location of production). In identifying this system, the analytical dilemma, as with all generalisations, is to identify coherence but without transgressing the reality of diversity. As 'reality' is intrinsically diverse, in the sense of each movement of capital having specific determinants, the identification of systematic change focuses on underlying determinants, and this makes 'restructuring' an explicitly theoretical question.

Diverse contemporary explanations of restructuring have made certain essential assumptions about the nature of the changes which have been characterised as 'recent internationalisation': that restructuring since the 1970s has been a response to an international crisis of profitability; and that restructuring can be understood as changing relations between national units. In combination, they propose that

45

restructuring is the process by which capital's response to crisis changes (amongst other things) the relations between nations.

Of course, not all explanations of restructuring are based on either or both these assumptions, and where these assumptions are apparent, there is still scope for fundamentally different interpretations of restructuring. But their widespread adoption, particularly in combination, warrants critical assessment. It will be contended that both assumptions have led to a restricted appreciation of the impact and momentum of international restructuring.

Some leading theories of restructuring which embody the dual emphasis on restructuring as a response to crisis, understood through a national spatial grid, will be looked at shortly. The New International Division of Labor thesis and theories of 'post-Fordism', perhaps the pre-eminent theories of restructuring, both express this emphasis. Before these theories are addressed directly, it is appropriate to consider the underlying assumptions in turn.

Internationalisation, Accumulation and Crisis

The characterisation of a phenomenon of 'recent internationalisation' in Chapter 1 was somewhat tentative — internationalisation certainly did not begin with the end of the long boom, and its relation to the end of the boom is not to be taken for granted.

Two issues arise here which are often, but should not be, conflated. One is internationalisation as the manifestation of capitalism's capacity to transform the forces of production: the way in which internationalisation expresses new opportunities for expansion, associated directly with the development of the forces of production — the technical conditions which have increased the need for extended markets and reduced the costs of traversing space, and, associated with it, the more global outlook of the managers of capital. In Chapter 1, the necessity of export markets for the efficient use of manufacturing technology was identified; as was the computer technology which permitted and, by the process of competition, necessitated the extension of movement of money capital. These developments created new potential for change in the spatial pattern of accumulation.

The second issue is internationalisation as the manifestation of counter-tendencies to crisis: that recent internationalisation has arisen in reaction to protracted international economic instability and slump (crisis for short), which has lasted since the end of the long boom. Here, the standard emphasis is on the shift of manufacturing to low wage countries, and the rise of internationally sourced credit. Certainly, to pose international restructuring as a 'response to crisis' imposes a causal and functional relationship which is by no means clear — that in the absence of crisis the tendency for capital to internationalise would have been qualitatively and quantitatively different: at the limit, unchanged from the 1960s. This is indeed a bold proposition, yet one rarely contested in theories of restructuring.

Of particular concern is that these theories of restructuring actually avoid investigation of the connection between crisis and restructuring. Reorganised (internationalised) accumulation is simply characterised as a 'new era', where the attribution of novelty too often suffices for an explanation of change. Indeed, by such formulations we lose perspective on the degree of change (as found in notions that the United States or Britain have been 'deindustrialised', when the reality is the closure of some industrial plants, albeit with profound regional consequences); and lose perspective on what is preserved and reproduced by means of the change.

It is nonetheless true that restructuring and the international movement of capital have been transformed with the end of the long boom, and that both processes can be understood in some part as a response to profit downturn. But these processes are also an expression of the development of the forces of production. There are elements of both rupture and continuity. There is need for an appreciation of the relationship between internationalisation of accumulation and crisis tendencies of capitalism which is neither functionalist nor deterministic.

In the analysis so far, and often in Marxist theory generally, capitalism has been understood as a system of expanded reproduction. This is indeed the partial orientation of the system, and it explains why capitalism, unlike all previous epochs, has expanded so rapidly society's capacity for wealth generation. Moreover, the orientation towards expansion is built into the system of capitalism. The mobility of capital, and the process of competition between capitals to increase their share of surplus value, both ensure that capital must expand in order to survive. In the process, the forces of production are developed, which gives capitalism its enormous wealth-creating capacity and adaptability.

Yet this is only a partial depiction of the orientation of capitalist accumulation,[1] for the expanded reproduction of capital is neither guaranteed nor self-sustainable, either for individual capitals or for capitalism as a whole. Experience since the 1970s, with continuing periods of stagnation and recession, has shown this empirically. (Broadly) Marxist theories of crisis (and there are many, mutually-reinforcing aspects of 'crisis') have argued the tendency theoretically. Thus the tendency towards crisis should be seen as equally much a component of the capitalist mode of production as is the process of expansion.

Marxism's focus on the contradictory relations of capitalism gives central attention to economic crises. Crisis may come from any source which interrupts the accumulation of capital — from a crisis of confidence in the money system, to social upheavals which impede production. They all cause the movement of capital to stall: in the first case by its 'failure' to convert from commodities to money; in the second case because of its 'failure' to convert from money to commodities and from commodities to production.

The form of crisis on which Marx himself focused was the tendency of the rate of profit to fall, associated with the rising organic composition of capital. The essential proposition here is that competition would 'force' capitalists to replace labor with machines in order to reduce their individual costs of production, but, in the process, the expulsion of living labor from production reduces the total amount of surplus value which the capitalists have to divide amongst themselves. Hence the search for individual profits causes the overall rate to fall.

Marx's particular interest in this source of crisis was that it is associated with the underlying dynamic of capitalist expanded reproduction, in that the 'ultimate' origin lies in the contradiction between the forces and relations of production: the development of the forces of production, manifesting in the rising organic composition, is in contradiction with the relation of capitalist production expressed as free wage labor rendering surplus value. Thus the 'law' of the tendency of the rate of profit to fall demonstrated capitalism to be unstable and ultimately unsustainable.

Yet this particular relationship was posed by Marx only as a tendency (that is, only under certain assumptions), and he also identified counter-tendencies which would help to sustain the rate of accumulation: in particular, increases in the rate of surplus value; wages reduced below the value of labor power; cheapening the elements of constant capital, and, notably in the context of internationalisation, foreign trade (1894 Ch.14). Marx attributes to foreign trade diverse capacities to increase the rate of profit:

> In so far as foreign trade cheapens on the one hand the elements of constant capital and on the other the necessary means of subsistence into which variable capital is converted, it acts to raise the rate of profit by raising the rate of surplus-value and reducing the value of constant capital. It has a general effect in this direction in as much as it permits the scale of production to be expanded (1894:344).

Both the tendency to crisis and the counter-tendencies must be understood as contingent issues of capitalist development — the organic composition of capital does not automatically rise, nor do the elements of constant capital automatically cheapen over time, although both are likely elements of the process of competition to reduce costs of production. Nonetheless, there is a clear message for the interpretation of accumulation: unless the counter-tendencies are occurring, it is likely that the tendency towards crisis will be realised.

Hence, what we observe of capitalist accumulation, both for individual capitals and for total capital, is not so much the falling rate of profit tendency, but the 'successful' operation of the counter-tendencies. For example, Marx says of foreign trade in the context of counter-tendencies that "it becomes the specific product of the capitalist mode of production ... through the inner necessity of this mode of production and its need for an ever-extended market" (1894:334).

The tendency for the rate of profit to fall may be critical to an explanation of periods of recession, but the so-called counter-tendencies appear as the 'norm' of capitalist development, in both boom and crisis. In booms, these counter-tendencies can increase the rate of profit. In crises, no matter what their cause, the counter-tendencies are required to increase the rate of surplus value and of profit. In this sense, the counter-tendencies are not simply activated at times of crisis. They are tendencies in themselves, with their own 'histories' and 'dynamics'. They assume the position of 'counter-tendencies' only by a theoretical juxtaposition with the movement of the organic composition of capital.

Contrary to deterministic interpretations and impressions, the particular forms of crisis cannot be generalised, beyond the most obvious manifestations such as a loss of profitability and rising unemployment. Nor are the counter-tendencies to be understood in a functionalist way as being triggered by the onset of crises. Each crisis has its own path and its own immediate determinants, and each 'recovery' occurs in the context of a different set of on-going 'counter-tendencies'.

The direct concern for analysis is how the contradictory nature of accumulation, and the crisis orientation of capitalism exhibited since the 1970s, relates to the internationalisation of capital. In relation to the two schools of restructuring theory which will be addressed shortly, two fundamental methodological propositions should be noted:

* the rejection of a deterministic and teleological interpretation of accumulation and crisis need not involve a rejection of the proposition that there is an underlying orientation of accumulation towards increasing the rate of surplus value by whatever means can be initiated and implemented. The international movement of capital provides a conduit for that process.

- the relationship between internationalisation and crisis is not exclusive. More than crisis is required to explain internationalisation and more than internationalisation is required to explain crisis.

Thus the question to be asked is not what is the role of internationalisation as an expression of or reaction to crisis, but how has a sustained period of crisis been expressed in the process of internationalisation? The latter is a much more open-ended question, for it leaves the form of internationalisation and the contradictions of internationalisation — in short, the political economy of internationalisation — much more unresolved. The former, by contrast, poses a functionalist role of internationalisation getting accumulation 'back on track', with all the implications of determinism and certainty about accumulation's long-term course.

Crisis in a National Framework

Analyses which attempt to understand recent internationalisation generally start from a conception of accumulation defined with reference to national units; an issue raised in Chapter 2. This starting point proves a fundamental constraint in understanding the current era, because it assumes what is most contentious — that the world is structured by a hierarchy of nations, and that any change must be understood within that hierarchy.

'Classical' Marxist theories of internationalisation — actually, the desire by many subsequent analysts to be seen as inheritors of the classical tradition — are largely responsible for uncritically imposing this framework. While spatial units should be historically defined, for the meaning of space changes over time, reverence to the classical tradition has seen national spatial units, and international relations of national dominance, defined as formal, ahistorical categories.

'Classical' Marxism has left to contemporary analysis two propositions which have come to assume the status of theoretical tenets in contemporary analysis of international restructuring. The first, which is most pervasive, is an understanding of international accumulation in terms of relations between national processes of accumulation. Central here is the notion of over-production in the advanced capitalist countries requiring an international outlet. This can be found in Bukharin (1915:96); and in the underconsumptionist tradition, most particularly Luxemburg (1951) and in the *Monthly Review* School (Baran and Sweezy,

1966 and the *Monthly Review* journal). The widespread acceptance of the *Monthly Review* approach has seen global developments since the end of the long boom frequently posed in terms of the inability of monopoly corporations to remain nationally constrained. This is a direct application of Lenin's analysis of early twentieth century imperialism (1917) to the present.[2] Internationalism, by contrast, appears not so much as a contemporary economic agenda of capital, but as the future political agenda of socialism, tied directly to the assertion of the international unity of the working class.

The second inheritance, which is the extension of the focus on the expansionist requirements of monopoly corporations, is the concept of finance capital, developed at the beginning of the twentieth century by Hilferding (1910) and popularised by Lenin. This concept expresses the unified interests of banks and large-scale industrial corporations. It has been central to the proposition that monopolies and conglomerates must outgrow the national economy, and that in some sense, these institutions have been central in ordering and reordering international accumulation. The understanding of recent internationalisation in terms of the unified expansion of large national banks and large national corporations has served to constrain the understanding of developments and especially contradictions in the relation between money and production in recent internationalisation. In particular, it leaves the relation between money and production centred on national constraints, in contrast to the integrative process of recent internationalisation.

The focus of 'classical' Marxism has dictated the fundamental conception of internationalisation which has dominated contemporary theories of restructuring. The contradictions of accumulation are conceived in national terms. International expansion is the bearer of those contradictions from capital's nation-of-origin, and there may be national rivalries over where capital can extend (as emphasised by Bukharin[3] and Lenin), but internationalisation of itself embodies no inherent contradictions for the expanded reproduction of capital. An appreciation of contradictions internal to international accumulation (as distinct from national contradictions which 'break out' as international expansion) is all but absent from contemporary notions of restructuring.

The contrasting proposition is that the contradictions of international accumulation derive from the fact that the conditions of accumulation are being secured by nation states, while capital itself circulates on a global scale. So the space within which the conditions of accumulation are secured is distinct from the space of accumulation itself, and within this lies the potential for crisis associated with the absence of systematic regulation of globalised accumulation.

Even where accumulation is recognised as a global process, most contemporary 'Marxist', and much non-Marxist analysis, has attempted to comprehend the process of international restructuring by a view of the world comprising a binary opposition of core and peripheral nations. The core is made up of the advanced capitalist countries in which accumulation is largely self-generating; the periphery is made up of those countries in which accumulation is, in some critical sense, externally driven. The essential relation here is that international capital movement involves the core in some sense exploiting the periphery.

The centre-periphery model has provided the means to construct the history of the modern world (world systems theory) and to identify the process by which wealth is drawn from the periphery to the centre (for example, unequal exchange theories); it is also the hallmark of a distinctive school of 'neo-Marxism', or 'dependency theory'. Within this framework, theories differ on how they interpret the determinants of core-periphery relations: the extent to which the core has 'created' the periphery to advance its own accumulation; and the degree to which individual countries are locked into their positions in the core-periphery relation. Yet within these debates over process, the conception of spatial structure goes almost unquestioned.

Much of the debate on 'the world system' as structured relations between centre and peripheral nations has remained unaffected by the profound impacts of recent internationalisation. Chase-Dunn (1981) identified the central dilemma in world systems theory: is the modern world dominated by "one logic or two"? Is it dominated by the logic of all-embracing, globalised accumulation, or by interaction between the independent realms of the process of capitalist development and competition between nation states? While this does indeed characterise the world systems theory dilemma, it is a false dilemma. The analysis in Chapter 1, in focusing on the developments in the internationalisation of money, suggests that this debate is somewhat restricted. It precludes a sustained analysis of the way in which nation states are transformed with international accumulation.

Hence there is no opposition between nation states and international accumulation, but an inability of each to adequately secure conditions of the other, manifesting as a contradiction both within international accumulation and within individual nation states. The limitations of the nationally-centred, centre-periphery models can be seen from a closer inspection of the two dominant theories of restructuring: the New International Division of Labor thesis, and theories of the French Regulation School. Neither is a unified body of thought, so there is no suggestion that there is a single theory of restructuring associated with each. But both, in their fundamental orientation, contend that capitalism has undertaken a qualitative transformation since the end of the long boom, and each emphasises, though to different degrees, the importance of internationalisation as central to this transformation. The explanatory capabilities of both theories are constrained by the assumption of the analytical primacy of national units in identifying the contradictions of internationalisation, and by a mechanistic appreciation of the impact of a crisis of profitability on the process of accumulation.

The New International Division of Labor Thesis

The new international division of labor (NIDL) thesis emerged in the late 1970s, particularly associated with the work of Froebel, Heinrich and Krye (1980), and it has remained an influential theory of restructuring, particularly within a 'world systems' framework. The thesis is based on a recognition that, with the end of the long boom in the international economy, capitalism was reorganising on an international scale.

The essential argument is that manufacturing, which had been at the centre of the protracted post-war boom in the industrialised countries, was being relocated to the low-wage, abundant-labor countries of the 'third world' (from the 'centre' to the 'periphery') in order to increase the rate of profit. As a consequence, many of the older industrial countries have been 'de-industrialised'.[4] Conversely, the recipients of the world's manufacturing industries were emerging, from the position of low-wage, agricultural producers, as the newly industrialising countries (NICs).

Some versions attribute the NIDL to developments in the forces of production (manufacturing labor process; transport and communications) while others attribute the NIDL to the decline in the rate of profit in the advanced countries, leading capital to look for production sites with lower wages.[5] In both versions, international differences in wages is central to the thesis (hence it is a division of labor, not a division of industry thesis). Within global restructuring, the countries which have remained at the top are those which advance beyond mass-production, relatively labor intensive manufacturing, and into control over finance and the frontiers of technology and specialist production.[6] These areas are the key means of control over international accumulation. Thus the NIDL is seen as a construction of capital (particularly TNCs) to re-establish the conditions of accumulation internationally within a period of crisis.

Clearly, there is some broad descriptive appeal in this depiction of the process of restructuring, but it remains constrained by a static, national focus while attempting to depict a dynamic, international process. It is static (strictly speaking, synchronic) in its conception of accumulation; as if one world order is overturned and replaced by another, fully-formed world order (see Lipietz, 1984). As such, the NIDL thesis underestimates the spatial and technical flexibility of capitalist accumulation — that national specialisation is not clearly delineated, let alone determined by direct labor costs. Since wages have always been lower in the periphery than in the centre, there remains the need to explain why the 'new' division of labor emerged when it did — why the relocation of manufacturing was not undertaken before the 1970s. The inability to explain the timing of the NIDL indicates the functionalist conception of internationalisation as arising in response to a crisis in accumulation.

Moreover, cheap labor in the periphery has been over-rated as the source of increased surplus value, to the neglect of processes to increase in the rate of exploitation in the 'old' industrial countries.[7] In some industries in the 'core' the rate of surplus value is increased by attempts to compete directly with low-wage countries on labor costs by means such as wage cuts, lengthened working hours, immigrant labor, casualisation of labor, and the operation of 'backyard sweatshops' and outwork. In other industries, an increased rate of surplus value is pursued by increasing the productivity of labour time (relative surplus value) by advances in technology and initiatives in the organisation of the labour process. This latter response is the focus of theories of 'post-Fordism', and is taken up by the Regulation School.

The critiques of the NIDL thesis as static and regimented is now widely recognised, not least by the Regulation School, most notably Lipietz, which shall be discussed shortly. But there is a further dimension to this critique, which applies in some measure also to the Regulationists, related to the status of national units in understanding the changing pattern of global accumulation. The NIDL thesis suggests that *nations* adopt functional positions in the international economy and that, following the end of the long boom, the international reorganisation of industry can be explained in terms of an amended pattern of national specialisation. When the object of analysis is to explain the consequences of international mobility of capital it seems odd to start with the primacy of national units as economic entities when they are precisely the spatial forms which the mobility of individual capitals has transcended.

It is this primacy of national units which dictates the political response of the adherents to the NIDL thesis, for the invariable political agenda of advocates of the NIDL thesis centres on advocacy of increased national autonomy from internationalised accumulation. The degrees and forms of such programmes are many and diverse, but for each particular nation a common agenda can be observed. Pre-eminent is the perceived need to establish (or re-establish) a diverse industrial structure, particularly its manufacturing base, and a domestic supply of capital to restrict the national outflow of profits and interest payments.

Thus, the NIDL thesis, while having some roots in certain currents of 'classical' Marxism, does not advance the classical political agenda of internationalism. While Lenin saw international 'uneven development' as giving rise to nationalist movements in the 'oppressed', colonised countries as an early stage in the development of capitalism, we now see left-nationalism as re-emergent, and not as a potentially progressive force towards socialist internationalism, but advancing parochial, and hopefully thriving, capitalism, conceived in the name of social democracy and *real politique*.

The French Regulation School

The so-called Regulation School developed in France in the 1970s. Its objective was to identify the structure and patterns of capitalist accumulation in a way roughly consistent with a Marxist framework, but devoid of the determinism thought to be found in the general, eternal laws associated with Marxism (see especially Aglietta 1978; Lipietz 1985, 1987; Boyer 1990). The Regulation School has attempted to show how the dynamics of both the business cycle and major crises depend on the particular forms of productive structures and social relations (Boyer, 1990:viii). By means of historical country studies, particularly of the United States and the major European countries, the Regulationists have sought to establish what is distinctive about the downturn of the 1970s and 1980s, compared with previous downturns, and to understand why different countries have had different experiences of and reactions to the current downturn.

Central to their argument is that the post-war era of mass production and consumption was centred on manufacturing and extractive industries. These were industries in which technology and control over the market made large-scale production of standardised commodities essential. The production process in these industries is idealised as 'Fordism'. It is associated with the concentration of capital, and managerial control (a separation of ownership and control), with the associated ascendancy of a managerial, administrative class and the application of the principles of 'scientific management' ('Taylorism') — in short, the Galbraithian corporation.

The Regulation School contends that the Fordist regime of accumulation in the advanced capitalist countries went into decline with the end of the long boom. The explanation for this is not critical to our understanding. Suffice to say that it was in part associated with the saturation of the market for mass-production goods (see Boyer 1990:89-90) and in part because of the globalisation of capital. Since the mid 1970s, the restructuring of capitalism has led to the ascendancy of a new regime in the advanced capitalist countries and the export of Fordist production to the periphery in search of lower production (wage) costs and to penetrate markets protected by customs barriers.

This new regime in the advanced countries is popularly referred to as 'post-Fordism', although, consistent with the anti-determinism of the French Regulation School, there is a clear reticence to 'over-specify' and 'over-generalise' the regime which replaces Fordism (Boyer 1990:xviii; Clarke 1988:67; Jessop 1988:160). For 'post-Fordism' the hallmarks are flexibility rather than economies of scale and specialist production for niche markets rather than long production runs of standardised goods. Of particular importance is the development of computer technology. This has permitted reduced fixed costs of production, in both plant and equipment and in stock management, and reduced reliance on large supplies of semi-skilled production-line workers in favour of a distinctly segmented labor market: a smaller number of educated, multi-skilled workers and a rump of low-paid, casual workers.[8]

Within the Regulationists' framework, the contradictions of capitalist accumulation are posed in national terms, and this serves to leave an incoherent explanation of the international determinants and pattern of accumulation. It is first necessary to establish the nationalist agenda before the international incoherence can be identified.

Accumulation within each nation is understood as the interaction of the regime of accumulation and the mode of regulation. Differences between nations and differences within nations over time are to be understood as different 'combinations' of regimes and modes.

A regime of accumulation is the conceptual basis on which capitalism can be broadly differentiated into its Fordist and post-Fordist epochs. It is defined as "the stabilisation in the allocation of the product between consumption and accumulation over a longish period" (Lipietz 1984:85), or "a macroeconomic principle which describes compatibility between transformations in production conditions, and in types of usage of social output" (Lipietz 1987a:3). It is to be understood as a scheme of reproduction. But reproduction does not secure itself. The compatibility of production conditions and use of output is only secured by a system of "norms, habits, laws and regulating networks" (Lipietz 1986:19), and this is the mode of regulation.[9]

A succession of different regimes of accumulation is associated with capitalist development, and at the heart of each regime is the labor process. But, in contrast with a deterministic base-superstructure model, there is no notion of evolution in the regime of accumulation calling forth a mode of regulation. Indeed, the mode of regulation may delimit or preclude certain possible regimes of accumulation. More importantly, the mode and regime stabilise together. History, as the combination of various regimes and modes has nothing inevitable about it — it is a matter of what combinations give, for a prolonged period, regularity and stability in the reproduction of social relations.

The mode of regulation centres on institutional processes which secure the sustainability of any regime of accumulation. Key here for the Regulation School is the nation state. According to Lipietz, the nation state "is indeed the archetypal form of any regulation" (1986:21); and the primacy of national institutions in regulating class relations is continually reiterated, for, as Lipietz continues, "it is at this level that the struggle of classes is regulated". Leaving aside the reality of international institutions, legal and economic, which clearly do exert impacts in the regulation of social relations within nations, there seems to be a basic conflation of the level at which the struggle of classes exists, and the level at which the struggle is regulated. We are reminded of the proposition of Marx and Engels that the class struggle is "though not in its substance, yet in its form ... a national struggle" (1848:59). This would suggest that the national-institutional emphasis of the Regulation School has led, in those terms, to the analysis of the form of class relations, and a neglect of their substance.[10]

But the national-centredness of the Regulation School does not rest simply on the conception of a mode of regulation which is defined in terms of national practices and institutions. It is also found in the conception of a 'regime of accumulation' which, it will be recalled, will exist historically only in combination with a 'compatible' mode of regulation. Thus regimes of accumulation are being defined in terms, including spatial categories, which provide for the possibility of consistency with modes of regulation. Thus regimes of accumulation also are defined nationally.

Aglietta, the school's leading theoretician, defines a regime of accumulation in terms of the 'value' creating process, and the circulation of 'value' — apparently directly following the Marxist agenda. But the value creating process is defined differently from Marx,[11] in terms of the wage relation, and his analysis of circulation centres on competition between capitals, expressed as 'competitive' and 'monopoly' modes of regulation. So production and circulation are conceived in institutional terms and not value categories. The purpose is to define the regime of accumulation and the mode of regulation in compatible categories, so as to clarify the terms of their interaction. But institutions invariably take a national form, and the compatibility of categories in the Regulationist framework depends critically on the institution of the nation state. The state is inserted directly into the regime of accumulation, in both the wage system and relations of competition,[12] and the effect is to construct a nation-centred theory of accumulation.

It is entirely appropriate to draw the interconnection between the wage relation and the state. But in a value theoretic form, it is the value of labor power, not wages which is the starting point. At this level of abstraction, the critical issue is not whether nation states exert impact on the value of labor power, which is undoubted, but the relation of a nationally-determined value of labor power to the determination of international commodity values.[13]

The effect is that the national-centredness which is embedded in the concept 'mode of regulation' is found in the same form, and for the same reason in the concept 'regime of accumulation'. The objective of making the categories interactive so as to avoid determinism has been to package them into the same spatial horizons.[14] The possibility that the space of accumulation and the space in which class relations are 'played out' may be different, and that this difference is itself critical to an understanding of both international accumulation and national class relations, is analytically precluded in Regulation theory. That is, the national focus of the theory is built into the categories of analysis and this can only be asserted dogmatically.

With accumulation conceived in national terms, the international economy is conceived only as the nation's "external linkages" (Lipietz 1986:22). These linkages are understood through a core-periphery model of the international economy. Lipietz contends that "the capitalist machinery of extended reproduction cannot be closed off at the core. The exterior brings to it a warm source (labor and raw materials) and a cold source (outlets)" (1986:27). But, different from the NIDL conception of core and periphery relations, the Regulationists contend that where each country locates in the international relations of dominance and dependence (what Lipietz calls its "mode of insertion into the global economy" (1986:24)) is not determined by the country's inherited position in that binary opposition, and that the core does not need to keep the periphery poor (Lipietz 1986:37). These propositions explicitly preclude the notion that a new global order has been 'imposed'. The international pattern of specialisation, as we observe it, constitutes a "find", not a deliberate construction (Lipietz 1986:23). The object of analysis in the Regulation School is the search for patterns and regularities in the conditions of reproduction of accumulation, and for crises or ruptures in those patterns and regularities. These are national patterns which have international expression only by aggregation.

Derived from this framework, the Regulation School contends that each country's response to the crisis of the 1970s was the product of its internal class relations. New regimes of accumulation and their attendant modes of regulation cannot be generalised. Thus there is a rejection of the determinism and functionalism (for the advanced capitalist countries) of the NIDL thesis, outlined above, which sees nations adopting a 'new' position in the international order so as to regenerate the international accumulation of capital.

The end of the long boom, which the Regulation School associates with the demise of the Fordist regime in the advanced capitalist countries, leaves the Regulation School's understanding of the nature of the international movement of capital unchanged. This outcome is not as a product of critical re-evaluation of the nature of capital movement and integration, but because the nation-centred categories of analysis mean that the question is not posed.

The consequence is that the Regulation School offers us a choice of extremes in understanding the global economy: either it must be understood as a system of interacting states, each state with its own regime of accumulation and mode of regulation, and its own 'mode of insertion' within the global economy; or, we must "declare that the world economy has been instituted from the start as a unique regime of accumulation with its forms of global regulation", and this would be to suppose that "on a global scale, economic exchange, social norms, codified procedures guaranteed by a unique sovereignty and eventually delegated to local states, have been instituted at the same time" (Lipietz 1986:21).

If this were indeed a real choice, the answer would be obvious. Hence Aglietta can confidently assert, apparently as self-evident, "the primacy of the national dimension" and that the world economy is to be understood "as a system of interacting national social formations" (1982:6). And Aglietta will countenance no debate:

> The main currents of thought on the world economy can be distinguished from one another, amongst other things, by the precise importance they attach to the national dimension. For neo-classicists, as well as for supporters of the 'globalist' ideology propagated by the multinationals and transmitted by the communications media, there is a one-way process of the unification of economic relations (1982:5).

But the choice is not real; indeed it shows the limitation of the Regulation School's conception of the global economy, for by definition there cannot be a global regime of accumulation and mode of regulation,[15] as these categories have been defined in terms of national institutions. We are cornered in a nationalist perspective, and a global dimension is simply dismissed.

The inevitability of this conclusion warrants reiteration. The Regulation School has set as its agenda the identification of long term patterns in accumulation. These patterns are defined in terms of the symbiotic relations between regimes of accumulation and modes of regulation. These regimes and modes centre on the nation state; the rest of the world is 'external'.[16] Thus there can be no pattern to international accumulation within this theory. Observations of international disorder then are to be understood not as historical or theoretical propositions, but as definitional statements.

Yet it follows, as Radice has emphasised (1984:114), that if the international economy is assumed to 'fracture' along the boundaries of nation states, then the contradictions of internationalisation can only be interpreted as disorder. Internationalisation, in its multiple aspects and contradictions, is beyond systematic analysis.

In order to challenge this national focus, we need not adopt its antithesis — the 'globalist ideology' of a homogeneous world economy, and the belief that the new international order is imposed on the world pre-conceived and fully-fledged. The range of possible understandings is surely more contentious than is provided by these extremes: it is that the nation state, and the national political form, is important to internationalised accumulation, but how it is important may change over time.

Thus the relation of national to international accumulation, and the relation between national 'regulation' and international accumulation must be understood as historical as well as methodological questions. In particular, this relation may change with the increased international mobility of capital, so that the understanding of the effects of this increased mobility cannot start with a preconception of the analytical primacy of national accumulation, without that analysis becoming self-fulfilling. Hence the possibility of nationally discrete analysis must itself be seen as a problem for analysis, not to be resolved *a priori* by the employment of nationally-centred categories.

Restructuring and Recent Internationalisation

The observed experience of international restructuring is all about industry and industrial change: industry closures, unemployment, and regional decline offset (though, particularly in recession, less than fully) by the emergence of new industries in new regions with new employment opportunities. Associated, there is observed in the advanced industrial countries the shift towards service industries, and thus new skills and new work practices. It is here that analyses of restructuring, including those considered above, focus.

But the observed experience of restructuring is not obviously the level at which the process of restructuring is to be explained. With the Regulationists, this analysis shares a rejection of search for a general pattern to the international movement of capital; not because of an *a priori* philosophical rejection of determinism, but because the contradictions internal to internationalisation have uncertain outcomes. The Regulationist retreat into 'anti-determinism' denies the challenge of characterising the process of restructuring, by contending that the outcome of the restructuring process is circumstantial.

Central to the contradictions which are internal to international capital movement is the leadership of money within recent internationalisation. In the context of sustained crisis in the profitability of industrial capital since the end of the long boom, the changes in the sphere of money capital have been profound, both in themselves, and in internationally integrating the investment and realisation calculations associated with industrial capital.

The mobility of money has served to subject all activities involving money to an international criterion of profitability. One outcome has been the international relocation of industries, as the NIDL thesis picks up; another is the pursuit of higher rates of surplus value by development of 'flexibility' in some industries and the development of 'Fordism' in some locations, as the Regulationists emphasise. But each of these explanations misses the comprehensive multiplicity of responses associated with international integration under the aegis of money capital, because each remains centred on the national location of industry.

The 'leadership' of money in recent internationalisation involves more than the proposition that the integration of commodity trade and production followed in its wake. It raises the question of the significance of money's leadership. Here it will suffice that three issues are noted, which are taken up in later chapters.

First, the integrity and effective operation of national money systems has historically rested on the functions of central banking, securing the quantity or price of money and sustaining popular confidence in the legitimacy of issued currency. But as money internationalises and diversifies its forms, it has increasingly expanded beyond national regulation. There exists no systematic international regulation of internationally-circulating money, while national systems of regulation exert only a partial impact on the (internationally-mobile) money which circulates within the national economy.

Herein lies a potential for crisis in the international money system which would flow directly into each nation's money system. The unregulated international extension of credit can generate, and has already generated, the insolvency of corporations, national treasuries and banks themselves. The more capital internationalises, the more likely that the insolvency of financial institutions will be on a scale beyond the capacity (or 'responsibility') of any single nation state to associate the legitimacy of its 'own' financial system with the costs of supporting such an institution internationally.

Second, and closely related, the potential for crisis lies not just in the repercussions of institutional failures, large and significant as these may be. It must also be situated in the relationship between money and production, and the primary function of money in facilitating the accumulation of capital in production. In Marxism, this problem is recognised explicitly: that the production of surplus value is the source of all profits — including those associated (in aggregate) with money markets. Money thereby 'depends' on production in a fundamental way.[17] But even outside Marxism's formal proposition, the problem posed historically is that the profitability which has been associated with the 'setting up' of internationally integrated and diversified capital markets has surpassed the profitability of industrial production, and that this is not sustainable.

Third, because of the creation of new sources of credit associated with new forms of international financial intermediation, the industrial relocation which has occurred since the 1970s has occurred without conspicuous financial constraint. The notion of industrial capital outgrowing its nation of origin, or finding a higher rate of profit from production in other nations has nothing particular to do with the lack of profitable domestic investment opportunities. Internationalisation has not involved the 'evacuation' of countries, for capital is currently diversifying its sites — the flow of money and the relocation of production has moved in all directions; both into and out of countries at the same time. While, for example, heavy industry may have been in decline in the United States, this has not been true of all capitals in those industries. Moreover, it has been profitable for capital situated in other countries to relocate to the United States, and since the 1980s, the United States has been the recipient of substantial direct foreign investment. That the 'new' industries may produce a lower level of output than the old, or employ fewer people, is a reflection of the broader nature of the changes in capitalist production in the context of recession, not the expression of capital 'outgrowing' the United States economy.

Thus a theory of restructuring which captures the distinctive characteristic of the recent period must have a number of critical elements.

First, there must be recognition that capital is permanently restructuring as conditions of profitability change. The period since the

1970s should not be posed in terms of (unchanging) old structure being replaced by new structures, but as a particular set of changes within a continuum of change. This continuum includes change in the composition of industry, its most general form being the relative expansion of so-called 'service' industries, and changes in the organisation of industry, its underlying determinant being the rising technical composition of capital.

Second, following the focus on money in the context of recession, there need be no general observable patterns to industrial restructuring, save that the international rule of profitability has become increasingly dominant, as the expression of both the rise of debt financing and internationally-mobile credit. Beyond this general determinant, the nature of change must be understood as historically contingent. Certainly, notions of a world structured by a delineated centre and periphery have only the most aggregate attachment to real processes. The emergence of Newly Industrialised Countries from out of those previously condemned to periphery status, and the transformation of the world's largest foreign investor (the United States) into the largest 'recipient' of foreign investment, are two clear developments which do not fit the formal models. Indeed, they should have been enough to see such models dispensed with entirely. It is surely only their broad descriptive perspective, not their analytical merit, that sees such models retain their theoretical standing within the study of international political economy.

Third, it follows, analysis of restructuring within nations must recognise the contradictory role of the nation state. The state's role cannot be assumed to be simply the pursuit of national efficiency, for restructuring creates so many winners and losers, all of whom look to the state to advance their incompatible causes. With more and more individual capitals having expectations of national policy that are informed by global rather than simply domestic agendas, nor can it even be assumed that nation state policy is determined purely in reference to domestically-based accumulation. The nation state's position in international accumulation must therefore feature centrally in any theory of restructuring. This issue is taken up in the next two chapters.

Conclusion

Chapter 2 identified the nation state as central to (internationalised) accumulation, but it is altogether another matter that this leads to a nationally-centred conception of accumulation. A nationally-centred conception of international accumulation would require two critical assumptions: the mobility of capital is uniformly affected by national borders; and the state's role in mediating the contradictions of accumulation always gives priority to domestically-centred accumulation.

Contravention of the first assumption means that the experiences of individual capitals in relation to international accumulation are different. If this is the case, there will be no coherence to domestic restructuring in response to international 'changes'. Moreover, and this moves into the second assumption, the agendas of different individual capitals for nation state regulation will be dictated by their international, and not just domestic conditions of accumulation. Contravention of the second assumption sees the nation state, and its role in mediating the contradictions of accumulation, as a sectional component in mediating internationalised contradictions, not as an exclusively inward-looking stabiliser.

For both the French Regulation School and the NIDL thesis, the identification of the end of boom conditions with the emergence of a new 'order' — a new 'regime of accumulation' in one case, and a 'new division of labor' in the other — has obscured both the continuities in accumulation, and the way in which change represents a development within past patterns of accumulation. Thus certain questions about the operation of the 'new order' are obscured or avoided simply by it being identified as novel. In particular, the role of nation states in regulating the process of internationalisation has been made analytically redundant.

These limitations of the NIDL thesis and the Regulation School cannot be 'blamed' on the national primacy found in classical Marxism. Nor can either particularly claim to be the 'logical' derivation of the classical tradition. But both remain confined within the problematic of that tradition, and the novelty they identify since the 1970s remains limited — in the case of NIDL because it identifies just a reallocation of industries between nations; in the case of the Regulation School, insofar as it has a supra-national perspective, because it remains preoccupied with the (re)allocation of labor process between nations.

In the process of its reproduction, capital, both individually and in total, is oriented towards expansion over both space and time. It may therefore be conjectured that internationality is in the nature of capitalism. It is not a general tendency towards internationality which requires explanation, but its particular form. A Marxist agenda suggests that the form in which capital internationalises is not to be understood as the integration of market processes, as in the conventional economic approach; nor the relocation of manufacturing industries between countries, as in the NIDL thesis; nor by the shift of 'Fordism' to peripheral countries, as the Regulationists contend. It is to be found in the developing relationship between money, production and commodities as they each, with their own (though inter-related) histories expand across space and time.

The response by capital to the period since the 1970s has been at one level no different from the path out of previous periods of downturn: extending markets to increase the mass of surplus value and increasing the intensity of labor to increase the rate of surplus value. Its particular form has been expressed particularly as the mobility of capital — both the spatial movement of industry, and the shift to forms of capital which have become inherently international — in particular, the entry of capital into the provision of credit, and other forms of 'capital market' investment. This has made possible (and the force of competition compelled) the movement of capital to wherever and whatever generates the highest rate of expected profit. In this sense, capitalism can be said to be 'advancing', at least in its own terms. In the process, individual capitals themselves are internationalising — not just by becoming transnational corporations, but by being integrated into international money and commodity markets. Capital breaks down the limitations of national barriers, making the integration of accumulation between nations increasingly complete.

Internationalisation therefore represents the intensification of competition, with all the implications for product development, technological innovation, reduced costs of production, and the intensification of surplus value appropriation which follow from capitalist competition. This makes any subsequent tendency of capitalism towards crisis increasingly universal. Moreover, it was emphasised in Chapter 2 that capital is not just a process of value creation and circulation; it is also a class relation, and international integration of accumulation may serve to internationalise the experience of class conflict. Nationality may continue to reproduce differentiated experiences of accumulation, but it no longer provides a buffer against international tendencies.

Notes

1 Here, of course, accumulation means not stockpiling, in the literal sense of accumulation which dominated classical political economy, but the contradictory process of wealth generation and distribution (Christian 1990).

2. See Olle and Schoeller (1982) for an excellent critique of this application.

3. Bukharin argued peaceful co-existence of the imperialist powers was logically feasible as a process of accumulation (Kautsky's conception of 'super-exploitation'), but precluded politically, due to unequal power in the international market and the differential exercise of that power by national economic policy.

4. For the United States, see Bluestone and Harrison (1982) and Bowles, Gordon and Weisskopf (1984).

5. This follows the distinction drawn by Jenkins (1984).

6. The more conspiratorial versions even suggest that these functional roles performed by nations in the NIDL are allocated by transnational corporations, seeking to hold technology and finance, the key levers of accumulation, under the control of the industrialised countries. This is an embellishment not central to the general thesis.

7. From a quite different paradigm, there is an emphasis on the non-price aspects of competition, such as emphasised by Porter (1990).

8. Comparable with this depiction of 'post-Fordism' is the concept of 'disorganised', as opposed to 'organised' capitalism (Lash and Urry 1987)

9. This should not be interpreted as the state 'regulating' the economy in the sense of 'intervening in' the economy. Regulation here, in the sense of the French word *regulation* "evokes cybernetics or the 'homoeostasis' of biological processes". It is the "ensemble of institutional forms, networks and explicit or implicit norms which assure compatibility of market behaviour with a regime of accumulation" (Lipietz 1985:*xvi,xvii*).

10. Indeed Aglietta claims on this point that Marx got it wrong (1979:31).

11. This is not a pejorative statement: indeed, the Regulation school claims its reformulation here to be central to their agenda.

12. Aglietta argues that "the state forms part of the very existence of the wage relation" (1979:32), and the wage relation cannot be defined outside of the state. The same point is made in relation to competition (for example 1979:19).

13. The tendency for the nationally-determined value of labor power to become internationally-determined in discussed in relation to Marxist theory in Chapter 4, and in the contest of the impacts of national policy for 'international competitiveness' in Chapter 9.

14. Teague (1990:40-41) contends that this imposes a functionalism into the Regulation School's understanding of the relation between economics and politics. Insofar as regimes of accumulation were roughly the same in advanced capitalist countries in the post-war period, different, nation-specific, modes of regulation must nonetheless have fulfilled the same functions with respect to the regime of accumulation. This perhaps understates the national differences the Regulationists claim for different countries' regime of accumulation.

15. As was noted earlier, Lipietz is prepared to use the terms descriptively in reference to stasis in international relations, but there is, at a global level, no process to reproduce that stasis.

16. This is not to be confused with 'excluded'. There is no suggestion that a 'closed economy' model is in use.

17. It is significant that the countries which have been most successful industrially in the 1980s, particularly Germany, Japan and the Asian NICs all have institutionally close relations between their financial systems and industrial systems. But this domestic success in managing the relation of money and production cannot translate systematically to an international scale, except as temporary international partnerships.

4

The Internationalisation of Capital and Marxian Value Theory

The rapid acceleration of international capital mobility from the 1970s (the term 'recent internationalisation' has been adopted to cover its multiple dimensions) has depended critically on the policies of nation states, but policies in relation to international capital movement have not been straightforward. Within conventional economic analysis, and in national policy circles, these global developments are understood as posing a constraint on national economic expansion, and nation state policy formation.[1] Much 'Marxist' and radical analysis of recent internationalisation has similarly focused on national constraints, although formulated very differently from the economic orthodoxy. International industrial restructuring, it was seen in Chapter 3, is generally understood to be structured by the relation between rich and poor countries. Similarly, 'imperialism', as the most conspicuous label applied to the international system, is tied inextricably to a conception of unequal power relations between nations.

The various prevailing analyses — Marxist, radical and orthodox economic — while no doubt facilitating some understanding of global developments, continue to pose the global economy as exogenous; as something outside the nation, which constrains national choices, and to which national policy must react. Yet the effect of recent internationalisation has been to transform the very notion of a 'national economy' as a discrete entity; an issue addressed in previous chapters.

Accordingly, national policy cannot be understood adequately in terms of the (internationally-constrained) management of a 'national economy'. The analytical task is to understand how accumulation within a national space is linked into international accumulation, and the role of nation state policy within this process. The national impact of recent internationalisation is more effectively understood as a contradiction: the contradiction between the internationality of accumulation and the nationality of state regulation. This contradiction was posed in Chapter 1.

But what does this contradiction imply for the formation of state economic policy? As posed, such a question is too broad to answer definitively — states have their own histories, and there is no sense in which the internationalisation of accumulation comprehensively circumscribes policy. The objective is not to define policy, but to elaborate why the contradiction, which has been posed so far largely as a spatial incongruity, is actually played out as a contradiction for accumulation.

The key is to identify the aspects of accumulation which are contingent upon certain functions being performed by the state. It is then possible to consider the implications for those state functions, when accumulation is conceived of as an international, rather than a national, process. Posed this way, there is no opposition between (international) capital and the nation state (in contrast with the TNC subordination thesis), and there should be no assumption that state policy is inherently parochial, pursuing an exclusively domestic agenda (in contrast with external constraint conception and most 'restructuring' theories).

Marxist value theory provides the starting point to cast the contradiction between the internationality of accumulation and the national regulatory capacity of the state. The conception of accumulation within the labor theory of value is of a process of production, circulation and reproduction of value, and integral to this conception is a number of minimal requirements for the state to perform in sustaining the value system.

A value-theoretic perspective is not without problems. In relation to the state, so-called 'capital logic' analyses which developed in the 1970s[2] imposed a determinism into the understanding of state policy: that the state knows capital's collective interest in a way that capitals individually do not perceive. The objective here is much less embracing than was the capital-logic analysis. It is also less deterministic, for it specifies no logic to state policies. There is, however some notion of determinism: that state policy is required to sustain accumulation, and this is what characterises the state as a capitalist state. But how (by what policies) and, subject to that requirement, in whose 'interests' is not pre-determined.

Accumulation and the State in an International Context

Accumulation

The conception of accumulation is developed most directly by Marx in Volume 2 of *Capital*, in the depiction of circuits of capital. Capital takes three different forms in the process of accumulation: money (M), production (P), and commodities (C). Accumulation is the process of capital moving between these forms, sometimes as a process of exchange between enterprises, sometimes as a transfer within enterprises. In passing through the form of production (C...P...C'), labor power and the means of production (both forms of commodity capital) are brought together and surplus value is created. The value of capital is expanded. In moving between the forms of money and commodities (M-C-M, or C-M-C), capital is circulated. As capital moves between these forms in the process of accumulation, it makes up the circuit of social capital. Within this circuit, capital is advanced as industrial capital, creating capital of expanded value (C'-M'-C...P...C'),[3] or as merchant's capital, engaged in buying and selling (M-C-M, etc.). Each of these circuits describes the movement of an individual capital and an aspect, or component, of the circuit of total social capital.[4] The circuits of individual capitals aggregate to the circuit of total capital.

As posed, there is no spatial dimension in the exposition of the circuit. The sustained development of that dimension was not the direct object of Marx's analysis. Nonetheless, the notion of capital as movement can be understood as a movement across space, as well as between forms of capital, and thus a movement across national spaces. It is critical to the spatial dimension that capital moves in the forms of money and commodities, while production, as a social process, can only be relocated via movements in the other two forms of capital (Marx describes production as an interruption in the circulation process, hence the use of dots in the depiction of C...P...C' (1885:118)). Internationalisation therefore relates to the expanding spatial movement of money and commodities, and the associated international relocation of production.

The priority given to commodities and money in this conception does not preclude the centrality of globally-integrated production as a major manifestation of recent capitalist development. But production processes are integrated only via the movement of money and commodities. International production is strictly an antilogy. This is not simply a semantic point: it poses production as qualitatively different from circulation, as something which must locate in a particular site (country). This has direct implications for the role of the nation state in the reproduction of relations of production, which is qualitatively different from its role in mediating the international movement of money and commodities.

The State

'The state' in Marxist theory has become a somewhat over-embellished concept. Somehow, the importance of states in history has become confused with the desire to capture them ahistorically in theory as a logic, or a prescribed set of processes. There are surely limits to this theoretical development, which most people would agree have widely been exceeded. It is, however, necessary to develop some broad propositions associated with understanding the state within a value-theory perspective. First, the analysis is not posed as a general theory of the state because there is more to states than their requirements of supporting the value system. Second, value categories, at least as they are applied here, operate at a level of abstraction which permit clarification of the functional requirements of the state with respect to accumulation, but cannot specify the policy agendas which follow from those requirements, or even the policy debates which may, on occasions, serve to obstruct those functions being met. Hence the analysis is addressing the minimum requirements of the state with respect to accumulation. There is no suggestion that this is all that states do, or even all they need to do in capitalist society; nor that there are pre-determined ways of meeting these requirements; only that if state policies do not maintain these functions, accumulation cannot be sustained.

There are two primary functions and a secondary function of the state, in relation to the accumulation of capital. The two primary functions are:
    securing the labor system, and
    securing the money system.
The secondary function is:
    the mediation of the contradictory interests of different parts of capital.
The characteristic of these primary functions is that they are critical to accumulation, but cannot be secured by capital itself (DeBrunhoff, 1976). For labor, the freeing of workers from serfdom and slavery makes the supply of labor power in capitalism a contingent issue.[5] For money, generalised commodification (and exchange) under capitalism creates the necessity of universal acceptability of a money system, and this requires some degree of centralised state supervision.[6]

The secondary function of mediating the contradictory interests of different parts of capital also cannot be secured by capital itself. Unregulated competition has no capacity to secure the conditions of reproduction of accumulation over time: the state must establish the rules within which competition occurs (and we know that the state's role in mediating conflicts extends far beyond this minimal rule setting role). What makes this a secondary function is that it is a historical rather than a logical requirement of accumulation. The necessity of the state in securing the labor system and the money system are given in the nature of capitalism, while the mediating role is only played out historically as a result of the anarchy of market-based interactions. Posing this function as secondary and historically constructed is not to diminish its importance — indeed, it suggests that this is the most imprecise and volatile of the states' functions, therefore requiring closest scrutiny. A consideration of the role of the state in mediating the contradictory interests of different individual capitals with respect to international accumulation is considered separately, in Chapter 5.

The primacy given to the labor system and the money system is directly associated with Marx's conception of capital as value, set out in Part 1 of Volume 1 of *Capital*. Here, Marx establishes both money and labor power as the principal units of value. (Socially necessary) labor is the unit of value, and money its unit of measurement (equivalence). Capitalist value relations are devoid of meaning in the absence of either. How the state secures both the money system and the labor system in the context of internationalised accumulation, and the contradictions associated with these agendas, is an issue not addressed directly by Marx. Marx's own exposition of the theory of value, and most formal developments within that theory,[7] remain disconnected from the globally-integrated nature of accumulation. As Marx posed these two roles in *Capital*, they applied to a national conception of accumulation.

By combining the spatial dimensions of accumulation with the primary functions of the state, the contradiction between the internationality of accumulation and the nationality of the state can be clarified. Production locates in specific sites, although it can be relocated. Thus a role for the nation state in relation to production is to secure the conditions under which production can profitably (by international criteria) be undertaken within a national space. This requires, at a minimum, that the value of labor power and the rate of surplus value adhere to international norms. In short, it requires that the nation state secures the national labor system in reference to international conditions of profitability of production.

The circulation of capital, conversely, is not site-specific, but crosses space, including national boundaries. The requirement of cross-national circulation, as integral to global accumulation, is that the value of commodities and money (which amounts to the value of money, since commodities are exchanged for money) is preserved across different currencies. Thus the role for the nation state is to secure the integrity of the national money system within the international money system.

Just as production and circulation are not separate, so these two functions of the state are not discrete: costs of production measured in (socially necessary) labor time may provide the (abstract theoretical) norms for profitable production, but these are always expressed as prices. The rate of currency conversion thereby always mediates the conditions of profitable production in an international context in a way not found in accumulation under a single currency.

The agenda for nation states with respect to international accumulation is therefore by no means straightforward, but by posing the (national) labor system as linked to the global system of production; and the national money system as linked to the international money system, the contradiction between the internationality of accumulation and the nationality of state regulation can be further developed.

Before looking in turn at the labor system and the money system in an international context, it is necessary to clarify the meaning of 'the law of value on an international scale'.

Value on an International Scale

Marx's theory of value was not formulated with reference to the global economy — its conceptual construction does not specify spatial units, only processes of value creation and transfer. Where Marx himself does refer to space, the references are usually just illustrations, and invariably space is constituted as nations. By implication, much of Marx's own analysis of the theory of value is understood to apply to national units, with supra-national issues posed as relations between nations.[8] Whether this is understood as a product of Marx's own era of (relative) immobility of capital and restricted capitalist development internationally, or is posed as a critique of Marx's formulation of the theory of value,[9] does not really matter.

As internationalisation has been defined in Chapter 1 in terms of global criteria of calculation, rather than just cross-national capital movement, a conception of value formation on an international scale requires only that Marx's conception of 'transformed' values, developed in Volume 3 of *Capital* are calculated by international criteria. Reference here is to the transformation of 'individual' values (c+v+s) into prices of production, in recognition of the role of competition in (tendentially) equalising the rate of profit on investment. These prices of production are determined by industry average c+v + inter-industry average rate of profit. Transforming these further to international prices of production requires that industry costs (the norm of c+v for any industry) which are consistent with profitable production are determined by international criteria, and that the rate of profit tends to equalise internationally, associated with the 'free' mobility of capital.

By implication, the value of all identical commodities is the same, irrespective of the technical and spatial differences in their costs of production. Hence individual capitals which can produce with c+v below the global norm, whether due to a low value of labor power or higher productivity (rate of surplus value), can achieve above-average rates of profit; capitals with costs higher than the global norm achieve less than average profits.

The critical assumption in this formulation is that there are no barriers imposed by space — barriers which prevent the equalisation of the rate of profit on an international scale for reasons other than differences in costs of production. The assumption is bold — indeed, it is in identifying the impossibility of the assumption that role of the nation state with respect to international accumulation becomes explicit. Two dimensions are important.

First, there is a spectrum of national state policies, involving border controls, monetary and fiscal policy, which are designed precisely to transform the conditions of international mobility. Border controls may be used to promote or retard the overall international mobility of capital, while other policies impact by differentiating the terms on which different individual capitals engage in international accumulation. These policies are addressed in Chapter 5, in the context of the way in which the nation state mediates the contradictory interests of different individual capitals with respect to international mobility of capital.

Second, within the theoretical framework which utilises the assumption of barrier-free capital mobility, there are ambiguities. The role of the nation state of securing the supply of labor points to the problem of whether the value of labor power is nationally or internationally determined. The role of the nation state of securing the money system points to the problem of exchange rates determining the commensurability of money and money capital denominated in different currencies, and thus the role of exchange rates in the calculation of international prices of production. By investigating each of these in turn, it will be clarified why the essential roles of the state, which are required to sustain accumulation, manifest as a contradiction between the globality of accumulation and the national impact of state regulation.

The Value of Labor Power

For Marxist theory, the value of labor power is determined by the costs of reproducing the supply of labor power at a socially (not just biologically) defined subsistence level of consumption (SLC). This level may be different in different regions: a point often recognised by Marx, and one which creates possible non-commensurability in the formation of international values.

The economic criterion of regional division is related to the space over which there is possible mass mobility of labor. This usually, though not necessarily, corresponds with national boundaries. Immobility provides the economic condition for the reproduction of unequal costs of reproducing labor power, and thus different values of labor power in different nations. It must be noted, however, that this socially defined level of consumption is not reducible to these (labor market) economic factors alone. There is also a socio-cultural element, which will be different in different countries, which imposes standards and conventions about minimum acceptable levels of consumption across individual laborers. This socio-cultural element signals that the value of labor power is a class, not an individual variable, but it is also nation-specific.

With the value of labor power determined nationally, but prices of production determined internationally, there is a contradiction within the value system. Marx himself addressed the international dimension of the value of labor power in a rather cavalier way, although this was not particularly a critical issue in the nineteenth century. The value of labor power in an international context receives greatest attention in Volume 1 of *Capital* — before a consideration of the transformation of individual values into prices of production, and this, it will be seen, limits the usefulness of Marx's analysis in this context.

On a number of occasions, Marx contends that the value of labor power varies between countries. For example, "[the value of labor power depends] to a great extent on the level of civilisation attained by a country. . . [It] contains a historical and moral element. Nevertheless, in a given country at a given period, the average amount of the means of subsistence necessary for the worker is a known datum" (1867:275). Three possible interpretations arise, when this is applied to international value formation.

One interpretation might contend that differences in the value of labor power between countries reflect different levels of skill of labor.[10] The difficulty for this interpretion is to explain why the SLC remains the same in all countries (how it is sustained systematically as the numeraire against which skill differentials can be measured internationally); and to explain why labor power with identical skill is well recognised to have a different value of consumption in different countries.

A second interpretation is that commodities produced in different countries have different values — there are no international prices of production, only international equalisation of the rate of profit. Marx also floats this proposition: "the different quantities of commodities of the same kind, produced in different countries in the same working time, have, therefore, unequal international values, which are expressed in different prices . . ." (1867:702). Marx then argues that this will be 'rectified' by changes in the value of money: the relative value of money will be less in the more developed nation, reducing the difference in the real wage between the two countries. (Here, there is clear illustration of the link between the two primary functions of the state: 'balancing' the labor system and the money system in securing the value system.)

The third interpretation is associated with the proposition that the value of commodities produced with labor power is international, even though the value of labor power may be nation-specific. Here, the equalisation of the rate of profit internationally would require that the organic composition of capital is inversely proportional to the value of labor power, so that national differences in the ratio of s/v are directly offset by differences in the ratio of c/v, and s/c+v is the same in all cases. This would indeed be a grand historical coincidence.

Perhaps there is no solution, and this is, in one aspect, an expression of the contradiction between the internationality of accumulation, and the nationality of state regulation. It is expressed as a non-commensurability in the system of international accumulation, but it also signals the contradictions which national policy formation must address.

To develop this proposition, it is necessary to pursue the implications of the third interpretation. This interpretation suggests that, with capital mobile, there emerges some general pattern of national specialisation, according to differences in availability of constant capital (not all techniques are applied in all countries) and the extent to which, for different production processes, the inter-national differences in constant capital can 'offset' differences in the value of labor power. Thus (for internationally traded commodities) any particular technology will not be applied in both higher and lower value of labor power countries; it will be applied in the lowest value of labor power (high surplus value) countries with access to, or capacity to adopt, the technology.

This signals some degree of trade-off within a nation between the value of labor power, and labor's capacity to create surplus value — particularly relative surplus value. Some countries can sustain a higher value of labor power (wages) than others because of the higher rate of relative surplus value which, for various reasons, have not or cannot be replicated on a broad scale in lower-value-of-labor-power countries. Conversely, in countries without a sufficiently high rate of surplus value, the only obvious way to produce at the international price of production is to lower the value of labor power.[11] The implication is that, while the value of labor power is nationally determined, the use value of labor to capital (its value in production as variable capital) is internationally determined. As a result, the value of labor power may be different in different countries, and it may have a distinct social dimension to its determination, as Marx contended; but the national value of labor power is also constrained by the capacity of labor in a nation to generate relative surplus value, relative to the production of relative surplus value in other countries.

From this formulation there follow implications for the role of the state in reproducing the labor system in an international context. Within any nation, the value of labor power and labor's capacity to create surplus value are positively related: the larger the rate of surplus value, the more likely is the value of labor power to increase over time. If a nation state is to promote accumulation, it can invoke domestic policies to increase relative surplus value. Additionally, it can invoke policies to reduce the value of labor power.

These are not mutually exclusive objectives. The countries which have developed most rapidly in the context of recent internationalisation have been those which have been able to concurrently hold down the value of labor power and increase relative surplus value.[12] But for the industrialised countries, the state's first (stated) objective is the expansion of relative surplus value: the vision of a high productivity, high wage country. The policies by which this strategy might be pursued have varied significantly between countries — from 'free market' cases for efficiency, to corporatist cases for industry planning. While these particular policies have had different effects in different countries, and have been associated with differing social policies in different countries, the high-productivity goal has been consistent.

Yet the objective of increasing the rate of surplus value may not, in itself, be sufficient to secure 'competitive' domestic costs of production within the internationalised system. If domestic policies to develop productivity are unsuccessful in achieving 'competitive' costs of production across a significant range of production processes, the 'alternative' is to increase the rate of surplus value via reductions in the value of labor power.[13]

Because such a strategy is not a popular alternative, rarely will it be a direct state policy. In few countries does the state exert direct control over the general level of wages, and even there, it is to be doubted that the state can impose wage cuts (or at least increases less than productivity increases) without broader social complicity. The pursuit of reductions in the value of labor power are much more likely to manifest through such things as fiscal contraction, leading to a lesser provision for welfare and public sector services (due to a lack of state revenue from accumulation) and policies to deal with a current account deficit, leading to high interest rates or higher import prices (due to a lack of export industries). In each case, a fall in the value of labor power becomes an integral component of macroeconomic adjustment. These issues are developed in later chapters.

Exchange Rates

The second issue raised by constituting value on an international scale is the impact of cross-currency movements of capital on the formation of international prices of production. For international prices of production, the role of exchange rates is to sustain the value of money capital as it moves between currencies. Non-equivalence in the value of money capital is to be understood in terms of state-imposed barriers to free mobility — barriers which create monopoly (the capacity of capital to achieve the international average rate of profit with costs of production above the international norm). Hence the exchange rate is a critical determinant of the distribution of surplus value amongst capitals.[14]

In the absence of a global currency which sustains the value of capital, the international monetary system is made up of the marketised interaction of various nationally-designated currencies. There are two aspects of this system which, in combination, reflect the contradiction between the internationality of capital and the nationality of state regulation. First, the international movement of capital involves the movement of money across currencies. This does not preclude currencies operating outside their nation-of-issue, but internationalised accumulation invariably involves a translation between currencies. Second, it is the nation state which secures the national monetary system (and individual nation states which secure the international monetary system), yet currency value cannot be regulated comprehensively within the nation of symbolic attachment (the nation which notionally issues that currency). National currencies are traded outside their country of issue. Privately-issued bonds in international financial markets are effectively currency issued outside the nation of symbolic attachment. As a result, national monetary policy can effect exchange rates, but not control them.

The contradiction is expressed in the fact that the nation state's roles of securing the national money system does not aggregate to the creation of a unified global currency system, as if it were a single currency with different national faces. In part this is because currencies have to a significant degree lost their links to their nation of origin, and are thereby beyond the capacity of nation states to finely control; and partly because nation states, in managing their national monetary systems, are meeting domestic as well as international agendas. The effect is that exchange rates will not be set with the purpose of securing continuity in the value of money capital across currencies.

As a result of this contradiction, there is no coherent explanation of exchange rates, either within the mainstream or Marxist economic traditions. But while the mainstream has posed exchange rates as a critical issue for analysis, there is no clear convention of a Marxist theory of exchange rates. With the conspicuous exception of Carchedi (1991) exchange rates have been understood purely as a price phenomenon, and injected into value analysis as a received rate of currency conversion.[15]

The objective here is not to rectify that gap; it is more to identify why that gap cannot be resolved within a formal theoretical framework. The absence of an explanation of exchange rates is to be understood as an expression of the contradiction between the international circulation of money and the national regulation of the money system; not as an undiscovered logic awaiting more advanced econometric modelling.

Hence, to cast the role of exchange rates in terms of sustaining the value of capital across currencies is a Marxist equivalent to the mainstream economic conception of a 'purchasing power parity' theory of exchange rates. This theory, which is discussed in detail in Chapter 6, contends that exchange rates will adjust to equalise prices in different countries. But both the 'Marxist' and the purchasing power parity models neglect two critical factors. The first is that exchange rates are not determined with respect just to commodity capital and the formation of prices of production.[16] Such a calculation ignores the dominance of internationally-mobile money capital which is independent of trade — which makes up about 97% of cross-border currency movements — for this capital movement has driven exchange rates away from any notions of purchasing power parity, or preserving value. The second factor ignored in these conceptions of the exchange rate is that currency values are not a direct reflection of their symbolic nation of issue — the value of the United States dollar is not simply a reflection of the 'performance' of the United States economy, but of non-United States uses for the United States dollar, too.[17]

In the absence of a systematic explanation of international movements of money capital, exchange rates must be recognised as largely beyond explanation, in value theory as well as in the economic orthodoxy. This inability to explain exchange rate levels is a direct reflection of the contradiction between the nationality of state regulation, expressed here as national policies which impact on 'national' currency, and the internationality of accumulation, requiring a sustainable rate of conversion between currencies.

There cannot be a conception of exchange rates which assumes that their role is to simulate a single global currency, just with different, nationally franked, currency units. But nor are exchange rates randomly determined by the collective whim of currency speculators. On the contrary, exchange rates, as an aspect of each nation's money system, are subject to some degree of state determination.[18] As such, exchange rate policy is an expression of the state's mediation of the contradictory interests of capitals. Moreover, as part of this mediation process, the value of currencies is 'traded off' against other elements of the money system: the level of interest rates and the inflation rate. Thus exchange rates cannot be understood outside of the political expression of contradictions between different parts of capital.

Conclusion

The mobility of money capital has added continuity to international accumulation which makes general 'laws of uneven development' and structured 'world systems' less satisfactory as a depiction of the pattern of accumulation. Even the most abstract of models of internationalised accumulation, which may succeed in internationalising prices of production of commodities, cannot construct a logic of money capital flows, short or long run. The relation between the national currency in which money capital is held and the national location of capital (money, productive, and commodity) is not subject to general trends, and the rate of money capital conversion between currencies cannot be taken to be (even tangentially) regulated by some underlying 'natural' value.

If one general conclusion comes out of an analysis of value formation on an international scale, it is that the international movement of capital should not be understood as the relation between national and international accumulation, for the mobility of capital across national boundaries has served to globally integrate accumulation. But global accumulation still rests on the role of nation states in securing the conditions of accumulation, particularly the value of labor power and the value of money. These roles are performed in neither a completely internationally isolated way, nor a completely internationally co-ordinated way. Essentially, this amounts to the proposition that the system of nation states does not and cannot secure on an international scale either the supply of labor power of consistent value or a system of money of consistent value. Hence, globally integrated accumulation does not transcend the role of national states, nor, therefore, of national units.

Consequently (and perhaps ironically), nation states must be at the centre of Marxist theories of internationalisation because nation states are critical in determining the commensurability of capital in its international movement, and also as a means to preclude the automatic presumption that nation states' policies are inherently nationalistic. An approach to analysing the role of nation states in these terms is considered in Chapter 5.

Notes

1. The implications of policy being formed within the precept of a balance of payments constraint are discussed in detail in Chapter 9.

2. See Holloway and Picciotto (1978) for a selection of this literature.

3. This is the circuit from the perspective of commodity capital, identified by Marx as the "general form of the circuit" (1885:177), because it presumes the existence of capitalist commodity relations at its commencement. Because capital is in continual movement between its forms, the presentation here of the circuit of commodity capital rather than productive or money capitals is not critical to the analysis.

4. Clawson (1977) seeks to periodise internationalisation according to the historical period in which each circuit internationalised. But these are not different circuits; they are different aspects of the one circuit of industrial capital. Thus commodity capital cannot internationalise before money capital, for both are required for international exchange. Kay (1975) more reasonably depicts the internationalisation of the circuit of merchants' capital (M-C-M') prior to the internationalisation of the circuit of industrial capital (M-C...P...C'-M').

5. Marx refers, in the context of primitive accumulation, to " unhappy Mr Peel" who could transport his wealth, and 3,000 servants to the Swan River Settlement, but was left with no-one to make his bed or fetch him water, because he could not export English relations of production to Australia (1867:933).

6. Marx's first mention of the state in *Capital* is in relation to the production and distribution of coins, which is "an attribute proper to the state". The same point is made in relation to paper currency (1867:223,227).

7. Kay (1975), Becker (1977), Shaikh (1980), Carchedi (1991) and, most notably, Palloix (1975, 1977) stand out as notable exceptions.

8. For example, Marx suggests that his theory of the formation of an average rate of profit is applied to one country, and that comparing different countries' rates of profit is quite a simple exercise: it rests on a comparison of variation in national rates of surplus value with variation in national rates of profit (1894:242).

9. According to Marx's own initial research agenda for proposed further volumes of *Capital*, international trade, the world economy and crisis, and the State were each deserving of complete volumes (Marx to Engels, 2 April 1858, in Marx and Engels 1975:104).

10. Here the analysis draws on the means established within Marxist theory to compare the relative value of skilled and unskilled labor power, in terms of the socially necessary labor time involved in the production of skills (see, for example, Rowthorn 1980 Ch.8; Devine 1989).

11. This is the Marxist critique of neo-Ricardian theories of unequal exchange; that the value of labor power alone is not a determinant of the rate of exploitation.

12. This is the consistent characteristic of the so-called 'newly industrialising countries'.

13. This policy agenda is developed in Chapter 9.

14. Marx argues (in the context of the division of profit into interest and profit of enterprise) that "there is no law of distribution, other than that dictated by competition" (1894:478). Applied to exchange rates, it suggests that the state's role must be understood as a political mediation, not an (attempted) economic 'solution'.

15. While Shaikh's (1980) seminal work on the internationalisation of the law of value gives central attention to the theory of money and international money flows, exchange rates receive no specific attention.

16. This is the form of calculation undertaken by Carchedi (1991).

17. The limited relation of the United States nation to the United States dollar, and its implications for balance of payments accounting, is considered in Chapter 8.

18. Even where there is a freely floating exchange rate, the state's impact on money supply and/or interest rates, as well as its general macroeconomic management, all exert impact on the exchange rate. This is an inherent aspect of the state's responsibility for securing the monetary system.

5

The Nation State and the Contradictions of International Capital Movement

The nation state is central to the internationalisation of capital because it is integral to all accumulation. As it stands, that is hardly contentious. In Chapter 4 the centrality of the state was developed through the proposition that the nation state has three minimum requirements with respect to accumulation: it must secure the labor system, it must secure the money system, and it must mediate the contradictory interests of different parts of capital. The first two of these were considered in Chapter 4. The third function which is considered in this Chapter.

It is necessary to develop a way to understand the spatial contradiction involved in nation states' role of regulating accumulation in what is an inherently international context. This is not so much a question of the relations between states within a hierarchical world system of states, as found in theories of imperialism and the core-periphery model. More conspicuously, the international mobility of capital occurs through diverse market processes, with money and commodities moving in all directions. Thus a critical question for understanding the nation state in an international context is not just relations between states, but also, and as a prior question, the relations between capitals, in the context of their differing requirements of nation state policy with respect to the international movement of capital.

This chapter uses Marx's circuit of capital to differentiate the points in the accumulation process where individual capitals are integrated into (or isolated from) international accumulation; and then poses these differences as the 'tensions' within accumulation which state policy is required to 'solve'. It is, therefore, a taxonomy of capital movements which helps to explain what are widely understood by economists as inconsistent or contradictory nation state policies.

What is meant here by contradictory and inconsistent policies? Conventional economic analysis poses policy as situated within an ideological axis which sees the policy choices as ranging from 'free market' at one end, to 'centrally managed[1]' at the other. But within the international arena, this spectrum would signal that the principal policy debates are a mass of inconsistencies. National governments advance policy packages which contain elements of both: for example, free international capital mobility, but central bank intervention; or free trade combined with domestic assistance packages.

The divide between the 'free market' and 'central management' is not false, but it is predominantly only an ideologically-defined dichotomy. It characterises policy with reference to economic textbook models, without an appreciation of the forces which move policy one way or another. 'Consistency' in policy must be defined with reference to social effects, not with reference to libertarian benchmarks. Hence, in relation to international accumulation, nation states maintain policies which are blends of ' central management' and 'free markets', with the underlying agenda of promoting particular forms of integration into international accumulation by means of a diverse range of policies.

This in turn involves a recognition that different individual capitals and different industries within a nation have different connections with the international economy and have different expectations of state policy. This is not new. The tariff, as a clear point of division between capitals, has been a post-war domestic policy debate in all industrialised countries. But the terms of this debate have become more complex with the widespread international movement of money capital.

Globally-integrated capital markets have brought the whole spectrum of monetary policy into the division between capitals. There are conflicts over the exchange rate and the interest rate. This is discussed in detail in Chapter 6, but some comment is warranted here also. The tariff debate is about a discrete border control, where the rate of protection is set as a deliberate policy decision. But with currencies floating, the rate of protection afforded by the tariff varies with the exchange rate. The deliberate calculations of tariff setting become swamped by the volatility of currency markets. Further, it is in the nature of tariff policy that the benefits are specifically targeted and the costs generally dispersed. But the same is not true of monetary policy. Monetary policy is not, like the tariff, a regulation targeting specific industries, nor is it explicitly a border control: the state must implement monetary policy, and its impact within the nation is pervasive. Even with a freely floating currency, the state's policies on interest rates and inflation rates directly effect the exchange rate. Thus the conflicts associated with state regulation of the money system are more complex than those associated with the tariff and trade policy generally, and thereby subject to more complex divisions between capitals.

In characterising the bases on which capitals divide with respect to state policy on international capital movement, the presentation in this chapter remains formalistic. Nonetheless, it is hoped to avoid an over-specification of 'the role of the state' as an ahistorical set of logical propositions about what states actually do. Rather, there is here an exercise of specifying some minimum conditions of what states must do, and the contradictions expressed in these imperatives; and posing a method by which to comprehend how these contradictions are expressed within the policy formulation of individual nation states. The method is then applied to particular policy issues in the next four chapters.

The Minimum Requirements of a Conception
of the Nation State: A Reiteration

In the context of international capital mobility, it was posed in Chapter 4 that, as a basic condition, the nation state must secure the conditions of accumulation through the reproduction of labor power at a value compatible with international accumulation, and it must secure a national money system which is compatible with the international money system. In so doing, it must mediate in the national space the vicissitudes of the (generally) unregulated international money and production systems.

Of course, nation states do much more. These requirements are just minimum logical functions specific to the international movement of capital. Yet even within these minimum requirements, there is ambiguity, for it cannot be assumed that state policy will be inherently nationalistic in its orientation. The criteria applying in the determination of state policy do not pertain simply to what will be appropriate for domestic growth, employment, inflation, etc. and external balance. They pertain more generally to the policy agendas borne by the capitals which are required to deliver the growth, employment, exports, etc., where these capitals have a view of policy which is informed by their own position in an internationalised process of accumulation. Hence it cannot be assumed that accumulation by individual capitals which have some presence within the nation equates to a programme of national accumulation. This is not simply because TNCs take jobs and production off-shore, but, more generally, because national space is only a partial consideration for internationally-integrated capital. An example, which will be developed in Chapter 6 will suffice to make the point. Capitals which have borrowed in international credit markets, might promote (directly or indirectly) high domestic rates of interest — higher than consistent with domestic growth requirements — to secure a higher exchange rate, to reduce the costs of debt repayment. Conversely, capitals which depend predominantly on export markets may prefer very low domestic interest rates to push the exchange rate down. The 'battle' is only played out historically. The simple point is that the participants in the battle are not deriving their 'positions' on exclusively domestic grounds.

This formulation involves two degrees of differentiation from the approach to national economic policy found widely in orthodox economics and political science:

- It involves a challenge to the conception of a distinct, 'correct' economic policy (leaving aside the impediments to the application of 'correct' policy). This rests on the proposition that social objectives, and thus requirements of the state, are divided. Even if there could be formulated consensual economic objectives of growth, low inflation, high employment, etc. there are clear divisions on how those goals should be achieved — who should bear the costs, and who should sustain the benefits. This issue forms the basis of social democratic critiques of the economic orthodoxy; indeed, it is a critique that has become so commonplace that it is now the accepted terrain of economic policy debate, with the laissez faire, minimalist state agenda distinctly out of fashion. Yet the social democratic 'new' orthodoxy, such as is expressed in the Clinton Administration in the United States, remains in the terrain of postulating an (alternative) correct path to achieving national economic goals in the 'national interest'.
- International accumulation exists not just as a 'constraint' on domestic accumulation (as is so often posed in the mainstream economic and social democratic orthodoxies), for the nation is, though with its own distinct significance, but a particular site of internationalised accumulation. Conversely, so-called 'interventionist' state policy should not be seen as an inherent fetter on the international movement of capital, but as determining the form in which capital internationalises.

The path into this contradiction is to pose the nation state's role as being that of formulating national policy through the mediation of the different and contradictory interests of different parts of capital. It could well be argued that it is reductionist to see the nation state's policy formation in terms of divisions between different parts of capital. If the analysis developed here were being presented as a comprehensive 'theory of the capitalist state', the criticism would be well founded. But the more modest proposal of this chapter is that divisions between capitals are significant, although just how significant the reader must decide. But if the division is attributed any significance, then the grid within which these divisions are constituted must be seen as a critical issue for understanding policy as a product of social processes rather than the application of textbook theories of national optimisation.

Division Between Capitals

The issue of how capitals divide over national policy on the international movement of capital is, for this chapter, the central issue. The political issue is how the state mediates the opposed interests of different parts of capital. The economic question, which is here the central concern, is how those opposed interests of capital are defined within accumulation.

There are two divides which are widely adopted in Marxist and radical analysis: between industrial, commercial and bank capital; and/or between foreign and national capital. A critique of both of these will be developed shortly, although it is appropriate at this point to signal the need for an alternative framework. In an analysis of the opposed interests of capital with respect to the international mobility of capital, it is important that the opposed interests be defined outside of the standard nationally-conceived categories of exporters, importers, foreign capital, local capital, etc.. To adopt these categories immediately inserts the primacy of a nationally-based division between capitals, while the object of the analysis is precisely to determine how and in what form nationality is important. It prejudges the issue by assuming that the substance of divisions within capital, even within the space of a nation, is determined by the national political form. In developing an alternative framework for understanding the divide, it is first necessary to contextualise the framework within Marxist economic theory.

'Capital', or total capital, does not have a coherent *a priori* common good which the state must secure, beyond the subordination of labor to the surplus-value-producing process. This is because total capital is but an aggregation of individual capitals, each with a particular path of accumulation. In securing the conditions of accumulation, the nation state will implement policies which advance the interests of some parts of capital at the expense of other parts of capital, and not out of some 'higher' aggregate good, but simply because competition makes capitals' requirements of state policy incompatible.

The divisions between capitals must therefore be identified with respect to the particularity of individual capitals, and not simply on the observation that capital is not a monolith. Marx's circuit of social capital, discussed in Chapter 4 provides the means to identify the particularity of individual capitals with respect to the international mobility of capital. The circuit can be used to characterise three aspects of accumulation: capital as a social relationship; accumulation as an on-going and potentially self-expanding process; and how the competitive interaction of individual capitals aggregates to the unity that is total social capital. Here is a brief clarification.

While the social relation of capital is most conspicuously understood in production, as a relation of surplus appropriation, the circuit shows that production and circulation cannot be isolated. Hence in the circuit M . . C - P - C' . . M' production (P) is but one phase of the circuit. What changes in the circuit is not only the value of capital (by the addition of surplus value in production) but also the form of capital (money, production, commodities). The social relation is present in all forms.

The circuit also shows explicitly two underlying themes of Marx's economic theory. One is that the reproduction of capital is essentially the on-going movement of capital through a circuit, with the 'flow' through the circuit potentially increasing with each 'round' via the addition of surplus value. The other is that the process of competition can be understood as the interaction of these individual circuits. As the work of Palloix clearly demonstrates, the circuits of individual capitals "cross each other" (1975:73) in the process of their individual reproductions. This interlinking takes the form of exchange between capitals: for example, the movement C' - M' of one individual capital is the movement C - M of another capital when the latter purchases its means of production from the former. This shows not only that individual capitals exist in a relation of competition, but that it is by means of competition that the internationalisation of total social capital is secured.

For individual capitals, value may be produced and realised over a small or a large spatial area — a city, a nation, or many nations. But individual capitals cannot occupy the same space as total capital, for their movements are just a component of total capital. So what makes total social capital global is not the existence of ubiquitous individual capitals, but that individual capitals, whose production and realisation is spatially constrained, enter into competitive exchange relations with each other so as to bring global continuity to the circulation of value. The circuit of the individual capital shows that there is a number of different phases in the circuit of each capital, and each of these phases involves the the impact of state policy, and thus the basis for division between individual capitals over state policy.

Four Forms of Accumulation

Four different forms of international integration, which help comprehend the divisions which must be mediated by nation states, will shortly be identified. Because there categories are somewhat schematic, three preliminary explanations and assumptions are called for.

First, a general theory of the division of capitals is not being advanced. The division pertains only to conflicting interests with regard to the international mobility of capital. Second, it must be assumed that each form of accumulation involves some process of production within the nation concerned.[2] Third, within the circuit of the individual capital (M - C . . P . . C' - M'), the movement M - C which 'begins' the circuit is not of distinct significance: M itself can be taken to be international capital, and whether the movement M - C occurs within a nation or across national boarders is reflected only indirectly in the analysis. Conversely, the movement C' - M' at the 'end' of the circuit is taken to have direct significance because it signals whether money capital, including 'newly-created' surplus value, is advanced internationally, or remains within the nation to commence the circuit anew. Thus there is concern only indirectly with the spatial origin of M in the movement M - C insofar as it is, in certain respects, the reciprocal of the spatial movement of M'.[3]

To reflect this emphasis, it will be clearer for the differentiation of spatial forms of accumulation to rewrite the circuit of the individual capital as C . . P . . C' - M' - C' so as to focus on the use of M' at the 'end' of the circuit as the decisive indicator of the reproduction of capital (that is, the spatial location in which M' is advanced for the purchase of labor power and means of production (C) at the commencement of a 'new' circuit). By earlier assumption, nor is the analysis concerned with whether C at the start of the circuit (means of production and labor power) is of domestic or international origin. The issues under consideration requires only that these inputs cohere within the nation in an act of production.

Within the circuit specified as C . . P . . C' - M' - C', the movement C . . P . . C' characterises the production of commodities; C' - M' characterises the realisation of commodities through the act of exchange, and M' - C' characterises the reproduction of capital (the allocation of revenue to new production). On this basis, four forms of international integration can be depicted in terms of different spatial combinations of production, realisation, and reproduction. They are the national circuit, the global circuit, the investment-constrained circuit, and the market-constrained circuit. Table 5.1 shows the classification of these circuits.

TABLE 5.1 Circuits of Capital and International Accumulation

	Production (C .. P .. C′)	Realisation (C - M′)	Reproduction (M - C′)
national	national	national	national
investment-constrained	national	international	national
market-constrained	national	national	international
global	national	international	international

The Circuit of National Capital

The circuit of national capital is defined by each movement within the circuit being spatially constrained to within the nation. Production, realisation and reinvestment all occur within a single national space. The historical conditions of existence of capital moving in this circuit cannot be generalised. However, capital in this circuit is likely to be small scale (not large enough to reproduce internationally) and will be somewhat associated with import-competing or naturally protected industries. Small-scale capital in service industries are conspicuous here.

This category of national capital should be distinguished from quite differently defined, though frequently conflated categories of capital. First, it is different from the concept of an import-competing or non-traded sector. While national capitals are likely to be concentrated in these sectors, the sectoral categories have no concern for the space of the reproduction of capital. Second, the category of national capital defined above should not be confused with the more common conception of national capital as nationally owned capital — the antithesis of 'foreign' capital. There is no attempt in an analysis of circuits of capital to include any reference to the location of company owners; indeed, in the following section, the use of reference to the national location of ownership will be explicitly rejected as a criterion relevant to an understanding of the different forms of internationalisation of capital.

The Circuit of Global Capital

In the global circuit, the comprehensive international mobility of capital is constrained only by the assumption that some part of production remains within the nation. Realisation (C′ - M′) and reproduction (M′ - C) will be located according to international conditions of profitability. This circuit is termed 'global' rather than 'international' so as to make apparent that the international movement of capital is not restricted to this particular circuit.

International realisation is not defined as the export of commodities (a distinctly nationalist perspective), but the production of internationally-tradable commodities. Some output may, therefore, be sold within the nation of production, but only if this is consistent with international conditions of profitability.[4] International reproduction means that money capital realised by the sale of commodities is internationally mobile, so that it can be advanced as money capital to commence a 'new' circuit in a location determined by international criteria of profitability. Thus reinvestment may occur within the nation of 'initial' production, not because it is constrained to do so, but because such investment is verified by international criteria of profitability. International reproduction depicts the activity of transnational corporations. It should not be confused with the concept of 'foreign-owned' capital. As already emphasised, the nationality of ownership is not deemed relevant.

The Circuit of Market-Constrained Capital

This circuit depicts the investment of capital on an international scale, and so, as with the global circuit, it depicts the activity of what are called transnational corporations. In contrast with the global circuit, the market-constrained circuit involves production for realisation only within the nation of production. Thus capital in this circuit produces non-traded and import-competing commodities. Conspicuous here is the production by transnational corporations of services (which are consumed at the point of production), of perishables which cannot be transported any significant distance (for example, the McDonalds restaurant chain), and of commodities which are not produced at internationally-competitive costs of production, but are protected by nation state regulations which restrict imports.

The state's tariff and exchange rate policy is therefore of central concern to many capitals in the market-constrained circuit. These policies form a critical divide between different sorts of transnational corporations in their expectations of nation state policies.

The Circuit of Investment-Constrained Capital

The investment-constrained circuit of capital involves international realisation (the production of tradeables) but reproduction is confined to within the nation. Capital in this circuit is therefore integrated into international accumulation at the level of exchange, but not the level of production.

The historical conditions of the reproduction of capital in this circuit are less clear than in the other circuits, particularly when the internationality of money capital is 'reinserted' directly into the analysis.

Nonetheless, the most conspicuous form of accumulation depicted here is smaller-scale capital which produces exportable commodities, but is not large enough to undertake production internationally. It is beyond the scope of the current analysis to explore the competitive conditions of existence of such capitals, but some clear conditions are apparent. One is where small individual capitals combine to undertake exports, such as has been undertaken in agricultural industries which sell to international merchants or to marketing boards. Another is where smaller companies, which compete domestically, combine to meet export contracts, such as has been widely extolled in the industrial resurgence of Northern Italy. Still another is the production of exclusive luxury goods where the location of production is either critical (for example, wine) or arbitrary but singular (for example, designer clothing).

Capital in this circuit has increasingly become the target for state policy initiatives, associated with national policy agendas to make 'national industry' more 'internationally competitive'. However, there are also individual capitals, more conspicuous in the 1970s than now, which can be considered to have achieved sufficient size and administrative capability to produce internationally, yet continue to focus their production within a single country. Critical here has been nation state intervention in the international circulation of capital which has secured for a particular set of individual capitals the availability of a range of profitable investment opportunities which precluded the need by these capitals to expand internationally in order to achieve profitable investments. This has conspicuously been the objective of national foreign investment controls. Particularly in smaller countries with few large companies, it has been left to a relatively small number of companies to undertake privileged access to large-scale investments preserved by the state for companies which have been classified as 'national'.

Thus for at least some part of capital reproducing in this form of accumulation, state restrictions on the international mobility of capital have been critical. But the progressive lifting of these controls in most countries since the 1980s has reduced the importance of this form of accumulation; in part because of the loss of protection associated with the decline of border controls on capital movement, and partly because of capitals themselves shifting into the global circuit as either they outgrow protected investment opportunities, or such opportunities dried up.

Of these four forms of accumulation, it is clear that the nation state is critical to their existence. Controls on imports of commodities and money capital, as well as monetary policy's impact on the exchange rate, all determine the relative size and fortunes of capitals engaged in each of these forms of accumulation. The movement over the past decade towards the free international mobility of money has seen the reduction of capital in the investment-constrained circuit, but the continuing international debate on protectionism, and the inability of the GATT to secure in practice the 'free trade' it advocates in theory indicates that capital in the national and market-constrained circuits still exert significant influence in the policy formation of nation states. Beneath it all, the exchange rate, on which nation states are directly and indirectly influential, remains a major, on-going, and irresolvable point of conflict between capitals engaged in different forms of accumulation. This conflict is considered in Chapter 6.

Some Qualifications

Having depicted, in schematic form, four forms of accumulation which give focus to the issue of the relation between state policy and the international movement of capital, there is need for some qualifications. For simplicity of exposition, the forms of accumulation have been defined with sharp boundaries. They should, however, be understood in terms of dominant tendencies and spatial patterns, rather than absolute conditions[5]. Moreover, there is the question of 'converting' the interests associated with a particular form of accumulation to the interests of an individual capital. In part, this is a question of how an 'individual capital' is to be understood in institutional terms. The closest equivalent is a 'firm' or 'company', and in many circumstances, this may be sufficient. But the tendency towards the concentration and centralisation of capital, particularly in the credit-glutted 1980s, means that amalgamated 'companies' frequently embrace two or more different forms of accumulation. In part also there is the broader methodological question of the relation between formalised, structural definitions and historical, political processes, an issue well understood in relation to the analysis of classes and class relations.

The nature of the exercise has been simply to give focus to the proposition that the interests of capital with respect to state regulation of the internationality of accumulation are contradictory, and that the nature of this contradiction, in its material foundation, can be understood in terms of a Marxist theory of accumulation. While the general proposition of contradictory interests is well recognised, the identification of those interests in the terms identified above is critical. To highlight this, it is important to look briefly at some other, commonly adopted, ways of characterising the contradictory interests of different parts of capital, and see the limitations with respect to the internationality of capital.

Alternative Formulations of the Division Between Capitals

Reference was earlier made to other, more frequently utilised conceptions of the divisions between capitals: between industrial, commercial and bank capitals; or between foreign and national capitals. These can now be critically evaluated.

Industrial, Commercial and Bank Capitals

A differentiation of industrial, commercial and bank capital is the most common division derived from Marx's economic categories. Most conspicuous in developing this approach are Palloix (1975) and Poulantzas (1975). As with the division developed above, this division is identified in the circuit of social capital, but at the level of total (aggregate) capital, rather than at the level of individual capitals. The basis of a segmentation at the level of total capital is that individual capitals are considered to specialise in one or other functional forms taken by capital (money, production and commodities) within the overall circuit. Each form is then posed in institutional terms, to give the appearance of social categories. Thus production becomes industry (industrial capital); commodities become commerce (commercial capital); and money becomes banks (bank capital). This segmentation is thought to constitute a basis of divisions between capitals because specialisation within the circuit prevents individual capitals from perceiving the overall need to reproduce the circuit: the interests of capital are based on a partial view (Clarke 1978:59).

Segmenting the circuit of social capital in this way provides an unsatisfactory basis on which to identify the contradictory interests of capital for two reasons. First, and most simply, even if the institutionalisation of each of the metamorphoses of the circuit is accepted, individual capitals cannot be said to maintain specialisation in one metamorphosis or another. Concentration and centralisation make the integration of metamorphoses within individual capitals very much the norm.

Second, the division between industrial, commercial and bank capitals is based on a conceptual confusion of the levels of individual capitals and total capital. It seeks to differentiate individual capitals by a criterion appropriate only to total capital. From the perspective of total capital, individual capitals may be seen to specialise in the spheres of: provision of money (for example banks); production of value (for example primary industry); and the circulation of commodities (for example retailers). But from the perspective of individual capitals, such specialisation is not apparent. An individual capital which, from the perspective of total capital, specialised exclusively in the provision of money capital, must still employ wage labor and undertake a labor process. It must also sell credit in the form of a commodity. The fact that this may not involve the production of value, but only the circulation of value, is the means by which total capital differentiates production and circulation, and identifies the functions of money, production and commodities. But this is a social judgment: it is not determined within the circuits of individual capitals themselves. For each individual capital, the circuit is the same, involving the same movement of capital between the forms of money, production and commodities. Hence the designation of one production process as involving the creation of value and another involving the circulation of value is a social identification, made at the level of total capital, and related to the differentiation of productive and unproductive labor. But it cannot be imputed on an individual capital in isolation.

The point is that money, production and commodities were seen by Marx as distinct forms taken by total capital within the process of accumulation; they were not seen by him as the basis on which individual capitals specialise and segment. Marx could not have been more explicit on this point when he stated:

> Money capital, commodity capital and productive capital thus do not denote independent varieties of capital, whose functions constitute the content of branches of business that are independent and separate from one another. They are simply particular functional forms of industrial capital, which takes on all three forms in turn (1885:133).

If the contradictions between different parts of capital with respect to internationalisation and the nation state are posed in terms of the contradictions between different metamorphoses in the circuit, the particularity of the contradictions of internationalisation cannot be identified. The spatial dimension of accumulation is absent, and the role of the state in securing the conditions of accumulation involves no dimension which is particular to the contradiction between the nationality of the state and the internationality of accumulation

Foreign and National Capitals

An alternative, popularly applied, basis for the differentiation of capital in the international context is nationality: a distinction between German and Japanese capital, or between foreign and national capital. There are two problems with this classification.

First, the basis on which capital is attributed nationality is dubious. Is nationality to be defined by the nationality of owners or of directors (and is this defined by citizenship or by residence?); or is it defined by the location of head office, or location of principal productive activity? And how much ownership by 'foreigners' must there be before overall company ownership is classified as 'foreign'? It would appear that the attribution of nationality is somewhat arbitrary. This is not a semantic point. Particularly with recent internationalisation, the attribution of nationality has become a conspicuous legal issue. The increased international movement of equity ownership and the potential for decentralised management associated with telecommunications technology which has come with recent internationalisation has involved several challenges to the attribution of nationality to capital. These are pursued in Chapter 7 in the context of national balance of payments accounting and the requirement of attributing capital a nationality.

Second is the issue of how 'capital' is defined. In the context of the nationality of capital, capital is generally understood to mean 'production' or 'fixed capital'. Hence, 'foreign capital' or 'foreign-owned capital' is taken to mean foreign ownership of the means of production — a distinctly neo-classical conception of capital as means of production, and quite distinct from a Marxist understanding. This is not in itself a criticism, for a neo-classical analysis contends that capitals' behaviour will be dictated by the rules of competition, and thus nationality of ownership *per se* of capital is not important.

Yet when non-neo-classicals address the ownership of capital, ownership itself is attributed significance: that in some way, the means of production will be put to work to pursue the higher dictates of the interest of the nation (or nationals) of ownership. But what are these distinct interests? Here, there must be recourse to international conspiracies — of which there are many cases, such as ITT and the Allende Government in Chile to name but one — but these cannot be said to represent the general nature of international capital. They are exceptional cases.

By contrast, a Marxist conception of capital as a social relation, and not just in production, but understood as a circuit of social capital, gives a much different interpretation. What 'drives' this circuit is not a 'national interest' but self interest. Capital is not patriotic, but mercenary, and it engages the capital relation as and where it is deemed profitable. The self-expanding nature of capital, not national rivalry, drives accumulation.

This conception points, therefore, to the problem of the economic significance of a foreign-national distinction of capital. In what sense will capitals have different economic interests, or different patterns of accumulation due simply and exclusively to the location of ownership? The answer must be that location of ownership *per se* cannot be attributed with responsibility for explaining the particular interests of capital. The economically important characteristic of 'foreign' capitals is not the location of ownership, for this is a politico-legal definition, but that they engage in international relocation of capital — money, production and commodities. Yet this is not exclusive to 'foreign-owned' companies; 'locally-owned' TNCs do this too. The only difference is that for a 'foreign' company, international movement is definitional.

Yet to leave the issue here, and label nationality as a 'politico-legal' rather than an economic distinction is not sufficient. There clearly is, throughout the world, a pronounced capital patriotism — the belief that local ownership is preferred to 'foreign' ownership. Nation states do distinguish between foreign and local ownership, as the foreign investment controls (or incentives) which apply in most all countries attest. Moreover, by the existence of such regulations, the patterns of accumulation of individual capitals do come to vary because of nationality of ownership. Foreign investment controls, for example, permit capitals which meet the criteria of 'local' ownership to expand into industries in a way legally precluded to 'foreign' capitals. To identify a category as legally derived does not make it economically irrelevant. But the critical point is that the economic dimension of capitals' nationality is but an effect of the legal classification. The nationality of ownership of capital has economic significance only once laws are passed which differentiate between capitals according to their nationality of ownership.

The underlying issue, therefore, is the explanation of the origins of 'patriotism of capital'. It is clearly a derivative of economic nationalism generally, which was discussed in Chapter 2, and patriotism is considered further in Chapter 10 as a key ingredient of macroeconomic policy. Here, all that needs to be added is that the issue of nationality of ownership, as a populist political issue, also exists as a pragmatic basis of alliance between individual capitals which can ride populism to their own advantage. The success of capital politically has been in creating an identification of local private ownership with local collective social benefit.

Circuits of Capital and the Nation State

Divisions on the basis of nationality and institutional specialisation are static. They are unable to embrace either the extended reproduction of capital, particularly the spatial expansion of capital, or the tendency towards concentration and centralisation. The alternative division proposed in this chapter is a means by which the spatial expansion of capital can be qualitatively depicted — as the transformation from one spatial form of accumulation to another. For example, historically dominant phases of national policy, such as the shift from import substitution to export promotion, can be understood succinctly in terms of these forms of accumulation.

Similarly, the process of concentration and centralisation of capital, while largely irrelevant to the foreign-national divide (except for the fact that 'foreign' companies are usually 'big'), cannot be handled within a distinction between industrial, commercial and financial capitals. The effect of the process of centralisation has predominantly been to break down that divide, with individual companies increasingly investing in all three 'activities'. It is surely a limited taxonomy which is dissolved by an inherent aspect of the process it is trying to classify! Within the four forms of accumulation identified in this chapter, the tendency towards concentration and centralisation does not involve a blurring of the divide, but a tendency for capitals to move towards the international circulation of commodities and/or the international relocation of production. A merger between a capital in the global and national circuits will see capital of the aggregate increasingly engaged in international circulation. History, it is therefore conjectured in these broad terms, is about the increasing subordination of individual movements of capital to a global calculation.

Within these four forms of accumulation, it is also critical that they are defined with reference to the state. (This is true also of the foreign-national divide, although a fact not embraced by its advocates.) That is, there is no sense in which the four forms of accumulation are first defined, and only then their relation to the state is posed. The nation state actually participates in the determination of the relative scales of these different forms of internationalisation by its various policy interventions, and this occurs because state intervention has been central to the specification of the four forms of accumulation. This has some important implications.

First, each form of accumulation is directly reliant on state intervention, perhaps not for the existence of all constituent individual capitals, but for its relative prominence within the nation. This is because interventions which advance one form of accumulation inevitably retard another.

Second, the concentration of capital may involve a change in the form of accumulation — for example, a small company in the national circuit moving into exporting, and thus the investment-constrained circuit. Thus capitals in the national circuit may advocate state policies to subsidise or otherwise assist exports. Similarly, policies to facilitate international investment may be advanced not just by capitals in the global and market-constrained circuits, but also by capitals in the investment-constrained circuit looking to expand into international investment. Concentration and centralisation means that the policies advocated by individual capitals (or groups of capitals) cannot be simply 'read off' from their current form of international integration.

Third, just as the imposition of controls on the international movement of capital is important in some circumstances, the lifting of controls is important in others. The current expansion within the global circuit, for example, has been facilitated by the reduction of state controls on the international movement of money, and expansion within the investment-constrained circuit is facilitated by state policies to promote exports. This analysis has not made the error of assuming the initial existence of a 'non-interventionist' state, and constructing different forms of accumulation as a consequence of cumulative regulation. It is only those theories which understand state policy within an ideological spectrum from 'free-market' to 'centrally managed' (as discussed at the start of this chapter) which reduce state intervention to the imposition of controls.

In general, the exercise of differentiating patterns of accumulation according to their form of integration into the international economy indicates that the tendency for capital to move internationally is not a linear, incremental process, as if like a spreading oil slick. The oil slick conception, apparent in debates on the state *verses* international capital, equates internationalisation with the growth of the global circuit only. Internationalisation, in this rarefied form, is posed as outside the sphere of the state, as a process to which the state can only respond.

Conclusion

The analysis in this chapter has no doubt cut corners in targeting an aspect of the determination of state policy for exclusive analysis. The focus on divisions between capitals with respect to state controls on the international movement of capital is, of course, not the exclusive, perhaps not even a dominant, determinant of state policy formation. But it is an issue, and one generally neglected in analysis which constitutes the nation state as the national economic manager, in which policy debate is based simply in the ideological discourse of whether the state should 'regulate' or 'deregulate'.

In highlighting the material contradictions between capitals which each nation state must mediate, attention has been directed to the differing forms in which individual capitals are integrated into (or 'protected from') international capital mobility, and the role of the nation state in securing these conditions of accumulation. State policy then is to be understood in two aspects. First, it is in some sense a product of the contradictions between different forms of accumulation. Second, because the state is not just a passive reflection of the balance between capitals, but state policy is required to secure the conditions of each form of accumulation, state policy actually also creates the conditions under which capital within a particular nation circulates internationally. In simple terms, the state is both determined by, and determining of relations between capitals. While this chapter has advanced a way to 'order' the relations between capitals, more detailed propositions than this must be the subject for concrete historical analysis.

Nonetheless, some basic attempt should be made to identify the 'logic' to the apparent incoherence posed at the beginning of this chapter — the mixed bag of 'regulation' and 'deregulation' expressed in international forums. The observed global pattern of promoting the (so-called) 'deregulation' of trade and the (so-called) 're-regulation' of exchange rates is a contradictory agenda only within a nationalistic economic discourse which poses policy coherence within the ideological spectrum of degrees of government intervention. The more critical question is what form of accumulation is such a combination of interventions likely to promote?

The essential answer is that this combination of policies is directly compatible with export promotion as a national policy priority in a world where the balance of payments is understood as the key to national wealth. Financial movements (credit or equity investment) are not particularly in need of exchange rate stability — in part because exchange rate movements are themselves a source of speculation for some participants in international money flows, and in part because the systems of insurance and financial swaps within the international money markets can secure their own forms of stability without the need for central bank intervention. But the viability of exporting rests both on legal access to markets ('free' trade) and security about prices in international markets (stable relative currencies). The pursuit of 'export-led growth' as a national economic policy is taken up in Chapter 9.

In these terms, what sense can be made of nations which are not ordered by this combination of policies — for example Britain's withdrawal from the European Currency Union, or Japan's and France's avowed protectionism? Clearly, these are detailed empirical questions, but the answer may be conjectured in general terms. In the case of opposition to fixed exchange rates, opposition will be prevalent from global capital specialising in finance, where movement on exchange rates is central to the movement of money internationally. Certainly, Britain stands out as a country where this form of accumulation is more pronounced than in other European countries. Britain's opposition to European monetary union, first in principle under the Thatcher Government, and then in practice under the Major Government may in significant part be explained this way.

Opposition to 'free trade' is to be understood as the relative dominance of capitals in the market-constrained and national circuits, which survive in an international environment only via protection. More than this, these are not just capitals which accumulate by securing control over the domestic market. To some degree, these may also be capitals seeking to survive or expand in the investment-constrained circuit (exporters), but which can only do so by securing export subsidies. 'Farm lobbies', such as in the United States, France and Japan are typical of this form of international integration.

So while the internationalisation of total capital may be associated with deregulation of border controls on capital movements, capital is not expressed within the state as a unified entity; as total capital. State policy in relation to capital therefore cannot be explained by recourse to some conception of the 'interests of total capital' or the interests of the 'national economy'. To promote international expansion within one form of accumulation, the nation state must intervene so as to restrict international expansion within another form. From this perspective, controls on the terms of capital mobility can be directly compatible with the promotion of the international expansion of capital, so long as total capital is seen as divided, not monolithic.

Notes

1. There is a temptation to use the term 'state regulated' here, but that term has now been redefined by the French Regulation School. Alternatively, the term 'state interventionist' is to be avoided because it suggests that 'free' markets are constituted without the state (or that the state is only present in the economy when it restricts the operation of supply and demand). Yet this ambiguity leaves us without a simple term to depict the spectrum of policies advanced within a social democratic politics, and opposed by neo-classical economics.

2. Note that, in this context, production is equated only with the existence of a labor process. There is no attempt to draw a distinction here between productive and unproductive capital. The latter is determined at the level of total capital, while the analysis at this stage involves a classification of the movements of individual capitals. Thus banks, for example, are deemed here to undertake 'production' because their individual circuit involves a labor process, even though the activity of banking, from the perspective of total capital, may be deemed to create no new value.

3. It is apparent here that particular attention is to M as retained earnings and equity, rather than as credit. Thus, within M' the concern is with the spatial movement of both the original capital advanced and profit of enterprise; surplus value in the form of interest payments is taken to be inherently internationally mobile.

4. Domestic sale consistent with international realisation may be for domestic consumption at global prices, or associated with the insertion of a circuit of merchant's capital (M - C - M') to within the circuit of industrial capital, such as occurs when a producer sells output locally to a trading company which pursues international realisation.

5. For example, an isolated international investment which does not become part of a general pattern of international reproduction should not cause capital to be labelled as involved in international reproduction generally, for the interests of such capital, with respect to state policy formation, remain centred on the conditions of national reproduction.

6

Internationalisation and the Contradictions of National Monetary Policy

Chapter 1 highlighted the role of money in leading recent internationalisation. Money markets are now to be understood as comprehensively internationally integrated, and this has enforced a conspicuous global calculation on investment and expenditure decisions. The leadership of money was also associated with the determining role of production of new value within accumulation, and this means that money cannot be understood as a distinct market with its own *modus operandi*. While the buying and selling of financial assets can be posed as a market interaction, money itself is not exchanged for its own usefulness. It is exchanged for its own change in price, and ultimately for what money enables its holder to do. It is calculations about the price of money and ultimately the uses to which money might be put which determine the market for money.

But nor does money play a neutral role in accumulation, simply transmitting value between the commodity and productive forms of value, and permitting calculations about the relative uses of resources. Changes in the value of money through the inflation rate, the real interest rate and the exchange rate each exert impacts on accumulation. The relationship between money and production has always been difficult to understand and explain, yet it is the direct subject of state monetary policy. It is therefore hardly surprising that monetary policy has been one of the more open and unresolved areas of debate in economic theory and in economic policy in many countries, and this has reflected in dramatic shifts in the role of central banking and in the theory which drives monetary policy.

In the last twenty five years, the relation of national money to international money has been difficult, if not impossible, for nation states to regulate. Monetary policy has shifted from being Keynesian informed to monetarist driven and, with the decline of monetarist fundamentalism in the early 1980s, there has been a number of significant shifts in the guide-lines which determine the immediate objectives as well as forms of central bank intervention. Within monetary theory, there remains debate about the 'transmission mechanism' between monetary aggregates and the so-called real economy, and about the determination and volatility of market-determined exchange rates. Economic models seem to have fared badly in *ex poste* explanations, let alone future predictions, of major exchange rate fluctuations in the post-Bretton Woods era (Meese 1990; Frenkel and Froot 1990)). Moreover, much of the more reflective literature on monetary theory and policy (such as by former head of research in the Bank of England, Charles Goodhart (1989), United States monetary policy theorist, Benjamin M. Friedman (1988) and the General Manager of the Bank for International Settlements, Alexandre Lamfalussy (1985) has observed a disjuncture between the direction being followed by monetary theory, with a focus on the formalism of rarefied models, and the direction being followed by policy makers, where there is greater emphasis on the subtleties of judgment and the pragmatism of discretion.

This all suggests that monetary policy, in theory and practice, lacks a clear conventional wisdom and a consensus. The experience of the 1980s shows that the economy and the exchange rate do not move towards a conventionally-understood equilibrium. It is argued that there is need for more discretionary intervention by monetary authorities (Goodhart 1989:335; Friedman 1988:69). Yet a proposition of the need for intervention does not provide an agenda of intervention; nor does it ensure that even the best formulated discretionary plan will solve the problems of instability.

On many of these issues, Marxism has little to say. Even for adherents to Marxism, Marxist theory of money has its own debates and ambiguities. Moreover, many of the current difficulties in monetary policy are not contingent upon a particular theory of money or accumulation, and so are not automatically clarified should Marxism be seen to offer a significant alternative perspective. Nonetheless, Marxism asks a different range of questions of the role of monetary policy, and so can add a different perspective to the dilemmas of current policy perspectives. In particular, the underlying momentum and the limitations of national monetary policy can be posed in terms of a non-national conception of accumulation and a conception of the state as expressing and mediating opposed interests of capital.

That national monetary policy cannot effectively address national policy objectives is to be explained by the fact that the opposed interests of capital cannot be 'resolved', and that the nation state is attempting to mediate these interests in a space (the nation) which bears only a partial relation to the (internationalised) space of accumulation. Twists and turns in policy (such as have characterised the last two decades of monetary policy) may then be interpreted not as prospective solutions changing with the circumstances, or with deepening understanding, but as the expression of a contradiction which keeps breaking through no matter how the policy makers seek to resolve it. In relation to monetary policy, it follows that the Marxist question is: what are the conflicts/contradictions which state intervention in the form of monetary policy is attempting to mediate ('solve')?

Money, Value and the State: A Reiteration

In unfolding this analysis, a number of propositions explored in earlier chapters should be reiterated.

First, within Marxist value theory, the essential functions of the state with respect to accumulation are of two orders. The primary functions are securing a supply of labor and securing a supply of money (DeBrunhoff 1976). A secondary function involves mediating inter- and intra-class conflicts by a system of regulation and revenue/expenditure programs. It has been emphasised that these functions need not be understood in a deterministic way; and that there is more to state policy formation than the direct requirements of accumulation. But by specifying the essential functions, and identifying the contradictions within them associated with international capital mobility, an understanding of the underlying contradictions of international capital movement is clarified.

The second proposition is that capital value exists in three forms: money (M), production (P), and commodities (C). The process of accumulation (for both individual and total capital) can be understood as the movement of capital (or its failure to move) between these three forms. The existence of money as a form of capital,[1] commensurable with capital in the commodity and productive forms, ensures that the internationalisation of capital has a distinctly Marxist interpretation. One aspect of this interpretation is that when money takes the form of capital (money capital) by being advanced in the circuit of social capital, it is itself the embodiment of value rather than the signifier of the worth of an asset. That is, money is not merely a standard of measure and unit of payment, as the orthodoxy suggests. Money has these roles, but money as capital does more than link 'real' processes: it is itself the representation of a social process. As such, it acquires some autonomy (theoretical as well as concrete) in its conditions of movement. Hence, the international movement of money is itself the expression of contradictions within the value creating process; it is not simply the representation of contradictions based in the so-called 'real' economy.

In this sense, international movements of money are not driven exclusively by the forces postulated in the orthodoxy: the reciprocal of international commodity flows, international flows of income, capital flows to equilibrate (long term) national balance of payments, or short-term speculative movements on capital assets which are thought to have a 'real' value on which the speculators gamble.[2] For Marxism, money as capital may be advanced on an international scale for the purpose of buying and selling (M - C - M) or for the creation of new value (M - C . . P . . C' - M'), and it moves within and between these processes according to criteria of profitability.

An additional aspect of a Marxist conception of money is that the rate of interest is understood as (regulated by) the price of *money capital* advanced within the circuit of social capital (resolved by the competition between different parts of capital — financial and industrial[3] — for the division of total surplus value). Here, there is a contrast with the Keynesian view which sees the rate of interest as the price of liquidity (resolved primarily in the market for old loans) (Foley 1986:34). For Marxist theory, the rate of interest is much less responsive to changes in the supply of liquidity than is perceived in Keynesian-based theories of interest rate determination. This will be developed shortly.

There are two critical factors which affect state mediation with respect to the monetary system. First, the interest rate, the inflation rate and the exchange rate, as different aspects of the monetary system, are interdependent, so that an adjustment in one will, *ceteris paribus*, exert an impact on the others. For example, increased interest rates will push up the exchange rate; a lower exchange rate will increase the inflation rate, etc..

Second, the interests of different parts of capital with respect to the interest rate, the exchange rate and the inflation rate are not the same: different individual capitals will prefer different levels for each. It was seen in Chapter 5 that these oppositions can be understood according to the different forms in which individual capitals are integrated into international accumulation. Importers and import-competitors want different exchange rates; capitals with loans in local currency want lower domestic interest rates, capitals with loans in other currencies prefer higher domestic interest rates, if the effect is to push up the exchange rate.

These are the dilemmas (contradictions) which the state's monetary policy must mediate. The nation state must secure the monetary system, within the limits imposed by national regulation, but there are contradictory interests of different parts of capital regarding securing the different components of the system. The fact that monetary policy may be formulated with respect to the 'national interest' and 'national policy goals' does not refute this mediating role of the state. Indeed, the political role for different parts of capital is to represent their specific policy interest as the 'national' interest.

In identifying the forces which determine the way in which opposed interests are mediated, a broad historical trend can be postulated. As individual capitals become increasingly international in orientation, associated with a tendency towards the concentration and centralisation of capital, then, for a growing part of capital, the requirements of the nation state's policies are to promote accumulation not with a domestic focus, but with an international focus. If this is the case, it follows that the objective of policy is not automatically the conventionally-understood domestic equilibrium. The spatial area on which state policy focuses will itself be an expression of the way in which the state mediates the conflicting interests of capital.

Contradictions of the Monetary System

Contradictions within accumulation are various and historically determined. Here there is identified just one, with multiple manifestations, which is central to the formation of monetary policy. It is a contradiction found within the two propositions above, that the state, which we currently understand as the nation state, must secure the monetary system for total capital, yet money itself is internationally mobile. Hence the internationality of money constrains the capacity of the nation state to perform its fundamental role in accumulation, both because nation states cannot directly regulate a national monetary system and, even if they could, the contradictory interests of capital with respect to national currencies leaves the nation state without a clear agenda for regulation.

As it stands, this is not a novel formulation. Nationally-issued currencies have moved beyond the nation-of-issue throughout the history of capitalism, and there have been periodic crises in the financial system. It was explained in Chapter 1 that the most recent major international financial crisis, leading to the demise of the Bretton Woods Agreement, was associated with the inability of a single national currency (the United States dollar) to operate, in a sustainable way, as an international currency.

In the current era, the contradiction, while the same in nature, is expressed differently, associated with the increased international mobility of money capital during the 1970s and 1980s, and developments in types of capital markets which break down the distinction between 'money' and (previously) less liquid capital assets. The effect of this development has been to eradicate any notion of a discrete *national* capital market, so that the monetary policies of nation states are being constructed with control over a decreasing proportion of the elements which determine the national monetary system (the amount of money in circulation and the rate of interest). If the rate of interest is conceived as the price of (internationally mobile) money capital (not to be confused with a notion of the value of capital assets), rather than the price of liquidity, it is apparent that a central bank has very limited capacity to affect the general rate of interest and, thereby, the exchange rate.

It is important to see how this contradiction has been understood in the conventional theory which has informed monetary policy. The analysis will look first at the manifestations of the contradiction in monetary policy, followed by a consideration of its origins in monetary theory.

The Contradiction Within Monetary Policy

In the post-Bretton Woods era and the resurgence of monetarism, monetary policy focused on the control of the national money supply, with the direct objective of managing the domestic rate of inflation. Over a decade later, much of the important analysis of that time looks naive and simplistic, precisely because the contradiction identified above was so blatantly ignored. That is, while advocating both the targeting of money supply growth and the 'freeing up' of money markets, this early monetarism failed to acknowledge the resultant international movement of money would undermine any conception of a distinct national money supply, let alone the policy task of regulating it. Hence, in many industrial countries, the policy of money supply targeting was found wanting.[4]

The abandonment of money supply targeting by the mid 1980s signaled the end of a reliance on the use of long-run monetary phenomena to secure the conditions of accumulation in the so-called real economy.[5] More fundamentally, it was a recognition that, in the context of internationalised accumulation, the control of domestic interest rates was not the universal concern of capital. Yet with the interests of capital divided, the political conflicts around the objects of monetary policy were not quickly resolved. Monetary policy became *ad hoc*. Noted American monetary economist, Benjamin Friedman, has observed that, in the 1980s, "the growing disenchantment with (monetary aggregate) targets has created a conceptual vacuum at the core of the monetary policy process in many countries" (1990:1186-7).

In most OECD countries, the rationale of targeting was replaced by a 'checklist' approach to monetary policy (Goodhart 1989; Batten *et al* 1990). The checklists, while nationally-defined, generally embraced a broad range of national indicators: past and projected; financial and 'real'. Inflation, expectations of inflation, interest rates, the exchange rate and the balance of payments feature in all checklists. This was an attempt to signal that all aspects of macroeconomic balance were within the purview of the monetary authorities, in contrast with a preoccupation with domestic inflation.

Yet what the checklist approach gained from recognising the complexity of forces which determine the national monetary system, it lost in a failure of policy specification and clarity. There was conspicuous incompatibility of components within the checklist: in particular, objectives regarding the interest rate, the exchange rate the inflation rate and the balance of payments. Attempts by central banks to increase domestic interest rates in response to balance of payments (current account) deficits were causing exchange rates to appreciate as a result of speculative money moving towards the currency with the high interest rate, in turn leading to a worsening current account.

The experience of irreconcilable objectives under the checklist approach offered clear evidence of a policy without direction. It was an approach which sought to create the appearance of solutions to problems by constantly displacing the problem. Thus the checklist can be understood as an implicit recognition that the interests of different parts of capital are contradictory, yet it offered no sustained policy resolution. It did, however, provide the conditions under which monetary policy was no longer formulated by reference to a set of theoretically-constructed, technical rules. In its place, the checklist approach made possible the political resolution of priorities within the checklist.

Such observations are alarmingly simple in their critique, with the benefit of hindsight. The generally unexpected aspect of this era, which can now make the policy debates of the 1970s and early 1980s appear comprehensively inadequate, was the extent to which movements of money capital severed a close connection with movements of commodity capital: the movement of capital was increasingly between different forms of money, without involvement of commodities or the production of new value.[6]

For this process to remain profitable for a sustained period,[7] either there had to be a substantial increase in surplus value production, a fall in the rate of profit on industrial capital, or a continuing increase in the availability of credit money. It was the latter which dominated accumulation in the late 1970s and 1980s. But the income derived from credit is a claim against future surplus value, and the failure for surplus value production to increase in proportion to the availability of credit inserted instability into the money system via the credit system. Thus the expansion of credit, the dominance of capital circulating within the money form, and volatile exchange rates were all part of the same process, and they all operated on a global scale, with scant regard for national borders.[8]

As it unfolded, the exchange rate emerged from within the checklist as the primary objective of monetary policy in most OECD countries in the early to mid 1980s. In the United States, this was reflected in the shift from a combination of a domestic targeting of M1 and a rigid hands-off attitude to the foreign exchange markets espoused during the first four years of the Reagan administration to the abandonment of M1 targets and a the orchestration of a series of *ad hoc* international exchange rate agreements, beginning with the Plaza Agreement of 1985.[9]

This shift showed further that the fundamental contradiction between the internationality of money and the national basis of monetary policy could not be addressed, for a focus on the national value of the national currency (preventing domestic inflation) could only be replaced by its antithesis, the international value of the national currency (the exchange rate); but the two could not be reconciled.

As exchange rates stabilised in the late 1980s, priorities within the checklist again shifted towards domestic inflation. Indeed, to some considerable extent the whole checklist conception has become rejected. In the European Union this is because the pursuit of monetary unification superseded previous policy agendas. In other countries, the checklist conception is seen as using monetary policy inappropriately as a short-term, counter-cyclical policy tool. The renewed focus on longer-term strategies of managing domestic inflation is seen as taking monetary policy back to its 'appropriate' objective. There has not, however, been a return to the targeting of monetary aggregates, such as preceded the checklist approach. Money is no longer conceived as 'neutral'. Domestic demand has become the immediate object of monetary policy, with domestic interest rates as the immediate tool of policy. The implications of this shift are discussed shortly.

The Contradiction Within Monetary Theory

Monetary theory followed a similar path to monetary policy, with the focus shifting from the nationalist monetarism of Friedman (1953; 1968) to the conception of 'open-economy macroeconomics' (Dornbusch 1980). As a result, the exchange rate, as the mediator of international and domestic money, acquired new attention.

In reconstituting the theory of national monetary policy in the context of floating exchange rates, the economic orthodoxy had a ready-made alternative. The Mundell-Fleming model, derived a decade previous, and in the context of quite different international capital markets, came to the fore. It contended that, with floating exchange rates and capital mobility, nation states could apply effective macroeconomic policy by addressing fiscal policy to internal balance and monetary policy to external balance. Its focus on the importance of exchange rates was clearly germane, and its conclusion that, with free capital mobility and flexible exchange rates, small countries can conduct effective domestic monetary policy was comforting for national policy makers. The model stood as a testimony to the belief that free international mobility of capital is compatible with effective nation state regulation.

Yet the empirical basis of the model was dubious. It was, after all, formulated in a world of fixed exchange rates, presenting a theoretical case for floating rates. In particular, the equilibrium formulation of the original Mundell-Fleming model demonstrated that free international capital markets combined with floating exchange rates would lead to self-adjusting balance of payments. This proposition has been without empirical basis in the post-Bretton Woods era. Nonetheless, according to Dornbusch, Mundell-Fleming "remains, with some adaptations, the backbone of macroeconomic models of the exchange rate"(1983:51).

This development in monetary theory has expressed the contradictions of internationalisation in two aspects: the analytical primacy of national units cannot explain international capital mobility; and the reliance on equilibrating capital markets cannot explain exchange rates.

The Primacy of National Units

The Mundell-Fleming model takes as its point of departure the conventionally-constructed IS-LM analysis of macroeconomic balance. Hence, the conceptual basis of the Mundell-Fleming model is discrete national economic units linked to the rest of the world by commodity and money flows. Specifically, with respect to commodities, the relative price of domestic goods in terms of importables is a determinant of the composition of domestic spending and net exports are a component of the demand for domestic output; and with respect to money, domestic and international interest rates are equalised via an integrated and competitive world capital market. The theory then unfolds via the conventional IS-LM formulation, with focus on these international linkages.

Within this framework, the exchange rate system (fixed or floating) has a significant bearing on the relative effectiveness of monetary and fiscal policy. In particular, monetary policy will be more effective under floating than under fixed rates and, in general, monetary policy will be more effective than fiscal policy under floating exchange rates (Fleming 1962).

Critical to this approach is the method of commencing with a closed economy and then introducing openness in the above forms. Even though the model operates with international commodity and money flows, the discrete national economy is constructed as *ontologically prior* to the international economy. Thus the global economy is no more than the aggregation of (interdependent) national economies: the whole embodies no characteristics or logic of its own. As a consequence, the model assumes that the international system will equilibrate for national units. An equilibrated world is made up of so many equilibrated national units.[10] These units may be interdependent, requiring simultaneous equilibration, but the national economy, not the international economy is the object of the equilibration process.

This conceptual approach means that two contentious issues of monetary policy are solved by assumptions of the model, without being addressed explicitly.

First is the issue of whether internationally-mobile capital can be said to have broken its national ties, such that the (assumed) cohesiveness of national economies is diminishing. In the conventional wisdom, international capital mobility remains defined in terms of national inflows and outflows, rather than a movement with its own international logic.[11]

Second, the model assumes that the object of (national) government policy is the equilibration of the domestic economy according to nationally-defined objectives. That is, the model assumes that the nation state is purely nationalistic in its policy formulation. By this formulation, it pre-empts debate about the international autonomy of national policy (that is, the existence of internationalised contradictory interests), because the issue is solved by assumption.

The theory of monetary policy formulated on the basis of the Mundell-Fleming model 'plays out' the contradiction between the nationality of the state and the internationality of capital. The conclusions of the model, which were appealing to monetary policy makers because they pointed to national autonomy in policy, must be seen as embedded in the assumptions of the model, not proved by it, for the model assumes a national process of equilibration and a nationalist objective to national policy.

There is required an approach which both does not constitute the national economy as ontologically prior to the global economy, yet also constitutes the centrality of the nation state as having some autonomy as a mediator in the conditions of international accumulation. It is a fine, but critical, balance.

Exchange Rates

While the Mundell-Fleming model has remained the backbone of theories of open economy macroeconomics, the model itself rests explicitly on a purchasing power parity (PPP) conception of exchange rates. While the conventional analysis which has followed in the Mundell-Fleming tradition of open-economy macroeconomics has had to grapple with why PPP theory does not 'work' empirically, that theory remains, according again to Dornbusch "an essential element of open-economy macroeconomics" (1989:1083). A central role of applied monetary theory, therefore, has been to amend PPP to make it consistent with the historical movement of exchange rates.

PPP contends that the exchange rate between two countries over time is determined by their relative prices. Thus the price of identical goods in two different countries, when converted at their exchange rate, will be equal. As it stands, this 'absolute' PPP is hypothetical, and contingent upon a model of perfect competition. A more realistic version must allow for the effects of impediments to trade and information costs which will not be arbitraged away, and the problems of comparing aggregate prices in different countries.[12] Its weaker, but still significant proposition is that a domestic monetary disturbance will lead to an equiproportional change in all prices (including the exchange rate) if the 'real equilibrium' remains unchanged. This signals the close conceptual link between monetarism (the quantity theory of money) and PPP theory, developed in the 'monetary approach to the balance of payments'.[13] This connection will be returned to shortly.

The PPP thesis, in some form, has been the ruling orthodoxy of floating exchange rate determination since the nineteenth century. It was (and still is) understood as only an idealised approximation of 'real world' exchange rate movements, (either a rough guide at any point of time, or a long-run tendency). Deviations from PPP were believed to be confined to narrow limits. Nonetheless, and critical for the current analysis, among such disturbances, shifts in the international movement of capital were frequently cited, because they prevent the exchange rate moving to reflect trade in goods and services.[14] But pre-Bretton Woods, such movements were of limited significance, and the analysis lay dormant during the Bretton-Woods period of fixed exchange rates.

So by the time the Bretton Woods Agreement was terminated and leading international currencies were being floated, PPP theory was the means by which the new era was to be comprehended. Yet by the 1970s, and especially the 1980s, 'history' provided large movements in exchange rates inconsistent with even an approximate PPP thesis. So the object of the modern adaptations of the Mundell-Fleming model has been to seek to explain why the exchange rate has not performed the expected equilibrating role.

For example, the contributions of Dornbusch *et al.* on asymmetrical information in international markets, and the application of theories of 'rational expectations' (Dornbusch 1976) are embellishments of the Mundell-Fleming model which are able to derive the exchange rate volatility approximately consistent with what we see in the 'real' world. This argument here is posed in terms of deviations from the behaviour and structure of perfect competition explaining deviations from PPP. It is argued that different parts of national economies adjust at different speeds to exchange rate changes. Asset markets are internationalised and adjust quickly to exchange rates, while goods markets and labor markets are dominated by an oligopolistic structure, and so are much slower to adjust. For Dornbusch, "a model of imperfect competition is essential because the less-than-perfect degree of substitution is a key ingredient in PPP deviations" (1989:1079).

Such embellishments of the PPP theory reflect an alarmingly simplistic conception of the nature of theoretical abstraction: that a theory based in perfect competition comes more to approximate 'reality' the more assumptions of uncertainty and imperfection are substituted for assumptions of 'perfection'. Beyond epistemological issues of what constitutes adequate theory, one might suggest that such an approach has the effect of turning conceptual problems into technical problems, with the suggestion that there are technical solutions. Asymmetrical information suggests a solution through improved systems of information. Imperfect competition suggests the need to deregulate markets (particularly labor markets). In this respect, the model is fundamentally limited for its object. It remains tied to the proposition that 'reality' has its base in perfect competition,[15] and that the ability to predict the possibility of volatility by means of changing assumptions in an ahistorical model is a sufficient basis for policy formulation.

This framework has determined that developments in the theory have generally lacked cohesive direction. Indeed, it was history, rather than the development within monetary theory, which demonstrated that the original Mundell-Fleming model had not resolved the contradiction between the internationality of capital and the nationality of state regulation. Volatile exchange rates, and the severance of a clear equilibrating link between the nation's exchange rate and its international trade balance were the evidence that, with free capital markets, national monetary policy could *not* permit the nation state to secure the monetary system.

It is apparent that developments in 'refining' the Mundell-Fleming model coincide with what a number of eminent figures have noted as a separation in the development of monetary theory and monetary policy (for example, Goodhart 1990). It would suggest that theoretical developments in explaining instability were not proving useful in preventing instability. Again, this is *prima face* evidence of what has been identified as a contradiction as distinct from a problem. Hence, it was history which dictated the direction of theoretical developments. The object of theory came to be to 'catch up' with unfolding historical evidence, with the underlying theoretical approach remaining unchallenged: the theoretical agenda remained within the precepts of the Mundell-Fleming model, leaving its underlying assumptions about the world economy to pass without conjecture.

National Monetary Policy in a Global Context

With the global integration of accumulation, national monetary policy is required to meet international agendas, and at the same time secure domestic accumulation. How are these needs being reconciled, so that one is not being subordinated to the other? There are two dimensions here. One relates to the role of national monetary policy in contributing to a stable international money system, for it could be argued that an unstable international monetary system is detrimental to the overall global level of accumulation The other dimension is the role of monetary policy in contributing to making 'local' production more internationally competitive.[16]

Exchange Rate Co-ordination

An aspect of monetary policy can involve central bank intervention in the international currency market in order to adjust the national currency's exchange rate. Such intervention adds stability to the international money system when the central bank's long-term perception of the market exchange rate is used to over-rule short-term speculative volatility. But exchange rates are only relative prices, so that central banks cannot fix their own currency's exchange rate in isolation. For any one currency to appreciate, all other currencies must depreciate.

For currencies which are relatively minor within the international currency-trading system, such interventions are generally absorbed by the market, and are not perceived to upset the overall exchange rate balance. But this is not the case where there is direct interdependence between particular currencies, either because they are major international currencies, or because of a disproportionately large volume of transfer across two or more 'minor' national currencies. In each of these cases, central bank intervention to adjust the exchange rate will not be absorbed by the market, but is likely to lead to competitive interventions by other central banks to realign the relative price. If this is the case, central bank management of the national currency value may require cross-national co-ordination of exchange rate intervention, based on agreed adjusted relative currency values.

Yet exchange rate co-ordination is anything but a widespread and long-term process, despite its apparent logic for securing a stabel global monetary system. There exist two sources of opposition to such a regime. For one source, particularly capital in international finance, it is the fractures and discontinuities in the global capital market which provide the space for profitable manoeuvre. For the other source, a stable international system exists as an ideal, but there is opposition to the requirements placed on national monetary policy in order to defend that system; that the costs of those domestic policies required to stabilise the currency may be too high. From this perspective, the requirements of international co-ordination of exchange rate 'locks in' the terms on which different parts of capital engage with international accumulation. In these circumstances, national monetary policy no longer *actively* mediates the conditions under which different parts of capital engage in international accumulation.

The countries which are (or have been) most actively involved in exchange rate co-ordination are those with the most highly integrated processes of accumulation — where there is the greatest presence of comprehensively internationalised individual capitals (what in Chapter 5 were defined as capitals in the global circuit); and where movement in third-party exchange rates are least likely to upset the achievement of co-ordination. Those most closely fitting these conditions are the G3 countries (the United States, Germany and Japan) on the one hand, and the countries of the European Union on the other.

The G3 are the world's largest international investors and financiers as well as traders. For this reason, most of their cross-border trade and investment is with each other, and their currencies are seen as close substitutes as a form of international wealth-holding. A movement in the value of one G3 currency has sufficient impact on the other two to bring about a direct adjustment of their currency values also.

For the G3 countries, the issue of exchange rate co-ordination first arose in the mid 1980s. From 1982, the United States' current account deficit started to grow. While monetary theory would have predicted the value of the United States dollar to fall, it in fact increased rapidly.[17] Despite the Reagan Administration's earlier hands-off approach to the exchange rate and the balance of payments, by 1985, there was widespread recognition that the United States balance of payments position was unsustainable. United States Treasury Secretary James A. Baker sought to initiate an internationally-orchestrated devaluation of the United States dollar by means of monetary policy co-ordination between the world's major industrialised countries.[18] The first such initiative was the Plaza Agreement of September 1985, and the more substantial Louvre Accord of 1987.[19] The agreements involved policies by the German and Japanese states to appreciate their currencies, and reduce their current account surpluses, as the precondition of the depreciation of the United States dollar. The longer-term measures agreed in the Louvre Accord posed the operation of target ranges for exchange rates, which each country's monetary policy would seek to maintain; and fiscal policies which would assist to balance trade flows.

This was not just altruism by the German and Japanese states. A high United States dollar not only affected the United States balance of payments, it also reduced the relative value of the Yen and Deutsche Mark as internationally circulating money capital and increased the cost of repayment of loans denominated in United States dollar. But there were also costs in Germany and Japan in participating in policy co-ordination to alleviate the United States crisis. Japanese fiscal expansion to encourage imports worsened the long term state debt. Bundesbank cuts in interest rates reduced the value of the Mark, but at a cost of domestic inflation. Moreover, with policy directed to stabilising the United States dollar, the Deutsche Mark/Yen exchange rate became unpredictable. By early 1989, the Yen had appreciated 22% against the Deutsche Mark, despite Germany's relatively higher current account surplus (BIS *Annual Report* 1989: 167).

With the fall in the price of the United States dollar, and the rectification of the current account deficit,[20] the costs of exchange rate co-ordination became more conspicuous. In each of the G3 countries, monetary policy was 'reclaimed' by domestic policy agendas and formal co-ordination terminated.

The second example of co-ordination is the European Union (EU). Of the industrialised countries, the nations of the EU are the most comprehensively integrated. The development of free mobility of commodities and money within the EU has led to the 'Europeanisation' of industry (Rosewarne 1990; see also Bressand, 1990), whereby industry has restructured to produce for an integrated European economy. Further, European productive investment is generally financed from within Europe itself (Smith and Walter 1991).

In 1979, the European Monetary System was established to provide exchange rate stability for the main European currencies (excluding Sterling). The implementation of the European Monetary System, intended to lead to a single central bank, a single currency, and a unitary monetary policy can be seen, and is widely advocated, as the logical development of the integrated accumulation process. Yet the 'logic' of such a development focuses on the role of the state in securing the international money system, superseding the role of the nation state in mediating domestic monetary conflicts. These conflicts arise between capitals (and with direct implications for their 'attached' workers) according to the form in which their individual accumulation is linked into European accumulation.

The agreement by nation states of Europe to move towards monetary union involves acceptance of a given exchange rate, and the need to invoke domestic policies to defend that rate. But insofar as the monetary policy which supports exchange rates is an integral part of national politics, it is ultimately impossible to conceive of monetary unification without political unification. Political unification, in which the Maastricht Treaty is a step, and currency union, of which the Exchange Rate Mechanism is a step, cannot be developed separately.

The combined development of currency and political unification implies that nation states in Europe can abandon the role of mediating the terms on which different parts of capital engage in international accumulation, in the name of some higher 'logic' of accumulation. To be sure, the largest, and most Europeanised of individual capitals are somewhat indifferent as to the exchange rates at which individual currencies enter monetary union. They hold assets in all major currencies. They also have the most to gain from currency stability, irrespective of the rate of entry. But for the majority of other capitals, which have only partial links with other European currencies (as exporters, importers, and cross-currency borrowers), as well as (immobile) workers, the exchange rate at which national currencies are absorbed into the Exchange Rate Mechanism is critical. Yet these different domestic interests want different rates. No matter what rate of entry is negotiated at peak level, there are sources of domestic resistance.[21] Hence the so-called 'Sterling crisis' of September 1992 (which was also a crisis for the Italian Lira, the Spanish Peseta and the French

Franc; and hence a systemic crisis for the European Exchange Rate Mechanism)[22] and the widespread popular opposition to the Maastricht Treaty, particularly from within Denmark, Britain, and France, are to be understood as expressions of the fact that nation states reflect balances of sectional interests. This is not to suggest that non-co-operation reconciles domestic interests, but it does permit smaller, and more locality-confined capitals to play out the conflicts in a space in which they can expect to exert some impact.

European monetary union, should it arise, will be a reflection of the *political* dominance of the most internationalised individual capitals within each member country; it will not follow simply from the unimpeded and increased movement of capital within an economically-integrated Europe. Nonetheless, the more volatile and unsustainable are exchange rates, the more capital within each nation will perceive the costs of volatility, and the more likely will be the adoption of arrangements of co-ordination. But as perceptions of the costs of volatility, and of sustaining co-ordinated exchange rates change, so the national politics of co-ordination changes.

Monetary Policy and Wages Policy

While the determination of exchange rates is the explicitly international dimension of monetary policy, it is not the only dimension. Insofar as all accumulation is internationalised, the 'domestic' dimension of monetary policy, as a branch of macroeconomic management, is no less international in its implications. In a world with increasing emphasis on the international competitiveness of industry, national monetary policy has a role to play in securing the internationally competitive costs of local production.

The cost competitiveness of local production relates to the the rate of surplus value within each country. The rate of surplus value, it will be recalled, depends on three factors: the length of the working day (absolute surplus value); labor productivity within the working day (relative surplus value); and the value of labor power, which determines the proportion of the working day allocated to surplus value generation. An increase in absolute or relative surplus value, or a decrease in the value of labor power within a nation, can make accumulation more profitable and, in an international context, make production within that nation more profitable.

There are two ways to reduce the value of labor power. One is to make labor more productive so that the consumption needs of labor can be met more cheaply. Such initiatives are beyond the scope of monetray policy; they are considered in Chapter 9. The other way is to reduce the level of consumption of labor. To this end, national monetary policy in most OECD countries, formulated in the name of the conventional national objectives, has, in the past few decades, adopted high domestic real interest rates, increasing the proportion of the working day going to surplus value — in the form of interest payments on housing loans and consumer credit.

While monetary policy in the 1970s sought to manage domestic inflation by a targeted growth of national money supply, the new approach targets short-term domestic interest rates as a means to regulate domestic demand (Batten *et al* 1990), with monetary theory focusing on the transmission mechanism between interest rates and demand (IMF *Annual Report* 1991:105-08), in contrast with the former theoretical focus on the transmission mechanism between money supply and prices.

When first advanced, the regulation of demand via domestic interest rates was advocated by policy makers as 'non-discriminatory', unlike the differential impact of fiscal tightening. Of course, monetary policy is always discriminatory between those who borrow internationally, and those constrained to borrow at domestic interest rates. High domestic interest rates and constrained national demand involves a particular intervention between interests of different parts of capital — between those subject to the constraints and those immune from or indifferent to them. In general, those subject to the constraints of high interest rate policies are the smaller, domestically oriented capitals, which are also predominantly the national sources of employment.

That form of 'discrimination is inherent to monetary policy. The problem with reliance on monetary policy to regenerate domestic accumulation was that interest rate policy could *not* successfully discriminate between classes: capitals subject to domestic interest rates as well as labor faced the same contractionary effect. In pursuing international competitiveness of local production, national monetary policy could be seen to be generating domestic recession.

If inflation is to be reduced without an investment and employment crisis, demand must be cut by labor but not by capital. Wages policy becomes the new complement of monetary policy. Hence it is of no surprise that in many countries the effectiveness of national monetary policy is increasingly being linked explicitly to wage restraint and labor market deregulation. The role of the nation state is being cast in terms of the labor system supporting the monetary system. This issue is developed in Chapter 9 in relation to national strategies for international competitiveness.

Conclusion

The management of the money system, in theory and policy, has been profoundly affected by the global integration of capital markets in the last twenty years. It is therefore something of an irony that the conventional wisdom which condoned and advanced that tendency should have such great difficulty in comprehending and harnessing the processes to which it has given rise. It is more of an irony, indeed a profound limitation, that this conventional wisdom, while not without its debates, continues to appreciate internationalised money through the analytical grid of national units.[23] The spatial movement created by the historical process has superseded the spatial dimension of the analytical categories.

That monetary policy remains bound by national categories is not surprising, for it addresses the policies currently implemented by nation states. Where it remains oriented to a *nationalist* perspective, this is a limitation of understanding. It is an understanding derived from monetary theory, which remains tied to a nationalist perspective only by convention.

Yet while money itself has internationalised, monetary policy has not, beyond particular cases of exchange rate co-ordination. Indeed, in a world structured by nation states it cannot. The contradiction between the internationalisation of accumulation and the nationality of regulation of accumulation is experienced as national monetary policy which cannot meet international and domestic requirements at the same time. What remains systematic in nationalist monetary policy is its gravitation towards constituting labor as the principal obstacle to the achievement of national economic objectives. Through national monetary policy, the contradiction between the internationality of capital and the nationality of state regulation expresses the class contradiction between labor and capital. This issue is developed further in a consideration of balance of payments policy.

Notes

1. Of course, money does not always and in all circumstances take the form of capital. Money becomes money capital when it is advanced in the process of accumulation. See Brewener (1989) for some discussion of this point and some raised in the remainder of this section.

2. This conception of tied money is found clearly expressed in a recent study by the Research Department of the International Monetary Fund (Goldstein et al 1991). In defining international capital movements, it contends:

> Net capital flows, which serve as the financial counterpart to the transfer of real resources through a trade or current account imbalance, arise only when saving and investment are imbalanced within countries. Gross capital flows, which allow individuals and firms to adjust the form of financial claims issued and held, can be important in improving the liquidity of portfolios and diversifying risk. Since gross capital flows can be mutually offsetting across countries, they need not involve a transfer of real resources.

Note the emphasis that capital flows are understood with reference to 'real' resource movements, and that the whole process is understood by reference to national units. It is hardly surprising that the study concludes that "it has proved difficult to obtain stable empirical relationships between (gross or net) capital flows and their underlying determinants" (Goldstein *et al* 1991:1)!

3. As the rate of interest is determined by competition between different parts of capital, there can be no general laws governing the relation between the rate of interest and the rate of profit (Marx 1894:485).

4. In some countries, this was in part because of inappropriate definitions of money supply, associated with the arbitrary delineation of banks and non-banks; and partly because targeting was not formally adhered to. But, as the experience of other countries shows even when these factors were not an issue, the policy of money supply targeting was abandoned (see Goodhart 1989:300-05).

5. The distinction between monetary and real aspects of the economy has no meaning in Marxism, as money, production and commodities are just different forms taken by capital as it moves through its circuit.

6. In national balance of payments terms, the capital account was no longer driven by the balance of trade; capital movement developed a logic of its own. This is developed in Chapter 7.

7. This derives from the earlier proposition that interest payments, the (net) profits of buying and selling, and profit of industrial production must all come out of the surplus value created in the process of producing new goods and services.

8. There are two important aspects of this process which relate to the tendency towards crisis. First, the increase in the profitability of buying and selling capital assets compared with producing new value was unsustainable, since it is only the latter which produces the surplus value on which the former depends for its profitability. Second, while credit operated as a counter-tendency of a crisis tendency insofar as it increased the supply of money capital advanced and reduced the turnover time of capital, it could only do so by bringing

forward the profitability of capital, not by regeneration new conditions of profitable production.

9. The United States balance of payments crisis which led to the exchange rate agreements is the subject of Chapter 8.

10. This is clearly true of the 'original' open-economy macroeconomics of Dornbusch (1980) which is entirely partial in its construction. It remains true of the more recent and elaborate versions which construct an array of multiple national interdependencies.

11. It is ironic in this context that Mundell's own analysis (1961) contends that an optimum currency area (ie the space within which a single currency regime permits most effective economic management) should not be defined by reference to political units (nations), but by reference to the mobility of factors of production. An optimum currency area is one in which factors are mobile, and this could be a section of a nation; multiple nations; or sections of multiple nations. The basis of this argument is that immobility across space restricts the possibility of changes in industry mix in response to currency revaluations. While the theory applies to all factors, the principal barriers to mobility are associated with natural resources and labor.

12. There is a dual problem here: the shift from a global single price for an individual commodity to the aggregation of national price levels, including for non-traded goods; and comparing prices internationally when different bundles of goods are included in price indices.

13. This approach was popularised in the early 1970s, along with the broader re-emergence of monetarism. See in particular Mundell (1968; 1971) and Frenkel and Johnson (1975).

14. See Chapter 9 for a discussion of this in the context of balance of payments accounting.

15. This is not to be read as a rejection of some conception of 'perfect competition' as a hypothetical abstraction, useful for understanding real processes. The concern comes when the hypothetical abstraction is converted into an achievable reality, to be actualised by means of appropriate policy.

16. The concept of international competitiveness is by no means self evident. It is subject to critical evaluation in Chapter 9. At this point, it can be equated with securing the internationally average rate of profit in internationally-exposed markets.

17. See Chapter 8 for a detailed discussion of these circumstances.

18. For a useful summary of this and other forms of international macro policy co-ordination, see Webb (1991: 329-40).

19. The Plaza Agreement and the Louvre Accord were developed at meetings of the G7 countries. All participating countries were signatories the respective agreements. But there is no doubt that they applied most directly to the G3 countries: Germany, Japan and the United States.

20. See Figure 8.1, page 138.

21. See De Cecco (1989) for a useful, brief discussion of the divergent industrial interests within European nations, and the difficulties for a unified monetary system.

22. One of the criteria for exchange rate co-ordination is that third-party exchange rate movements do not upset the stability of the co-ordinated rates. In this regard, there is an inherent difficulty which comes from Germany being both a member of the European Exchange Rate Mechanism, and a G3 country.

23. International state financial institutions such as the World Bank and the International Monetary Fund are understood as a separate sphere of analysis, occasionally 'intervening' in national domains.

7

Balance of Payments as
Nationalist Accounting

Balance of payments figures have status as a primary economic indicator, called on by national policy analysts and international market speculators to signal how a nation is performing in the international economy. Moreover, there was once something predictable about a country's balance of payments position. The distinction between countries which ran a current account surplus and those which ran a current account deficit was close enough to the difference between rich and poor countries. Poor countries had to import more than they export, and they paid with capital inflows — foreign investment or debt. The pattern of balance of payments figures was, in short, a financial summary of imperialism.

But over the last twenty years, particularly since the 1980s, that standard story has been changing with the accelerating international mobility of capital — both commodities and money. From the First World War up to 1982, current account imbalances of the industrialised countries were small. If all the imbalances (surpluses and deficits, irrespective of sign) are added up for the fourteen largest industrialised countries, the figure was never above $US100 billion per year, and usually below $US50 billion per year. But from 1982, this figure climbed rapidly, stabilising at around $US300 billion from 1986 onwards (Turner 1991: 9). Indeed in but a few years in the early 1980s, the United States was transformed from the largest surplus country to the largest deficit country in the world.[1]

The 'free market' theory which inspired the policy of exchange rate floats predicted that exchange rate movements woulds rectify balance of payment current account problems. But this has not been the case. Rather than resolving current account imbalances, private capital flows have tended, if anything, to leave deficit countries and enter surplus countries, causing volatility of exchange rates, and accentuating balance of payments 'problems'. While the US was undergoing the change identified above, the exchange rate 'should' have been falling; but instead it was increasing, because of capital inflow. The fact that exchange rates were not moving to offset surpluses and deficits has left a difficulty in understanding what is determining the financial flows which appear on a nation's balance of payments.

Yet the more confusing balance of payments data are, the more important they become to national analysts. More and more levers of domestic policy are being allocated to tame the balance of payments. Economic theory has been set the task of solving the riddle. With balance of payments trends looking as messy as tea leaves in the bottom of a cup, so economists and bankers come forward as mystics, purporting a capacity to read the tea leaves, predict the future, and resolve the mess. We are told, as nations, how competitive we all are, how indebted we all are, how much harder we must work, what industries we must develop (and abandon), and what rewards will come if we are successful.

Within this sophistry, there is unquestioning reliance on the balance of payments as a data source. Certainly, the balance of payments tell imports and exports of a nation, but beyond that there is ambiguity, for the system of balance of payments accounting is predicated on the proposition that global accumulation can be understood, both in itself, and in its national expression, through a system of national classification of capital.

This chapter looks at the structure of balance of payments accounting as an expression of a nationalist conception of accumulation. It argues that balance of payments categories give a particular, ideological construction of accumulation. While recent internationalisation has made economic processes increasingly globally integrated, balance of payments accounting attempts to disentangle the integration into discrete national processes. This has two sorts of implications. First, the accounting requirement of allocating each part of internationally-mobile capital a unique nationality is technically flawed. The system's taxonomy reveals logical inconsistencies and arbitrary, but critical classifications.

Second, the national aggregation found in balance of payments accounting provides the analytical framework for the constitution of a shared national experience of the international economy. It is by means of balance of payments accounting that individual interactions in international accumulation are socialised as national interactions. But they are socialised in a class-based society, structured by the subordination of labor to capital. While the individual international interactions are predominantly those undertaken by capital, the process of (national) socialisation sees the responsibility for rectifying international payments imbalances transferred to labor. Compared with capital, labor is internationally immobile. While national policy cannot impose burdens on capital which are different from those in other countries, this is not the case with respect to labor and it is labor, through its consumption and its productivity, which is the ultimate object of national balance of payments policy.

The consequence is that balance of payments data come to appear less as a description of a nation's position in international accumulation, and more as a nationalist ideological construct, drawn on to legitimate national redistribution away from labor and towards capital. This chapter develops this proposition in the context of the formal principles of balance of payments accounting. The case of the United States' balance of payments in the early 1980s will be looked at in Chapter 8, as a particular, and historically critical, case. Chapter 9 shows how the post-war evolution of economic theory and policies with respect to the balance of payments has moved increasingly towards targeting labor as the key to 'national success'.

The System of Accounting

The balance of payments measures the movement of capital (commodities and money) between countries. It comprises two accounts: the current account, measuring inflows and outflows of commodities and income over an accounting period; and a capital account, measuring changes in international asset holdings over an accounting period. Hence the current account measures flows, in which all transactions, inward and outward, are shown, and the capital account measures stocks (for example, the level of direct foreign investment) for which only a net figure is shown (investment by foreigners less withdrawal of investment by foreigners).

The system of double entry book-keeping ensures that the balance of payments always balances. Even when the exchange rate does not move to balance the current account, a surplus or deficit in the current account has a counter-entry in the capital account, showing respectively as a build-up of foreign reserves, or as increasing foreign debt. This accounting process has created the impression that the capital account 'compensates' for imbalances in the current account; although whether this describes a real process, or just an accounting construction, is a recognised debate which will be considered shortly.

The accounting system that is the balance of payments has two orders of problem: the accuracy of data, and the imposed nationalist classification system.

128

The Accuracy of Balance of Payments Figures

Because of the complexity of the data to be assembled in this account, balance of payments figures are always of limited accuracy. Some indication of this is that, on a global scale, the transfers should sum to zero, but they do not. In fact, the inaccuracy has been large. The world went into deficit in 1974. A global deficit of around 2% of world trade was maintained from the mid 1970s until 1980. From 1980 to 1982, the deficit increased to 6% of world trade, but steadily declined over the second half of the 1980s to again stabilise at under 2% (BIS *Annual Reports*). While now small compared with the early 1980s, the statistical discrepancy remains sufficiently significant to warrant hesitancy about reliance on any single nations' trade balance.[2]

Some explanation of inaccuracy arises from the technical problems of data gathering, which have increased as countries progressively deregulated their foreign exchange controls. These controls, while not existing so as to record international payments, nonetheless could provide national statisticians with relatively accurate data on outflows and inflows. With the dismantling of controls, data have had to be derived more from survey techniques.

A further dimension in the inaccuracy of trade data is found in the rapid growth of transnational corporations in the 1980s. Transnational corporations can corrupt national data in a number of ways, due to the fact that cross-national transactions can remain intra-corporate. In particular, a corporation can price its 'internal' exports and imports differently from 'market' prices, so as to relocate financial assets internationally, especially for taxation minimisation. This is the process called 'transfer pricing'.

Transnational corporate structures can corrupt national balance of payments data in other ways, too. For example, in a payment system called back-to-backs, a company in country I exports commodities to a country II, generating an export entry in the balance of payments of country I, and an import entry for country II. But the payment from country II is not made directly to the company in country I, but to a subsidiary of the company in country III (a low tax country). The subsidiary in country III then lends the value of the exports to the company in country I, where the interest payments on the loan (to itself) are tax deductible. The company in country I is thereby 'paid' for its export. Country I's balance of payments records an export in the current account (but for which there is no direct receipt) and an increase in foreign debt recorded in the capital account.

The extent of such practices is inherently difficult to determine, although they are thought to be a substantial part of the explanation of why many countries show growing foreign debt, even though corporate leverage has been falling. To the extent that these practices are motivated by the minimisation of taxation obligations, they are invariably 'hidden'.

But accuracy is not the central concern of the current analysis. The question to be addressed here is not so much the techniques of data collection, but the theory implicit in data classification, and the politics and policies which follow from that classification.

Ontological Primacy of National Units

The system of national accounting provides the primary data on which national, macroeconomic analysis and policy are formed. The balance of payments, as an associated construct, provides the data on a nation's financial relations with the rest of the world. Combined, these data signify a fundamental proposition of macroeconomic theory and policy: that the 'national economy' is the primary economic entity, with the rest of the world exerting an exogenous (although not insignificant) impact.

Earlier chapters have already addressed how the assumed ontological primacy of the nation, while always a partial understanding, has become increasingly incoherent in the face of recent internationalisation. In relation to balance of payments accounting, the presumption of ontological primacy manifests as a nationally-defined taxonomy of capital movements: that transactions between individuals (either people or companies) which happen to cross political boundaries are recorded as transactions between nations (the nation's export income, foreign equity holdings, debt, etc.). This creates the impression that money and commodity movements are determined by reference to national units; that is, that money movement and commodity exchange takes place between countries and by reason of the national form, rather than between/within corporations. Yet for the corporations themselves, nationality may be quite arbitrary, and there is no analytical sense, let alone legal sense, in which 'the economy' is owner of capital.[3] So it must be asked whether the balance of payments really describe national economic performance, or whether the adoption of a national taxonomy of capital based on the assumption of national coherence in resource flows in itself creates the very notion of national economic performance.

While it is indeed important to determine how this (global) movement of capital appears within the space of a nation, the critical question is the appropriate spatial configuration from which to perceive this process; or at what point in the analysis is national unity constituted. Export income does not accrue to the nation as a whole; and foreign debt does not involve a national, *per capita*, liability; but they do have national impacts.

Analysis must start from the international perspective and then move to the national unit understood as a segment of the global process — a segment with some autonomy, but generally structured by the international logic. By starting with a model of national interaction, the cohesion of the national economy, and thus its responsiveness to domestic policy initiatives, is established by assumption, not by analysis.

A contradiction has thus emerged for national economic policy. Developments in international transactions have increased the popular concern with international economic processes and national state economic policy is being determined significantly in reaction to developments in international transactions. Yet the information source (the balance of payments) from which the national state's response to these developments is determined is itself unable to depict those developments. Therefore, all national state economic policies based on balance of payments data must be profoundly questioned.

Capital Mobility and the Balance of Payments

While the internationalisation of capital has been a crucial economic development of the last two decades, balance of payments categories fail to capture the characteristics of this development in two basic respects. First, the structure of the balance of payments cannot permit an adequate recording of the international movement of capital. Second, in an era of international mobility, the attribution of a nationality to capital becomes an increasingly arbitrary, and thereby purposeless exercise.

Can the Balance of Payments Record the Internationalisation of Capital?

At first thought, we might look to the capital account of the balance of payments to find evidence of recent internationalisation. But the capital account provides little useful evidence, for it has been constructed as an accounting category to meet quite a different need: the increase/decrease in the level of foreign equity and debt within the 'national economy'. An international perspective on data is thereby obscured by the demands of nationalist interpretation.

There are two essential ways in which the capital account of the balance of payments is unable to depict critical dimensions of the international mobility of money.

First, the capital account is not a recording of international financial transactions in any complete sense. It does not record the flows of money capital (debt and equity) in and out of the country over time; it records only changes in stocks of capital at a particular point in time. It is the integrated flow of capital into, out of and within nations which reveals the process of internationalisation of capital — the rate at which capital moves spatially over time in the process of international accumulation. Any given change in stock of capital may occur on a large or small turnover, but this latter dimension is immaterial for the capital account. So the capital account of the balance of payments does not reveal the rate at which money capital enters and leaves any nation, how long it stays or what it is used for.

Some information on the flow of capital is found in the current account, in the form of profit and interest inflow and outflow. Yet these are only partial indicators for there is but a loose connection with credit and equity flows. Moreover, the two accounts combined make no recording of the movement of money unassociated with credit and equity advanced for productive capital: most conspicuously, short term speculation in commodity and money markets, even though these speculative currency movements have the largest value per unit of time of all international transactions, and may in effect enter and leave a national accounting space multiple times per day. Indeed, since national currencies, national-currency-denominated bonds, and equities in 'national' companies are now widely traded in international markets (outside the nation-of-origin), these flows may or may not have contact at all with the nation's external accounts.

The second problem which arises from the international mobility of capital is how the international expansion of industrial capital relates to a nation's balance of payments. While it is clear that exports and imports of commodities fit clearly into national accounts, it is less clear as to how the non-national operations of national firms are to be treated. If, instead of exporting commodities, a company exports capital (it becomes a transnational corporation) its treatment in nation's balance of payments becomes a critical issue. With an increasing degree of international capital mobility, it must be asked whether the nation's 'external accounts' should be measuring the interactions of the nation in the international economy, or of the nation's companies (including its transnational companies) in the international arena.[4]

Can Capital Have a Nationality?

The question, therefore, is which capital movements are to be included in which country's balance of payments.[5] In this question, the limitations of the assumed ontological primacy of national units are clearly expressed. The division of international capital between different countries' accounts requires that formal rules exist by which nationality is determined. As will be discussed below, a fundamental problem arises in this requirement. Because capital is international in orientation, the rules by which nationality is attributed must be imprecise and arbitrary. They must be imprecise in recognition that there are diverse ways that capital may be attached to its 'nation-of-origin'; and they must be arbitrary because rules of definition require that shades of grey be classified as black or white. As a consequence, the balance of payments (particularly the capital account and income flows in the current account), are as much a reflection of definitions as of 'real' processes.

Balance of payments categories demand that each individual and enterprise be allocated a nationality and a residence. The category of residence is sufficient for commodity exchange (exports and imports), for these are classified with reference to the place of production of the commodity, irrespective of who produces it. For this purpose, an enterprise incorporated in more than one country is divided into separate enterprises, each with its own nation of residence (IMF 1977:23). From this point, data collection treats a foreign 'resident' the same as a 'local' producer.

But for money capital movements (the capital account and income flows in the current account), 'residence' is not a sufficient criterion. Capital must have a 'nationality'.[6] How nationality is defined within the balance of payments will be addressed shortly. First, it is important to determine why the attribution of nationality is essential to the structure of the balance of payments.

For movements of money capital, 'residence' identifies the side of the ledger on which an international money movement is located (an entry or exit of capital), but not the account in which the entry is located. The recording (such as it occurs) of the international movement of money capital is spread across both accounts: foreign investment and credit/debt being recorded in the capital account, while the associated income flows of profit and interest are recorded in the current account. Yet there can be no clear differentiation between income (current account) and investment (capital account) when the only recorded information is an international movement of money.

In the balance of payments, the difference between foreign investment (capital account entries) and profit or other income flows (current account entries) is identified only on the basis of the nationality attributed to the enterprise which initiates the flow. That is, foreign investments are defined as international money flows which emanate from the nation of origin, while income is defined as international money flows received by the nation of origin. This is the only criterion by which the balance of payments can differentiate income from investment.

For this reason, if not also a broader economic nationalism, the allocation of nationality to each enterprise is crucial to the structure of the balance of payments. So the definition of nationality within the balance of payments must be seen as an important conceptual issue. But how is nationality to be defined? It could be by reference to the nationality of major stockholders (but what constitutes 'major', and should their nationality be defined by residence or passport?); by the dominant nationality of directors, or by the location of corporate head office. There is no reason for any of these to correspond.[7]

The criterion used in the International Monetary Fund's *Balance of Payments Manual* (by which all countries construct their balance of payments) is an individual's or enterprise's 'centre of interest'. No conceptual category in the Manual has undergone greater transformation than this one. In the first edition of the *Manual* (1950), nationality was defined by reference to an individual's and enterprise's 'centre of interest'. Each country compiling its own balance of payments could decide how to define 'centre of interest'. By the fourth (and current) edition of the *Manual* (1977), increasingly detailed, though conspicuously arbitrary, rules of thumb are included for defining 'centre of interest' in terms of threshold proportions of share ownership which might determine 'foreignness'(IMF 1977:Chs.3&18). In most cases, 'centre of interest' will equate to the location of head office, although in some decentralised transnational corporations, autonomous subsidiaries will be constituted as discrete 'centres of interest'.

The more precise these rules are, the more arbitrary become the defining boundaries of nationality — a minor share transaction can change nationality even though the operation of a company remains unchanged. Two cases illustrate the point.

If company A based in country I has a minor subsidiary in country II, the capital flows of that subsidiary are audited through the balance of payments of country I, defined as company A's 'centre of interest'. If that subsidiary grows to become a discrete locus of accumulation, it may be redefined as having a 'centre of interest' in country II. When a subsidiary requires the attribution of a discrete 'centre of interest' is clearly arbitrary, but it has significant balance of payments implications. The capital transactions of the subsidiary would then leave the balance of payments of country I (except as they relate to financial flows with the parent company) and be recorded in the balance of payments of country II.

A company with head office in country I may choose to move head office to country II for taxation reasons or to gain insider access to a large market, such as Europe. If this company is centrally financed, such that subsidiaries do not constitute discrete 'centres of interest', the effect will be to relocate all capital account entries from the balance of payments of country I to country II, even though there may be no actual change in the spatial pattern of accumulation of the company. The assets in country I will now enter that country's balance of payments as foreign investment, while its foreign assets, such as in country II will disappear form country I's balance of payments. The company's debt will disappear from country I's foreign debt and become country II's foreign debt — unless country II was the source of the debt, which itself raises accounting complexities.

The only sense in which the I.M.F. *Manual* recognises the existence of a conceptual problem in relation to nationality is in the handling of retained earnings (now widely renamed 'reinvested earnings') on foreign investment: that part of income on foreign investment not remitted to the parent company. In the case of retained earnings, there is no cross-border flow of funds. If the balance of payments recorded simply cross-border flows, retained earnings would not be entered; yet they appear in the current account as a profit outflow and in the capital account as new foreign investment. The 'foreignness' of investment is not determined by the (re)location of capital (an economic process) but by the ownership of capital (a politically defined issue). The exceptional treatment of retained earnings reflects a nationalist political priority in data gathering (a concern to document foreign ownership).

The case of retained earnings illustrates the fact that economic space and political space are not coterminous, and the structure of balance of payments accounting is designed to meet national political agendas, not to track the international movement of capital. For balance of payments accounting generally, the treatment of retained earnings is illustrative of confusion as to whether the balance of payments measure cross-border movements of money and commodities, or the international flows associated with companies of different (attributed) nationality.

Conclusion

The use of balance of payments data to understand the national expression of international accumulation must be questioned. Accuracy of data collection aside, entries on the capital account are particularly in need of caution, for accounting procedures require that relations between capitals be converted into relations between nations. One aspect of this is that individual capitals (and hence financial movements associated with these capitals) be attributed a contrived nationality in order that international movements be divided up between the different nations' accounts. Another aspect is that all transactions are converted into the domestic currency, even though the 'real' transaction may involve no such conversion. Hence national currency movements are given exaggerated importance in the balance of payments. These sorts of issues are not just statistical anomalies. They call into question the whole use and interpretation of balance of payments data. This will be considered further in Chapter 8, looking at a critical period in the United States' balance of payments.

But balance of payments data are recognised as a received wisdom, and national economic policies are being formulated explicitly with the balance of payments as an objective. In the process, nation states formulate policies which entrench uncritically the nationalist aggregation. This leads to a limited range of policy debates, even to a particular policy agenda. A current account deficit is taken to mean that 'the nation is living beyond its means'. Austerity, through government budget cuts and reduced disposable income, is the policy solution. Foreign debt is similarly posed as a national problem, even when it is private (corporate) debt. Nationalist taxonomy creates the appearance that, while the credit flow was initiated and expended for private purposes, the recorded debt is socialised, being a burden for all nationals. It is the 'national debt'. State policy then becomes the socialised responsibility for corporate liability.

The problem for state policy, as was seen in Chapter 5, is how to socialise this responsibility. There are multiple strategies by which nations can export more and import less, but different strategies affect different parts of capital differently: exchange rate depreciation through direct interventions in currency markets, or reduced domestic interest rates; export subsidies; import restrictions; and contractions in domestic demand all can reduce a current account deficit, but with very different impacts.

Here is the class dimension of balance of payments accounting as the data source of policy; an issue developed in Chapter 9. By assuming national cohesion, and thereby denying class divisions, policy plays out systematic class interventions, presented in the 'national interest'. As for monetary policy in an international context, the contradiction between the internationality of accumulation and the nationality of state regulation is seen here also as an expression of the contradiction between labor and capital.

Notes

1. See Chapter 8 for a detailed consideration of this development.

2. See BIS *Annual Report* 1983:86-90 for a discussion of the basis of growing statistical inaccuracy.

3. See Chapter 5 for a consideration of the category of 'foreign' capital.

4. A recalculation of the United States current account based on the international exports and imports of United States companies rather than on exports and imports of the United States itself is discussed below, page 142. See also Julius (1990).

5. A parallel issue issue relating to monetary policy can be noted here. In Chapter 6, the difficulty for national monetarism in 'managing' the national money supply was noted. In significant part, this was associated with unregulated international credit flows. But there is also the measurement problem of which financial flows make up the national money supply. See Bryant (1980) for a consideration of these issues.

6. The problem in balance of payments accounting of allocating capital a nationality was first noted in 1895 by W.P. Sterns, observing the United States data on international payments for 1879 (Sterns, 1895 cited in Wasserman and Ware 1965). He noted the impact on United States indebtedness of the migration of William A. Astor to England, and the marriage of Miss Vanderbilt to the Duke of Marlborough. With the current degree of mobility, this becomes a more prevalent and less clear issue. This point is not just a technical anomoly, particularly in small countries. In Australia, for example, in the late 1980s, there were several companies which each held around 8% of recorded national debt.

7. See Chapter 5 for a discussion of the concept of 'foreign capital'.

8

The United States Balance of Payments in the Mid 1980s: The National Burden of Global Change

The issues raised in the past two chapters point to developments in the United States in the mid 1980s as critical for an understanding of global developments in national monetary policy and exchange rates. Reference has been made to the failure of money supply targeting, the re-emergence of the exchange rate and balance of payments within monetary policy and a balance of payments 'crisis' which led to the United States moving from the largest creditor nation to the largest debtor nation in the world in just a few years. This was also the period in which Eurobonds 'took-off', and transformed the nature of international finance, stamping the 'speculative decade' label onto the 1980s.[1]

The 'crisis' in the United States' international payments is therefore not just a period and process of historical curiosity: it illustrates the difficulty of inserting the impact of international financial developments into a country's balance of payments; and the 'real' consequences which follow from that process. The United States international payments 'crisis' is also, in key respects, the history of the end of United States' hegemony within the world economy. Developments in the United States' balance of payments at this time express statistically some fundamental changes: the loss of United States' global dominance of manufacturing industry, as imports started to encroach into the United States' market; the loss of dominance of international investment, as foreign investment in the United States comes to surpass United States' investment abroad; and, most symbolic of all, the loss of United States' capacity to determine its own balance of payments and exchange rate viability, and the need to call on other currencies to support the dollar.

But the loss of hegemony was not about the United States being on the slippery slope to economic and political obscurity. By the end of the

1980s, the trade flows, investment flows, and the exchange rate had stabilised. Fears that the United States had lost its 'competitiveness' were allayed, but its singular dominance of the post-war world economy had gone. This was a critical expression of the global integration of accumulation which is the characteristic of recent internationalisation. The unresolved question is, therefore, not so much the general direction of change, with the United States 'coming back to the field', but why that change manifested so rapidly and chaotically.

The underlying 'facts' to be explained are as clear as they are incongruous. There is general recognition that the United States was losing its industrial pre-eminence throughout the post-war period, with Germany and Japan in particular gaining ascendency in international markets[2]. As a result, there occurred from the late 1970s a divergence in these countries' balance of payments current account figures: while Germany and Japan were acquiring increasing surpluses, the United States' current account balance was declining rapidly. From a current account surplus of $5bn in 1981, there was a deficit of $99bn by 1984 (see Figure 8.1).

In itself, that is not incongruous. But the conventional wisdom would suggest that an increasing United States' deficit would be associated with a falling exchange rate. Yet the United States dollar appreciated in real

FIGURE 8.1 United States: Current Account and Exchange Rate, 1979-1991

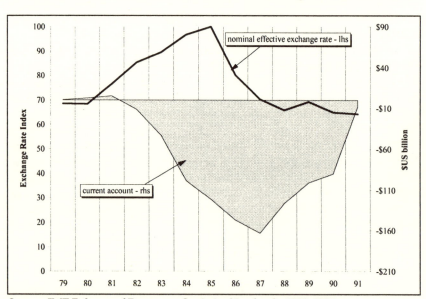

Source: IMF Balance of Payments Statistics Yearbook, 1980-1992

terms by about 50%. In Figure 8.1, the current account balance and the exchange rate 'should' have been moving in the same direction; yet they moved in opposite directions. Conventional analysis of these 'facts' looks to domestic, United States explanations, supplemented by the exogenous impact of foreign interest rates and exchange rates. Yet the developments expressed in the United States balance of payments during the mid 1980s is the expression of an inherently global process, which cannot be explained as a domestic problem. At the beginning of the 1980s, the United States was carrying the majority of the world's financial transactions on its books (balance of payments), both because of the predominance of the United States dollar in international financial markets, and because the bulk of financial intermediation took place under the auspices of institutions which are classified, for balance of payments purposes, as United States' companies. Dramatic changes in the international financial system were inevitably going to impact on the United States' balance of payments, no matter what happened to accumulation within the United States itself.

These financial developments impacted both directly in the United States' balance of payments as credit flows, and indirectly, through funding international reorganisation of corporate ownership, in foreign investment flows and even trade patterns. So the question, which makes this historical period worthy of close consideration, is how the system of balance of payments accounting gave a particular representation of these financial market developments as a United States' phenomenon, and so represented a long-term restructuring of the global economy as a short-term national crisis.

A consideration of both the current and capital accounts shows that the recorded change in the United States' balance of payments is not a straightforward representation of the impact of a process of global 'equalisation' (a loss of United States' hegemony). The structure of balance of payments accounting, discussed in Chapter 7, has served to misrepresent global historical developments, and so showed up in the United States' balance of payments as an exaggeration of national change. But because balance of payments data are believed to be a 'real' description, the exaggerated description generated an exaggerated response.

The evidence provided in the balance of payments is not therefore to be dismissed as a fantasy, but nor should these figures be seen as 'objective' evidence on which analysis, let alone national policy, can be based. Certainly, the widespread contemporary analyses which focused simply on a (inexplicably sudden) loss of competitiveness of United States' industry could not account for the increase in direct foreign investment coming into the United States, and particularly in association with an appreciating dollar. Nor could they account for the rapid 'rectification' of the United States' external position by the end of the 1980s. The United States policy debate which arose in the context of this international exchange crisis expressed little recognition that the data themselves may be a significant source of the problem, rather than representative of a 'real' problem. As such the policy debate was partial and *ad hoc*, and incapable of grasping the international dimensions of the aggregates they were seeking to 'rectify'. While the prominence of the debate waned with the (apparently self-) rectification of the balance of payments, this period remains in recent history as a largely inexplicable aberration; yet it is symptomatic of a fundamental development in global accumulation.

Before looking at this policy debate, this chapter documents how capital flows on a global scale, particularly the development of international financial markets and changing locations of industrial capital, manifested in unexpected and incongrous ways in the United States balance of payments. These manifestations are predominantly found in the capital account, but some also are in the current account.

The Current Account

TABLE 8.1 United States: Current Account, 1980 - 1990 (US billion)

	80	81	82	83	84	85	86	87	88	89	90
Merchandise Exports	224	237	211	202	220	216	223	250	320	362	389
Merchandise Imports	-250	-265	-248	-269	-322	-338	-368	-410	-447	-477	-498
Trade Balance	**-26**	**-28**	**-36**	**-67**	**-112**	**-122**	**-145**	**-160**	**-127**	**-116**	**-109**
Other goods, Serv.& Inc: Credit	120	144	150	150	172	164	175	195	230	268	292
Other Goods, Serv. & Inc.: Debit	-84	-99	-108	-109	-137	-141	-154	-176	-205	-228	-241
Balance on Goods & Services	**-25**	**-22**	**-28**	**-62**	**-113**	**-127**	**-144**	**-159**	**-123**	**-99**	**-89**
Income Payments	44	55	58	55	72	70	76	88	111	130	129
Income Receipts	80	94	92	91	107	98	97	107	131	154	160
Balance on Income	**36**	**39**	**34**	**36**	**35**	**28**	**21**	**18**	**21**	**24**	**32**
Current Account	2	5	-11	-44	-99	-122	-147	-163	-127	-101	-90

Source: IMF *Balance of Payments Statistics Yearbook*, 1980-1992.

The current account for the 1980s is shown in Table 8.1. Most of the contested data in this account are found in the income flows. But it is worth looking first at the whole current account, to get a full picture of how this period was recorded.

Balance on Goods and Services

Within the current account, the balance of trade on goods and services, which had been in continuous small deficit, increased from a deficit of $22bn in 1981 to $159bn in 1987. Import growth accounted for over half the increase,[3] the other portion was declining exports. As will be discussed below, some observers were associating this change with evidence of a loss of long-term 'international competitiveness'. But clearly there were also some short term factors, particularly the appreciating exchange rate, high domestic growth (leading to growing import demand,[4] and recession in traditional export markets (Canada and Latin America); although, by 1984, with the dollar still appreciating, export volumes started growing.

The balance of trade on goods and services is the least contentious section of balance of payments accounting; yet even here, global processes have a profound impact on data recording. Two limitations stand out: the increasing inaccuracy of current account data; and the question of whether trade flows can be understood in terms of national calculation.

The statistical accuracy of world current account figures was raised in Chapter 7. It will be recalled that the world's deficit tripled in the mid 1980s, before declining over the rest of the 1980s. There was, therefore, a close parallel between the cycle of the global deficit and the cycle of the United States' deficit. Of course, it cannot be known how much of this deficit is associated with the United States' current account figures. But if, as an estimate, fifteen percent of the world deficit was United States related, this would have moved the current account back into surplus in 1982, and reduced the 1983 deficit by twenty five percent; nonetheless, still leaving the deficit growing rapidly in 1984. The accuracy matter should not be over-stated; but nor should it be ignored (Cooper 1985).

More significant for the current analysis is how the international movement of capital served to transform the trade data. It will be considered later how the growth of 'foreign investment' in the United States related to developments in international financial markets, for the link is important. For the balance on goods and services, the concern is with how the growth of 'foreign' TNC investment in the United States and United States' investment abroad transformed the pattern of exports and imports. Each is considered briefly in turn.

142

The mid 1980s saw rapid increases in investment by 'foreign' transnational companies, particularly marketing subsidiaries of German and Japanese manufacturers, seeking to establish a position in the United States' domestic market.[5] During the 1980s, these 'foreign' companies increased their imports to the United States, and decreased their exports from the United States.[6] The trade deficit attributable directly to foreign investment corporations alone rose from $24bn in 1980 to $95bn in 1987 — well over half the growth in the total United States' trade deficit (Turner 1991:41-44). This is one dimension of the impact of the international movement of capital on the balance of trade.

Conversely, it is possible to pose the export of money capital as a substitute for the export of commodities: that, throughout the post-war period, the 'international competitiveness' of many United States' companies has been expressed by their capacity to produce around the world, rather than to export from the United States.[7] If the United States' trade performance is calculated in terms of companies classified as of United States' origin, rather than in terms of exports from and imports into the United States by companies of all 'national origin', the United States' trade balance would look remarkably different. DeAnne Julius (1990) has attempted to recast the current account for the year 1986, measuring exports and imports by nationality of company, rather than site of production. There is no doubt that this is a dubious exercise for, as has already been emphasised, the attribution of nationality to companies is too arbitrary to give significant results. Nonetheless, the results are interesting. The bottom line is that, on a world-wide scale, sales to the rest of the world by 'United States owned' companies exceeded conventionally-defined United States' exports by a factor of 5, and purchases from foreign companies were 3 times greater than United States' imports. When the official national current account deficit of $147 billion is recalculated on an ownership basis, United States' companies globally generated a trade surplus of $57 billion!

There is a general implication for an understanding of national trade figures, which is still more pronounced in relation to the capital account. While the balance on goods and services does indeed measure national inflows and outflows, the global calculation of individual capitals generates patterns of national trade (and an absence of trade) not directly determined by economic conditions within the nation.

Balance on Income Payable

The other component of the current account is income flows. This part of the current account is associated predominantly with past capital movements (recorded in past capital accounts) which have generated

FIGURE 8.2 United States: Balance on Income Payable, 1980-1990

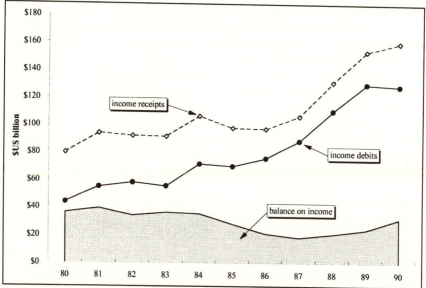

Source: IMF Balance of Payments Statistics Yearbook, 1980-1992

both inflows and outflows of profits and interest payments. The history of the United States as a capital exporting country, particularly in the post-war period, had meant that this component of the current account had been in continual surplus; yet this surplus fell from $39bn in 1981 to $18bn in 1987 (although it did increase in subsequent years). Figure 8.2 shows the pattern of income inflows and outflows, and the balance on income payable.

The most conspicuous change is the increase in income outflows, and this is partially attributable to the increase in capital inflow at the beginning of the decade, which then commands reciprocal income flows in the form of profits and interest payments. But this component of the current account is also misleading. The United States' balance of payments accounting conventions require that changes in the dollar value of stocks of United States-owned foreign assets are recorded as an income flow in the current account — even though there is not an actual flow of income. Thus the appreciating United States dollar meant a reduced value of foreign assets (expressed in United States dollars) showed in the current account as falling foreign income. With private foreign assets of the United States estimated to be $915bn in 1984 (BIS *Annual Report* 1986:67), an appreciation of the dollar on a trade weighted basis by 21% in 1982, 14% in 1983 and a further 20% in 1984 had profound effects on the invisible balance in the current account.[8] Of course, once the dollar started to fall in 1985, the invisibles surplus rose again. Here, too, is a dimension of the United States' current account which is unrelated to changes in accumulation in United States' economy, even though such data were used to depict the United States as having a current account 'problem'.

In aggregate, data recorded in the current account relate to processes in which the national space of the United States is but an element. The economic processes which give rise to these data cannot be explained by recourse to a conception of the United States as a discrete economic entity, for the recorded flows are structures by the international expansion of industrial capital; they are not simply exchange relations between nations.

The Capital Account

The entries in the capital account embrace the international mobility of money capital, and this was where the most unpredictable and dramatic transformation in the United States' accounts occurred (see Table 8.2). It is also where the principles of balance of payments are most misleading.

The capital account records a large increase in net capital inflow to the United States between 1983 and 1989. This served to transform the United States from the largest creditor nation to the largest debtor nation in just a few years. The impression created is that money was flowing into the United States, lodging with financial institutions of all varieties — banks, stockbrokers, the Federal Reserve, etc., and it was all recorded as foreign debt. Yet it must be questioned whether this was actually a flow into the United States, or just into international institutions designated, for balance of payments purposes, as of United States'

TABLE 8.2 United States: Capital Account, 1980 - 1990 (US billion)

	80	81	82	83	84	85	86	87	88	89	90
Direct Investment	-2	16	13	6	14	7	19	31	42	39	12
Portfolio Invest't	3	3	-1	5	29	64	72	31	40	44	-33
Other Capital	-37	49	-41	10	31	32	8	49	8	33	34
Reserves	9	1	-2	4	-1	-6	34	57	36	-17	30
Net Capital Flows	-28	-30	-30	25	73	97	132	168	127	99	43

Source: IMF Balance of Payments Statistics Yearbook, 1980-1992

nationality; and whether it was a flow relating to the United States' economy, or just to the United States dollar as a leading international currency.

The standard explanations for these capital account developments point to the combination of an appreciating exchange rate and high interest rates,[9] economic growth within the United States, and the relaxation of national controls on investment outflows in other countries, particularly the UK and Japan. These were the nationally identified indicators, which provide only partial explanation. The more profound, underlying processes related principally to the development of internationalised capital markets, whose activities and transactions are not particularly amenable to conversion into national data.

The development of these capital markets exerted impacts on the United States' balance of payments data through two related avenues. One was direct foreign investment flows; the other global credit markets, particularly Eurobonds. The relationship, most conspicuously, was that money raised on Eurobond markets funded much of the direct foreign investment. Of these two, the changes relating to credit markets exerted most, and most contentious, impact on the United States' balance of payments, but it is most straight forward to deal first with direct foreign investment.

Direct Foreign Investment

The change relating to direct foreign investment (investment by TNCs) was not only that it increased rapidly throughout the world in the 1980s,[10] but that the origin and target of this investment changed. Companies of United States origin had dominated post-war international investment, and this had generated a sustained and large net outflow of direct foreign investment. Recent internationalisation has involved a reversal of that trend, as seen in Figure 8.3, for the United States became the object of large inward direct investment. In the process of the world achieving a more globally-uniform pattern of TNC investment, at least within the advanced capitalist countries, the United States became the new frontier for expanding global capital.

From 1981 to 1984, the United States received about half the world's direct investment in industrial countries; a three-fold increase from the late 1970s.[11] The outflow of direct investment from the United States was about $10bn per annum between 1981 1984 (50% lower than in the late 1970s), and has not significantly increased since then (see Figure 8.3).

While the fact of this investment turnaround was significant, it is also the case that the balance of payments gave a distorted depiction of what was happening. The critical issue here is how direct foreign investment

FIGURE 8.3 United States: Direct Investment Flows, 1970-1990

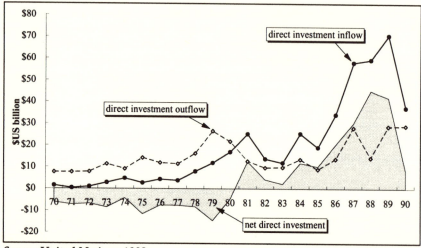

Source: United Nations 1993a

was being funded, and how differences in funding between direct foreign investment inflow and outflow impacted on the United States' balance of payments.

The rapid development of the international bond market was central to the funding of international investment (Benzie 1992). In 1983-84, the funding of investment changed rapidly, with debt replacing equity as the source of new investment funds, and leveraging (debt to equity ratios) increased throughout the world, particularly in association with the expanding Eurobond market. While total net funds raised in the United States scarcely increased, net new equity issues, which had been low but, on average, positive in the preceding years, suddenly became negative, and large, due to an increase in equity retirements.[12] Conversely, net borrowing tripled (Shoven and Waldfogel 1990:7).

There were two implications of increased corporate leveraging for the capital account. First, with United States' interest rates high, there was recourse to foreign borrowing, generating capital inflow. This was a straightforward entry in the capital account. Second, as part of the growing utilisation of debt funding of investment, there was a rapid growth of corporate mergers, especially leveraged buyouts.[13] Prevalent was the rapid growth of cross-border mergers and takeovers.[14] With the United States a long-term investment objective of many newly-internationalising capitals, these debt-driven mergers and takeovers were a critical avenue for foreign investment.[15] For many 'foreign' companies only newly arrived in the United States, they had no United States assets against which to borrow. Hence their investment was in large part by equity (direct investment), albeit funded increasingly by off-shore credit (a fact not relevant to the United States' balance of payments data). For balance of payments purposes, the debt-driven foreign mergers and takeovers appear as direct foreign investment.

But for outward direct investment, the balance of payments recorded exactly the opposite impact of increasing leveraging. Companies registered, for balance of payments purposes, as United States' companies were far and away the world's largest holders of 'foreign' assets, and these 'foreign' assets too were subject to increased leveraging.[16] United States' foreign investors could fund foreign investment by borrowing against overseas assets, without recourse to increased equity and, in the process, bring United States' overseas capital in line with new international norms of corporate funding. Borrowing recorded through head office on these assets therefore shows in the United States' capital account as a capital inflow, while the assets against which borrowing was undertaken had been recorded as previous capital outflows, perhaps decades before.

Moreover, high domestic interest rates had led TNCs from the United States to raise funds from their overseas, particularly financial, affiliates. In the balance of payments data, borrowing abroad by United States companies through Eurobonds issued by their foreign (particularly Netherlands Antilles) subsidiaries were recorded as a reduction in United States direct investment claims on foreigners. So in contrast to the debt-driven equity purchases of foreign investors in the United States, United States asset holders were borrowing abroad; thereby appearing in the United States' balance of payments as an increasing foreign debt. When financial transactions came back to the United States from the Netherlands Antilles in 1984, it was recorded as an increase in the claims of foreigners on the United States. While this did not effect the size of the capital account deficit, it exaggerates the decline in United States' outward direct investment.

Insofar as increasing leveraging was occurring on an international scale, the issue of which country's balance of payments recorded the growing debt, and which recorded the investment which flowed from the debt raisings, proved an ambiguity for the United States' balance of payments, and more than for other countries. The net effect is that, for reasons of differing historical patterns of international capital expansion, the one, international, process of increased leveraging had exactly the opposite expression in the data on direct investment inflows and outflows in the United States compared with other countries. This accounting construct manifested, in balance of payments terms, as a massive turn-around in the United States' international investment position not directly commensurate with the 'real' pattern of capital accumulation.

Credit Flows

In the overall capital account, movements in direct investment were rather small, and predominantly derivative of the main action, which was found in credit markets. The change relating to international credit was the rapid growth of Eurofinance, and particularly Eurobond markets. Because international finance had historically been dominated by companies of United States origin, developments in these markets repercussed directly in the United States' capital account.

In the United States' data, the increase in capital inflow was due to two factors: foreign borrowing by United States corporations, and net foreign purchases of United States' securities (excluding shares). The former, it has already been seen, is in large part to be explained by the historical pattern of international asset acquisition, not simply a build-up of domestic debt.

The foreign purchases of United States' securities followed United States interest rates, with the banking sector, and particularly United States' banks, reversing the net deficit to a net surplus on the capital account.[17] Critical here was that the external assets of United States' banks fell to a quarter of their 1982 level, while their liabilities to non-residents decreased only a minor amount (BIS *Annual Report* 1984:87). The decline in assets was due in part to 'real' forces (reduced lending to developing countries and the narrowing of the differential between the three month Eurodollar rate and United States' short term rates) but also to balance of payments accounting practices.

The accounting change was associated with the establishment of International Banking Facilities (IBFs) within the United States in late 1981 and early 1982. As IBFs were established, both assets and liabilities were shifted from the books of bank offices abroad to bank offices in the United States. This served to inflate the growth of both United States banks' claims on foreigners and United States banks' liabilities to foreigners in 1981 and 1982, with the resultant effect of accentuating the decline of both these levels in 1983 and 1984 (Isard and Stekler 1985).

Concurrently, banks in the United States took up large amounts of money in the Eurodollar market, mainly through their foreign offices, where there was excess liquidity due to the relatively high rate of interest on the United States dollar. This led to large interbank flows from the foreign offices of United States' banks into the United States. The effect was the recorded evidence that the external assets of United States' banks fell more than their liabilities; but it is also clear that this 'evidence' is as much about book keeping conventions as actual resource flows.

Capital Inflow, or Just Demand for Dollars?

In 1984, as the interest rate differential between the United States and the rest of the world disappeared, net bank inflows declined and private non-bank financial institutions became the source of increased capital inflow recorded in the United States balance of payments. These institutions increased their inflow from $9bn in 1983 to $57bn in 1984 (BIS *Annual Report* 1985:94-5). The question is whether these are really to be understood as flows into the United States, or just as flows transacted through United States classified institutions and in United States dollars, but with no particular connection to the United States' economy. The explanation is to be found predominantly through developments in the international bond market, and Figures 8.4 and 8.5 provide some perspective on this issue.

It is important to recall the overall growth of the international bond market in the 1980s, illustrated in Figure 8.4. International bond offerings in 1980 were $20bn; by 1984, they were almost $100bn. Virtually all the growth in international bonds issued until 1985 was in bonds denominated in United States dollars. This, it will be recalled, was while the United States current account ran deeper into deficit, and it was demand for dollars for international bond purchases which kept the United States dollar increasing in value. It was not until 1986 that bonds denominated in non-United States dollars were growing faster than bonds denominated in United States dollars, and this coincided with the falling value of the dollar.

The extent to which the United States dollar's domination of the growth of international bond issues up to 1986 was a reflection of borrowing by United States residents is shown in Figure 8.5. It is apparent that bonds issued by United States institutions and residents in international capital markets were exceeded by bonds issued in United States dollars by a factor of two to three times for each year until 1987, when the factor started to increase! For example, in 1984, a year at the centre of this perplexing period, the equivalent of $81bn of bonds were issued in international markets; $65bn of them (80 per cent) were actually denominated in United States dollars. Of these $65bn, only $23bn (35 per cent) can be attributed for balance of payments purposes to United States 'residents'.

150

FIGURE 8.4 Currency of Eurobond Issues, 1979-1993

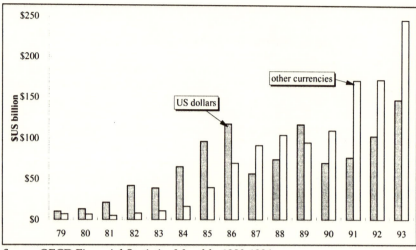

Source: OECD Financial Statistics Monthly 1980-1994

Thus there remained (and still remains) substantial holdings of assets raised in Eurodollar markets which are denominated in United States dollars, but with no practical connection to the United States' economy, and these holdings continued to grow over the 1980s, including while the dollar depreciated.

This is, clearly, a process of only limited attachment to the United States' economy; indeed, it is an area where the accuracy of national accounts (which dollar claims are to be counted as inflows to the United States?) are most vulnerable.[18]

Eurobonds, and particularly those denominated in United States dollars, were also being widely issued and traded as international gambling stock, with no more than symbolic attachment to the United States nation. In a period of both uncertainty in international currency markets, and innovation in forms of debt funding, there was some safety for market dealers in bonds denominated in United States dollars. Even if the currency value was uncertain and volatile, its status as the world's premier trading and investment currency was not yet over. It is impossible to imagine any other currency value climbing so rapidly in the face of such a mounting current account deficit! The perception of the relative security of the United States dollar was not a reflection of the current United States' national economy *per se*, but is better understood as the last vestige of the United States dollar as the proxy global

FIGURE 8.5 Bonds Issued in International Capital Markets: US Residents and US Dollars, 1980-1990

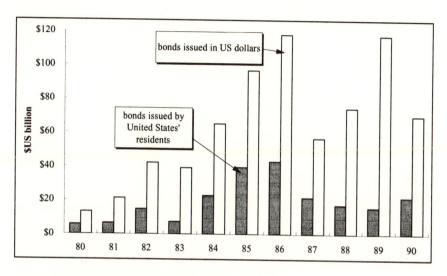

Source: OECD Financial Statistics Monthly 1980-1992

currency, as established at Bretton Woods. While this status had been relinquished in 1971, with the end of stable gold convertibility of the United States dollar, its *de facto* status remained in the era of floating exchange rates because of the failure of floating rates to secure a stable monetary system, and, as an alternative, the absence of another national currency to play the leading role. It was not until the politically orchestrated devaluation of the dollar in 1985 that the United States current account could move back towards balance, but at the cost of being relieved of its former premier currency status. But nor was this just a 'gentlemen's' agreement. The dethroning of the United States dollar was only made possible by the Japanese and German trade surpluses (due in part, as we have seen, to penetration of the United States domestic market) reflecting the growing importance of Yen and Mark in determining the international value of money capital.[19]

Domestic Policy Responses

How were these developments in the United States international payments position being interpreted in policy debates? It was seen in

Chapter 6 that the state's monetary policy changed dramatically. The hands-off approach to the exchange rate changed in 1984 with the development of the 'checklist' approach to monetary policy. The 'checklist' approach involved targeting a range of economic indicators, including the exchange rate and the balance of payments. The exchange rate could only be turned around by international agreement, for a fall in the United States dollar requires other leading currencies (the Yen and Mark) to appreciate. The Plaza Agreement and Louvre Accord were the means by which this was achieved.

But apart from exchange rate management, which is inherently an international exercise, domestic debate about the balance of payments was cast entirely in terms of revitalising the competitiveness of United States industry, with virtually no concern for the international transformations which had, in large part, constructed the balance of payments outcomes. This framework, it will be contended here and in Chapter 9, was the basis on which labor within the United States, has borne the burden of the nationally-constructed response.

The domestic debate about rectifying the balance of payments expressed a spectrum of positions, from recourse to market solutions, to various policies for intervention.[20] For some, the problem of the mid 1980s was short term macro policy settings,[21] in particular, fiscal expansion requiring high interest rates, pushing up the value of the dollar, despite the growing current account deficit (Lawrence 1984).[22] Different policy settings could rectify the problem (Bergsten 1983).

But for most contributions, the developments of the mid 1980s were the expression of a longer term trend towards United States' decline in the global economy. A Presidential Commission was appointed[23] to report on possible policy responses to the decline (United States 1985). One position in the debate posed the decline as the consequences of falling national productivity (or labor costs being too high) (for example IMF 1985), with the decline interpreted through either a comparative advantage or a New International Division of Labor view of the world. For the latter, the 'deindustrialisation' of the United States (Bluestone and Harrison 1982) was posed as a direct consequence. Either way, the United States could not compete on costs as it had before.

The other (related) explanation of the apparent decline of the United States focused on the inability of advanced countries to remain adaptive to structural change on an international scale. Deriving their understanding largely from Shumpeter and later Kindleberger, there emerged various explanations for economic atrophy as a distinctly American problem. This was explained variously in terms of: the loss of technological momentum (Kindleberger 1978; Porter 1985); the dominance of conservative interest groups blocking policy initiative

(Olson 1982), or class relations no longer consistent with accumulation (Gordon *et al.* 1982)

These explanations of cyclical and long-term downturn led to 'interventionist' policy proposals of 'over-ruling' the market forces which had led to the United States' international decline. Hence there was advocacy of protection from some quarters, but also a more 'positive' policy package of state assistance in industrial reorganisation (for example Magaziner and Reich 1983; Phillips 1984). The President's Commission, by contrast, reported in favour of policies to "improve the context for competition rather than intervene in it" (cited in Thompson 1989:46); a proposition which guided the Reagan Administration's policy formation.

It hardly needs saying that each of the positions in the debate represented a different set of interests, and it was on the basis of these interests that the debate was 'resolved' in policy formation. But all positions in the debate had two premises in common:

- United States' trade data and structural change are generally constructed as a national problem.[24] All positions in the debate consistently associated data on cross-national resource flows with the performance of nationally-based industry, and the performance of nationally-based industry with a conception of national well-being.

- There was at best a restricted appreciation of the internationality of money, and the way in which 'innovation' in international financial markets was manifesting in the United States external account.

The way in which strategies for 'international competitiveness' have been constructed as a policy 'solution' are considered in more detail in the next chapter. Here, there is a simple point to be concluded. The debate which formed the response to the United States' balance of payments and exchange rate 'crisis' remained almost entirely uncritical of the data on which the perception of crisis was based.

In part, this is because economic analysis has for generations accepted the ontological primacy of national units, and thereby had unquestioning recourse to structuring analysis in a national framework. The logic of how this framework explicitly posed the burden on labor (and not just in the United States) is the subject of Chapter 9. Here, it is useful to look at the evidence of broad economic aggregates over the period of the balance of payments 'crisis'.

Figure 8.6 shows for the United States the relationship between real wages and a number of other national indicators: economic growth; the current account deficit; average real wages; gross operating surplus, and labor's share of national income.

FIGURE 8.6   United States: Growth, Current Account and
Income Shares, 1980-1989

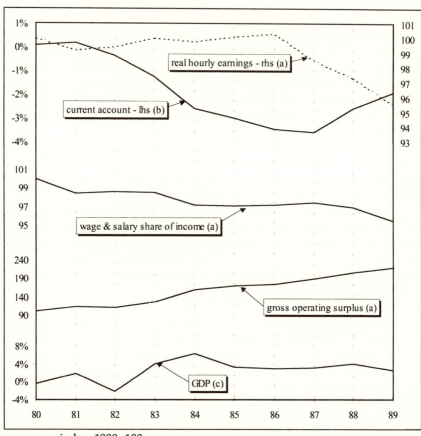

a index: 1980=100
b precentage of gross domestic product
c percentage change on previous year
Source: IMF *Balance of Payments Statistics Yearbook* 1980-1991
OECD 1993

While the period from 1982 saw the current account move into growing deficit (see Figure 8.1), the growth of real GDP continued at a high rate: the domestic economy was booming. Accordingly, net operating surplus as a percentage of value added (a proxy for profits) also increased, reaching its highest level since the long boom. Nonetheless, real wages and salaries fell to 97% of their 1981 level and the share of national income going to wages and salaries also fell from

66.0% in 1981 to 64.3% in 1989. Hence real wages were not reflecting domestic growth, or increasing profitability, but were associated directly with the current account deficit.

In the mid 1990s, there has emerged a debate as to whether United States trade performance and the current account deficit in the 1980s caused the decline in real wages (and increasing domestic wage dispersion). Two related explanations have been prevalent. One has been an emphasis on the declining relative productivity of United States manufacturing, and capital formation abroad, generating a tendency for wages to equalise internationally.[25] The other has focused on the trade deficit in manufactured goods, causing workers to shift from high paid jobs in manufacturing to lower paid jobs in services.[26]

These interpretations have been criticised essentially on the basis that the the trade deficit makes up such a small proportion of domestic GDP that the impact of the deficit was negligable on wage determination.[27] This debate continues, focusing particularly on how the international impact can be measured.

Two brief comments on this debate are warranted. First, the impact of trade on domestic wages should, in a neo-classical framework, be understood through the production of tradables, and thus price effects, not actual trade quantities (and not the size of the deficit). The global discipline of price determination, not actual resource flows, constitutes the neo-classical agenda for understanding global market integration, as discussed in Chapter 2.[28] Yet the debate about wages in the 1980s continues to focus on a national-interaction model, where nations are defined in terms of factor immobility. Second, and most importantly, these debates have neglected the impact of the nationalist, ideological construction of balance of payments accounting. Participants in the debate have looked for statistically significant, quantifiable relations between the current account deficit and wages. There has been no recognition that a nationalist concern for the current account deficit, its political construction as a collective, national liability, and a collective anxiety about United States external viability, may, for good or bad 'technical' economic reasons, have exerted a significant impact on wage determination. The role of wage cuts in nationalist programs for 'international competitiveness' is considered in Chapter 9.

This experience in the world's largest deficit country can be contrasted with comparable data for the largest surplus countries: Germany and Japan. Both show rapidly growing current account surpluses, and identical patterns of real wage growth. The pattern of wages growth diverges from that of the United States only from around 1985 — a full two years after the divergence in their current account 'performances', and long enough for these balance of payments data to become established domestic 'knowledge', exerting an impact on actual wage determination. In both Japan and Germany, net operating surplus as a percentage of net value added was growing at a rate comparable to that of the United States,[29] and in Japan, the share of national income going to wages was increasing, from 57.9% in 1981 to 59.3% in 1989. In Germany, the wages share fell slightly, from 58.6% to 57.2%.

So while all three countries were growing rapidly, and all three had increasing profit rates, their wage levels follow their current accounts.[30] Of course, the explanations for this pattern could simply be that wages followed labor productivity, and it was divergences in labor productivity which generated divergences in current account performance. Yet United States' productivity had been declining relative to Japanese and German productivity throughout the post-war period, and, while productivity is notoriously difficult to measure, and varies widely within countries, it is generally recognised that the productivity gap was closed by the end of the long boom. Productivity differences cannot be the primary explanation for the wage divergences of the 1980s.

To the extent that the differing wages growth is instead related to the balance of payments and the national agenda of pursuing international competitiveness, balance of payments data can be called on to develop a broader class politics of economic policy. Because policy makers, commentators, and most of the representatives of organised labor believe the balance of payments to provide information of the 'real' state of affairs, a deficit in the current account and growing 'foreign indebtedness' becomes the pretext to place downward pressure on wages, even in periods of real economic growth.

Conclusion

The 1980s was critical for developments in international capital movement. The divergence between surplus and deficit OECD countries in the early 1980s, in which the United States' current account deficit was central, coincided with profound initiatives in the role of financial markets (the growth of debt funding of investment, associated with the expansion of international bond markets). The combined effect was a period of extreme volatility in financial flows and exchange rates; the opposite of the stable equilibrium which had been predicted by economists to be the outcome of 'free' capital mobility. The contemporary, and subsequent, attempts to explain the observed volatility were therefore somewhat *ad hoc* and invariably superficial.

With awareness of the danger of simplification, it is useful to highlight the elements found in the United states balance of payments data for the mid 1980s, which cannot embrace the globalised nature of accumulation:

- The growing trade deficit was significantly due to international capital movement. On the one hand, 'United States' industrial competitiveness was increasingly being expressed in the competitiveness of United States-derived TNCs producing outside the United States. On the other hand, international capital, especially of German and Japanese origin, was establishing branches in the United States, and these capitals themselves exerted a significant impact on the balance of trade. This was a long-term change associated with global equalisation of direct investment flows, not a short-term pattern dictated by the exchange rate or national cost structures.

- The declining surplus of income flows in the current account was, in significant part, due to the accounting practice of revaluating foreign assets in line with exchange rate changes, and this has no relation to 'actual' income flows between nations.

- On the capital account, the relocation of the site of transactions had a profound impact in balance of payments figures. Moreover, the emergence of a large net inflow was in significant part due to changing debt-equity ratios on an international scale. For historical reasons, the result was that direct investment flowed into the United States as equity, and out of the United States as debt.

- The rapid development of the international bond market in the mid 1980s privileged the United States dollar for reasons other than the 'performance' of the United States' economy. Because United States registered banks and non-banks were prominent in their issue, they nonetheless generated a capital inflow for balance of payments purposes.

The underlying, long term, pattern of accumulation in the mid 1980s was the 'free' international movement of capital, creating an increasingly uniform global pattern of trade and investment flows. Within balance of payments data, the general picture which emerged was that, because the United States already had the most internationalised currency, and the most extensive international assets, the volatility which came with the extension of international capital markets was 'drawn into' the United States' data beyond its relevance to the United States' economy. The growth of international bond markets and of debt funding of investment which, for historical reasons, centred on assets and a currency denomination emanating from the United States, all showed up in the United States' balance of payments, and in the United States dollar, in a way not particularly related to the United States' domestic economy. Much of the data by which this period is analysed is more a reflection of the accounting conventions by which location of ownership is determined, than of 'real' changes in accumulation.

Nonetheless, these data are attributed significance, and national policy does take responsibility for rectifying balance of payments 'problems'. This is one central form in which the 'national economy' is constituted as a coherent entity within the process of global accumulation. It is by the constitution of this national coherence that the burdens of policy response can be socialised, and the contradiction between the internationality of capital and the nationality of state policy can be played out nationally as the contradiction between labor and capital. This proposition is developed in Chapter 9.

Notes

1. See Figure 1.1, page 14.

2. See above, pages 14 and 15.

3. This was despite a reduction of $26bn in expenditure on oil imports between 1981 and 1983.

4. Domestic demand from 1982 to 1984 was growing at twice the industrial countries' average.

5. This is a predictable expression of international competition, as post-war national differences in productivity were disappearing. While the timing of the move into the United States by German and Japanese manufacturers was no doubt facilitated by the exchange rate, its implications were clearly more permanent and determined by a more fundamental process, for the pattern continued even after the dollar had fallen.

6. Bonturi and Fukasaku (1993) identify the high proclivity for Japanese companies with subsidiaries in the United States to import wholesale goods from their parent companies.

7. Lipsey and Kravis (1985, 1987, 1992) are notable for their emphasis that United States-derived global capitals were holding their share of world trade even when the United States was losing its share. Also, Peet (1987) discusses the decline of the United States' supremacy as a trading nation in terms of the history of capital export.

8. The size cannot be calculated because of the uncertainty of the currency in which the foreign assets are held.

9. During the period under consideration, the increasing exchange rate, in spite of the current account deficit, was being explained predominantly in terms of interest rate differentials (the latter itself explained in terms of the high United

States growth rate). Yet by mid 1984, interest rate spreads in favour of the dollar had disappeared, but the capital inflow continued. The IMF, which had been explaining the capital inflow in terms of asset market transactions, was left without explanation (IMF 1985:4).

10. See Figure 1.2, page 19.

11. This was despite the fact that the rate of return on such investment was, on average, low and falling (Turner 1991:41-43).

12. This was primarily through share re-purchase programs and cash mergers.

13. Mergers and acquisitions in the United States had a value of $25bn at the end of the 1970s, and climbed from $50bn in 1983 to over $200bn by 1986 (Blair and Litan 1990:46). Leveraged buyouts were virtually non-existent until 1983, when they rose to fifteen percent of the value of takeovers.

14. The figures which were clearly inflated by a rush of very large takeovers, for example, the Royal Dutch-Shell purchase of publically-held shares in U.S. Shell Oil Co., and the Japanese entry into the United States steel industry.

15. Even when the dollar depreciated in 1986, the share of United States assets in foreign private portfolios (especially Japanese) continued to increase (Dealtry *et al* 1989:16), indicating a longer-term adjustment in international accumulation which was to some considerable degree immune from the vicissitudes of the dollar exchange rate.

16. To leave a company with a low debt burden at this time was to invite takeover, so that a buyer could use the company's assets to raise further credit.

17. The movement of the capital account into surplus between 1982 and 1983 was dominated by a turnaround in banking flows, from net outflows of $45bn in 1982 to net inflows of $26bn in 1983.

18. There were direct implications of this flow for defining national money supply, and hence for any policy of national money supply targeting; an issue considered in Chapter 6.

19. See above, page 16 for a discussion of the impact on Japan and Germany.

20. See Norton (1986) and Thompson (1989) for reviews of this debate.

21. See particularly the contributions from within the Brookings Institution.

22. Such a proposition was consistent with the early period of the current account deficit; although disproved by mid 1984 when interest rate spreads in favour of the dollar had disappeared, yet the current account deficit and capital inflow continued to increase.

23. The Commission was made up of business and labor representatives, academics and former civil servants.

24. For most, there is not even a regional dimension — that different regions of the United States are effected differently by the changes of the 1970s and 1980s.

25. See Lawrence and Slaughter (1993) and the associated discussants for some review of this debate

26. This interpretation is found in Thurow (1992); but see Krugman (1994).

27. See in particular Borjas, Freeman and Katz (1992), Bound and Johnson (1992), Lawrence and Slaughter (1993) and Lawrence (1994).

28. See especially, page 28. Studies with this emphasis have shown an impact of the price of traded goods on wages, for example, Ravenga (1992).

29. For Germany and Japan, this rate was still significantly below the rates of the 1960s, unlike the United States, where rates in the late 1980s were comparable to those of the 1960s.

30. The comparable data for the other two G5 countries, the United Kingdom and France is less clear, but following the same general pattern. Both these countries started the period with significant current account surpluses and ended it with large, but stabilising deficits. But it was not until 1988-89 that these countries started to record a 'net' deficit for the whole period 1982-1989 — a sign that current account deficits had become entrenched only late in the period under consideration. In both cases, real wages increased early in the period. In France, wages scarcely increased after 1984, while in the United Kingdom, wage increases continued to rise until the end of the 1980s. In both cases, the share of wages in GDP fell over the period.

9

Balance of Payments and Nationalist Policy

It was seen in Chapter 7 that the system of balance of payments accounting plays out in a statistical form the contradiction between the internationality of capital and the nationality of state power. The need by the nation state for a data source which describes the nation's position in international accumulation leads to the need for a national taxonomy of capital, and to squeeze what is essentially a global process into a nationally-defined grid. An effect of the contradiction is that balance of payments data can profoundly misrepresent the process of global accumulation and its regional (including a national) expression by constructing that national expression as a national product. One such case is described in Chapter 8.

Nonetheless, national governments and economic advisers around the world do place reliance on balance of payments data as a depiction of national performance. Central banks and national governments formulate monetary and fiscal policy with an explicit concern for the balance of payments; industry policy also is increasingly being formulated explicitly with reference to international trade. Currencies are traded on the basis of these figures, and even on predictions of what the figures might be! Belief in balance of payments data then sees that the contradiction between international accumulation and its national regulation is played out in national policy as a class contradiction, affirming the subordination of labor to capital.

Policies in relation to the balance of payments have changed dramatically over the last twenty years. Since the 1970s, but particularly the 1980s, the policy dilemma, particularly for deficit countries, has been how to reconcile the over-all policy momentum towards 'free' trade in money and commodities with the fact that current account deficits are not self-correcting via exchange rate movements. This has put the onus for balance of payments rectification back onto domestic policy (interest rates, demand management, industry policy and industrial relations). Fiscal and monetary policy have become increasingly formulated with the balance of payments in mind. For fiscal policy, 'appropriate' deficits are determined in large part by the anticipated effect on the exchange rate (will the money market approve?) and import demand, while monetary policy is formulated explicitly to balance the interest, inflation and exchange rates. Industry policy is being framed in terms of enhancing the flowering of (ultimately) 'unprotected', internationally competitive firms.

The policy process has by no means been straightforward. The agenda has shifted from some variation of Keynesianism,[1] to monetarism to the pursuit of international competitiveness as a 'solution' to the balance of payments. Increasingly, however, the underlying momentum of policy over the last twenty years has involved recourse to targeting labor as the means to manage domestic demand, reducing the costs of domestic production, and advancing the national trade balance. Labor, as the source of value, remains the one 'component' of production (and of costs) which is not (significantly) internationally mobile. Rightly or wrongly, labor can be imbued with the burdens of national adjustment to global accumulation, because it is the bearer, consciously and unconsciously, of 'nationality'.

But, of course, this class dimension of the pursuit of 'external balance' has not generally or consistently been played out historically as state policy based on an explicit assault on labor. On the contrary, 'Keynesianism' and 'monetarism', as the ruling liberal theories of the 1970s and early 1980s were unable to address the contradiction between the internationality of accumulation and the nationality of state regulation because they did not recognise the need to target directly the labor process and the production of surplus value.

This chapter looks at the contradictions of Keynesianism and monetarism in this regard, and then at the newer policy agendas of international competitiveness which have arisen since the 1980s. These new agendas see state policy targeting directly the rate of surplus value as the key to 'international competitiveness', albeit constructed as a liberal program for national success. Insofar as these new agendas take up the post-war successes of social democratic industry policy, this chapter also addresses the social democratic agenda in the era of internationally-integrated accumulation.

The Decline of Keynesianism ... and the Decline of Monetarism

The institution of maintaining national trading records is almost intrinsic to the concept of nationality. It reached its policy zenith in the post-war era when 'Keynesian' policy at least in its 'bastard Keynesian' form, ruled the world's policy fora[2]. Keynesian macroeconomics takes as its data source the national aggregates of consumption, investment, income, expenditure, etc., and policy centres on the management of (national) aggregate demand, primarily through monetary and fiscal policy.

Herein lies the centrality of the balance of payments data as the adjunct of national income and expenditure data. The current account of the balance of payments (in its simplified form, exports minus imports) specifies the extent to which the 'external sector' increases or decreases (national) aggregate demand, income, and expenditure. This is where the 'external sector' impacts on fiscal policy. The capital account of the balance of payments specifies the extent to which the 'external sector' increases or decreases national money supply. This is where the 'external sector' impacts on monetary policy.

In the 'Keynesian' economy, the equilibrating mechanism of the external sector derived from the accounting identity that a net outflow/inflow on the current account would be directly offset by a corresponding inflow/outflow on the capital account. This follows directly from the system of double entry book-keeping: a deficit in the current account balance is recorded as an automatic increase in national indebtedness in the capital account.

In the formalism of this identity lay the inability of the 'Keynesian' analysis to make sense of a world in which capital flows are not 'driven' by the current account, and do not systematically move the national economy towards 'external balance'. This issue, which became a conspicuous limitation in the 1970s, was well recognised in debates in the late 1940s and 1950s about the external sector in the 'Keynesian' system. It was characterised by Machlup (1943) as the distinction between autonomous and accommodating (sometimes called induced) cross-national transactions. The former are undertaken because they are profitable for the individual who initiates them; the latter occur where the former do not lead to an accounting balance — they are the residual international money flow (Machlup 1943; Meade 1948-49). A surplus or deficit in the balance of payments current account is equal to the accommodating flows required to balance the autonomous flows. Within this framework, short-term capital movements were reckoned to be accommodating (Meade 1951:11).[3]

But the distinction between autonomous and accommodating flows did not enter into the concern of policy makers for a long time. It was a hypothetical distinction only, and balance of payments data themselves cannot differentiate autonomous and accommodating transactions. In the 1950s, and even the 1960s, this was an anomaly which attracted interest only because, in principle, the two types of flows have different roles in domestic policy. But so long as capital movements were predominantly accommodating, and the capital account adjusted to the current account, it was an issue of no great practical import. In Meade's initial formulation, the understanding was that autonomous transactions were predominantly in the current account, particularly trade in goods and services. Accommodating flows were, correspondingly, in the capital account, being short-term capital flows and official reserve movements.

Yet by the 1970s, the anomaly was turning into a major problem of national economic management. With recent internationalisation, autonomous short-term capital movements grew rapidly; indeed, they are the overwhelming proportion of autonomous flows, far greater than the autonomous flows recorded in the current account. With autonomous international flows now predominantly in the capital account, there have been two critical effects for the 'Keynesian' agenda. First, accommodating flows in the capital account have been swamped by autonomous flows in that account, so that the capital account is not an expression of national state policy (reserve movements to offset a current account imbalance), but an unintended (from the national policy perspective) national buildup of international debt (or credit). The second effect has been that trade (exports minus imports) has become less of an indicator of the impact of the 'external sector' on the 'domestic sector'. Hence, the effect of the 'external sector' is felt less through 'real' domestic demand, where the 'Keynesian' policy focus lay, and more through the capital account, manifesting as changes in national money supply, leading to domestic inflation.

The shift of the balance of payments' domestic impact from demand for goods and services to changing money supply was the international aspect of the inability of the post-war policy framework to reconcile in the 1970s the concurrent growth of unemployment and inflation. Of course, there is more to the decline of 'Keynesian' policy framework than balance-of-payments-induced national impacts, but the flows recorded in the balance of payments data were no longer compatible with 'Keynesian' tools of national economic management.[4]

Accordingly, the new orthodoxy which replaced post-war 'Keynesianism' can be seen in part as a direct response to this international impact on national money supply. The emerging popular conceptual critique of 'Keynesian' policy took the form of national monetarism. While 'Keynesianism' constituted space with reference to one set of national aggregates (production, consumption, investment, etc.), monetarism constituted space with respect to a different, single aggregate: money supply. Its essential proposition was that control of the national money supply was the key to 'successful' domestic economic management. Within a nationalist policy focus, the focus on money was confirmed by balance of payments developments, expressed in the dominance of international financial movements over 'real' resource movements.

The inability of the 'old' 'Keynesian' policies to interpret the dominance of financial flows over trade flows was clear. But the appeal of national monetarism was entirely superficial. While international developments were shifting the focus to money, and its national manifestation as inflation, the nascent popular monetarism was predicated on the national control of money supply, even though the dominant momentum was international money movement.

According to its own formula, national monetarism required strict predictability of international money movements, as a precondition for stabilising domestic money supply growth. This predictability, according to its advocates, was to come from floating exchange rates, for it was believed that a market-driven exchange rate would adjust to transmit the 'right' international money flow — the so-called 'monetary approach to the balance of payments'. Yet in this monetary approach to the balance of payments, it is ultimately commodity trade relations which determine the exchange rate and speculative financial flows simply facilitate its equilibration. That is, the theory rests centrally on a purchasing power parity conception of the exchange rate.[5] Yet history instead provided volatile exchange rates because of the dominance of speculative money over commodity flows in the international payments system. This was directly incompatible with the requirements of national monetarism, but beyond the capacity of nationalist monetarist policy to resolve.[6]

Hence there was a fundamental belief in common with Keynesianism: that theoretical coherence requires the determinacy of 'real' resource flows (trade) over capital account flows within the balance of payments and exchange rate formation. This has precluded both theories from providing a sustained explanation of the domestic impact of recent internationalisation. In the terms of 1950s Keynesianism, national monetarism retained the assumption in that short-term capital movements are accommodating, not autonomous. The advantage Monetarism had over Keynesianism on this point was that the primacy of international commodity movements over international financial movements was more deeply buried within monetarist theory (found in the purchasing power parity theory of exchange rates), so that the contradictions for national policy formation were less obvious. Monetarism won the policy battle over Keynesianism because it nominated money as the critical lever dictating instability in the 1970s; not because it had a profound understanding of how that lever operated in an international setting.

So although monetarism posed a decisive break with respect to national management of monetary and fiscal policy, there were some important characteristics it shared with 'Keynesian' policy; particularly that each, though in different ways, constituted analytically the notion of discrete national economies as the object of policy, and the belief that 'correct' domestic policy settings could secure low inflation growth insulated from the experiences of the rest of the world.

Internationally-Oriented Macro Policy

The shift from the post-war version of bastard Keynesianism to monetarism as the guiding theory was based on theoretical critique (albeit a critique which served entirely to marginalise the interventionist traditions of the 'original' 'Keynesian' approach), supported by evidence of financial crisis. By contrast, the demise of monetarism was much more *ad hoc* and incomplete, for the laissez faire doctrine which underlies the monetary approach to the balance of payments and open-economy macroeconomics generally remains the starting point of the orthodox theory. Chapter 6 contended that it was historical evidence of the failure of national monetarism, not critique of its theoretical basis, which led to its formal demise as the ruling ideology of national policy. Indeed the critique is generations old, and had accompanied the (re)ascent of monetarism in the 1970s. The refusal of the economics discipline to invoke that critique lay more in the sphere of the libertarian doctrine which rules economic theory than in open debate about the possibility of new policy visions. The result has been an *ad hoc* approach to national policy formation, based on amended and adjusted monetarist theory, rationalised as an exercise of subtlety and balance, rather than theoretical dogma.

Within this *ad hoc* approach, policy and theory have moved towards recognition of the global nature of accumulation, albeit often still constituted as an intrusion into domestic processes. At various times domestic inflation, the exchange rate, the state's budget deficit, the balance of payments and industry structure have been different pre-occupations of state policy; all the time rationalised in terms of agendas of 'international competitiveness'.

The Balance of Payments 'Constraint'

As the gap between current account deficit and surplus countries widened in the early 1980s, the balance of payments has come increasingly to order the discourse of policy debate. Policy makers in the deficit countries were increasingly constituting the balance of payments as a 'constraint' on domestic economic expansion, and invoking policies to increase exports and reduce imports. It is necessary to see first how the balance of payments has been constituted as a constraint, and then at how the policies which are designed to overcome that constraint attempt to 'resolve' the contradiction between the internationality of accumulation and the nationality of state regulation.

The constitution of the balance of payments as a 'constraint' on national economic growth is not new. The debates at the time of the Bretton Woods Agreement, about the need for international adjustment mechanisms to facilitate rectification of domestic imbalances, was one way of constituting the balance of payments as a constraint. But with the end of the long boom, there developed a somewhat different and more general depiction of the balance of payments as a 'constraint'.

The term in its current usage is particularly associated with the work of Tony Thirlwall (esp.1979, 1992). His initial application was an attempt to explain the slow growth of the UK economy since the late 1960s.[7] Thirlwall argued that UK output could not grow as quickly as labor productivity should have allowed because the relative income elasticities of demand for imports and exports would have seen a growing deficit in the balance of trade. This situation is unsustainable, without a falling currency. Generalising from this proposition has come a much broader depiction of the balance of payments as a national 'constraint'. The constraint has been posed in several aspects.

One, as depicted by Thirlwall, focuses on the inability of a nation to expand exports as fast as it would 'like' to import. Hence, either the exchange rate must fall, causing either inflation or lower incomes, or the domestic rate of interest must increase to secure capital inflow to pay for imports, causing domestic economic activity to decline.[8] Either way, the national economy is constrained by a current account deficit.

A second aspect of the current account as a constraint uses national accounting identities to derive the 'domestic shortfall' which makes a current account deficit a direct corollary. In other words, the current account is a constraint only in the sense of manifesting an excessive domestic demand. This style of analysis has had two general versions. The first, which lasted only a short time in the policy debates, was the 'twin deficits' thesis. It argued that a government fiscal deficit automatically flowed into a current account deficit. This proposition had appeal because it revealed a possible policy synthesis between 'Keynesian' national income accounting and the monetarist visions of small government. It was, however an accounting identity only under highly restrictive assumptions about the funding of fiscal deficits, and was unfortunate to reach policy prominence at a time when, in many countries, falling fiscal deficits were associated with growing current account deficits!

The related, and more recognised formulation of this problem is that the current account deficit is associated with low national savings (private as well as public); and that the lack of savings has required capital inflow to fund investment.[9] For both the savings deficit and the twin deficits, the 'solution' is said to lie in domestic austerity, not in 'external' policy, so they will not be further considered in the current context.[10]

A third aspect of the balance of payments as a constraint is the concern for national debt and the spectre of 'debt traps' haunting nations with sustained current account deficits. In one interpretation, this is a variant of the shortage of national savings, leading to the call for national austerity and redistribution of income from poor to rich to supplement the portion of national income going to savings. The other variant, with a more neo-Marxist edge, focuses on the extent to which creditors (international banks) are able to extract a surplus out of indebted countries.

These different versions of the balance of payments as a national constraint involve different domestic policy agendas. But what they share in common is that, by privileging the balance of payments as the arbiter of policy, they constitute a national problem with national policy solutions. A common solution (perhaps not applicable to the neo-Marxist version) involves policies to decrease imports and increase exports. Even if trade is not considered to be the source of the national constraint, increased international competitiveness is considered to be the source of the solution.[11]

National Policy Within a Balance of Payments Constraint

With the emphasis on 'international competitiveness', the contradiction between the internationality of accumulation and the nationality of state regulation is approached in policy in a very different way from Keynesianism and monetarism. While the latter showed benign neglect of the growing complexity of international accumulation, policy agendas framed in direct reference to a balance of payments constraint involve an internationally aware nationalism. They address the international competitiveness of domestic production as the key to domestic economic expansion.

The agenda of 'international competitiveness' has been seen to offer a national policy vision in a world where adherence to 'free markets' leaves nation states powerless to rectify the balance of payments outcomes which the 'free market' has delivered. What is the scope for domestic policy initiative when policy itself has increasingly involved accession to the dictates of international market forces?

The answer lies at two levels. First, the policy dilemma as posed here reflects the contradiction between different parts of capital. Not all capital requires 'free' international commodity movements, as the battles in GATT negotiations continually attest. Nonetheless, the momentum towards 'free' trade is real, and reflects the increasing prominence of globalised individual capitals within international accumulation. In the context of 'free' capital mobility, the nation state has to develop other forms of 'supervision' for capitals dependent on the domestic market (in Chapter 5, these were characterised as capitals in the national and market-constrained circuits). State regulation of domestic industry structure and investment has been a form of 'supervision' practiced in the social democracies and in the so-called newly industrialising countries.[12] In the liberal democracies, subsidies, particularly schemes for structural adjustment, and non-tariff barriers have become a resurgent option. Patriotism is another dimension of economic policy, discussed in Chapter 10.

But the second level provides the more sustained and dynamic state response. While international market forces may be acceded to, these are only regulations in the circulation of capital. They impose no constraints on state policy in the sphere of production.[13] In an increasingly 'deregulated' international trading environment, the construction of external balance depends on domestic policy to facilitate individual capitals to produce locally under conditions which secure profits in internationally-exposed markets. State policy in this context is directed particularly to the expansion of investment-constrained and global capital to advance the balance of payments. The expansion of investment-constrained capital increases the domestic production of tradables (exports and import replacement goods). While global capital also produces tradables, the added requirement is inducements to produce these within one nation rather than another.

But the social democratic nationalist agendas of central industry and labor market policy, incomes policy and corporatist decision-making are proving less able to insulate domestic solutions from the force of international competition. International competition makes visible the costs of cross-subsidy which are inherent in the social democratic program. For the most internationalised of individual capitals, the costs of national consensual policy determination become too high.

From Comparative to Competitive Advantage

How particular nation states pursue the objective of creating internationally competitive companies and industries is very much a national question. The national policy debates play out universal themes (from free market cases for efficiency, to centrally co-ordinated strategies for growth), which result in nation-specific policy 'solutions'. The concern here is not the detail of those domestically-determined packages, but the constitution of the agenda those packages are required to play out.

In addressing the conditions of production required for the development nationally of internationally competitive industries, there has been a widespread shift away from 'comparative advantage' as the theoretical rationale for policy. The popular lexicon is now 'competitive advantage', not 'comparative advantage'. This is representative of an important development, for the shift away from reliance on the rationale of comparative advantage has come at precisely the time when the 'free trade' policies advocated by that theory are most widely recognised in national and international policy circles.

So what is the basis of this shift? It is that the notions of competitive advantage create a space for on-going national policy initiatives in the sphere of production, while comparative advantage does not.

The theory of comparative advantage assumes the domestic mobility but international immobility of capital (defined as factor of production). Domestically, therefore, it proposes an analysis in which the free market is the optimal mechanism for resource allocation, with the addition of international prices to determine what is profitable to produce in an international context. National specialisation according to comparative advantage is, therefore, not a deliberate strategy, but the logical outcome of reliance on 'free' markets, under the assumption of international capital immobility. On this basis, the postulation of global gains from national specialisation, and hence the potential for all nations to share in the global gains, follows as a logical derivation.

This theory, as the essential basis for modern trade policy, displays two problems. First, and obviously, the assumption of international immobility of capital is historically false. In the current era (and the future) it is not even a rough approximation. Yet it is a critical assumption for comparative advantage theory because immobility is what defines the domestic, as opposed to international, economy. As a consequence, comparative advantage embodies the implicit assumption that accumulation has a national cohesion (shared domestic mobility) and that the nation engages in international exchange as a unit (a shared international immobility).[14] This leads the theory directly to the specification of the rules for industry specialisation in national terms (national factor endowments; national factor costs). It follows that the gains of trade constituted in the theory are collective, national gains.

Second, comparative advantage doctrine leads to a set of national policies of laissez faire, with the promise that domestic efficiency and international exchange will both expand national income and balance the external accounts. Thus the theory gives no rationale to the nation state to formulate policies to address balance of payments 'difficulties'; simply because such difficulties can only be explained in terms of market distortions.

Combined, these characteristics create the problem that comparative advantage theory rests on the assumption of national unity and so collective benefit; hence precluding the space for policy to construct an explicit analytical basis for such a unity and collective benefit. So comparative advantage leaves nation states without an active policy rationale under conditions when the movement towards 'free trade' appears to not resolve the balance of payments constraint.

At the edge of policy debates, this dead-end has been the rationale to abandon adherence to free trade in favour of protection to domestic industry. But the momentum towards free capital mobility is too great to concede to this position recognition as representing anything but small, sectional interests. The dilemma for contemporary theory, in providing the rationale for policy, has been how to recognise the mobility of capital (credit and investment), which thereby negates the rationale of national cohesion found in comparative advantage theory, yet still derive the conclusion of collective national gains from 'free' international markets.

The mobility of capital eradicates the notion of a *nation* having factor proportions.[15] Instead, different industries, or segments of industries; or even individual companies must be constituted as discrete units, each with their own cost structure, and each with their own form of integration into international accumulation. They each have a different spatial circuit of reproduction.

With this recognised, it is apparent that comparative advantage theory 'prematurely' constructs a shared national experience of the global economy. There can be no explanation of how *individual* capitals can break free from their national factor proportions and expand into new industries, and thus no explanation of how national policy can rectify a trade imbalance when 'the market' will not do it. Policy makers

172

in an era of capital mobility need a theory in which national specialisation and international 'performance' is the outcome (or aggregation) of individual initiatives; not a theory which pre-allocates industries to nations.[16]

The theory of international trade in the era of widespread capital mobility has therefore had to return to such basic questions as "why do industries locate where they do?" (Krugman, 1991);[17] or "why firms from particular nations establish leadership in particular new industries?" (Porter 1990:17) — which can no longer be answered simply in terms of national comparative advantage. For policy makers confronting the balance of payments constraint, the equivalent question is how to get export growth-oriented industries and companies to locate within a country.

The new analytical question, therefore, is at what point and on what basis in the case for free international mobility of money and commodities is national cohesion constituted, in order to form the basis of nationally coherent policy responses to the balance of payments 'constraint'.

The alternative conception of *competitive advantage* is seen to address these issues; at least within the perspectives of policy makers. The conception of 'competitive advantage' was developed by Zysman and Tyson (1983) within the United States industry policy debate of the mid 1980s, although it is now most closely identified with the work of Michael E. Porter[18] (1985; 1986; 1990) from a management perspective, and Robert Reich (1991) from a political perspective. As a guide to policy formation, an emphasis on competitive advantage is said to be the key to the countries which successfully adapted their industrial structures, and have been increasing their share of world trade since the end of the long boom.

Competitive advantage starts not with nations, but with industries. Competitive advantage is an attribute of an industry within a nation compared with the same industry in other nations. By contrast, comparative advantage is a statement about the relative efficiency of an industry within a nation compared with other industries within the same nation. In terms of conventional trade theory, competitive advantage is comparable with absolute advantage (being able to sell at or below international price of production), Thus, for Zysman and Tyson,

> In contrast to the usual notion of absolute advantage, however, the notion of competitive advantage allows for the presence of economic policies that help or hinder the international performance of different firms. Thus the competitive advantage of the firms of a particular country in a particular market may be the result of either real absolute advantage or of policy-induced and hence distorted absolute advantage (1983:28).

But within this approach, absolute advantage has been reconstructed for a particular purpose. This purpose is to wrest the analysis of trade and efficiency from the conventional comparative advantage framework, in order to create a space for national policy. The need to challenge the conception of efficiency in terms of laissez faire is clear — it is the precondition of active state policy. But because comparative advantage postulates global efficiency gains, it is necessary also to show that national specialisation in contravention of comparative advantage will not lead to global efficiency losses — in other words, that one nation's gains are not another's losses.

Competition on an international scale is therefore about individual companies meeting international standards of costs, productivity, technology, quality and service in global, deregulated markets. The development of concepts like 'world's best practice' operates as the guide to internationally competitive production. The (alleged) global gains come not from national specialisation, but from intense global competition to innovate.

So this is a theory which explains the competitive position of individual industries, even individual capitals, not nations *per se*. There is no sense that individual industries or capitals are trapped by their national factor endowments. There is scope for individual (entrepreneurial) initiative. In the process, "competitive advantage has recognised that there is more to being competitive in international markets than specialising in line with [national] factor costs" (Porter 1990:6).

According to Porter, "[w]e must abandon the whole notion of a 'competitive nation' as a term having much meaning for economic prosperity". A nation's high standard of living "depends not on the amorphous notion of 'competitiveness', but on the productivity with which the nation's resources (labor and capital) are employed" (1990:6). This depends not just on increasing output per worker, but, in a more dynamic framework, in the ability of companies to move into more and more sophisticated industries, where productivity is higher. Hence, within this approach, the onus is on the individual firm to succeed in the international market — to be in the 'right' industries, and to be cost, quality and service competitive.

It might appear, therefore that this is an approach to international accumulation in which there are individual players, but no (national) teams. Far from it. Nations are central to this analysis — the critical point is where in the theory national aggregation becomes important. For comparative advantage, it is assumptions about capital mobility. For Porter, and the theory of competitive advantage, it is at the point of state policy formation. According to Porter,

> While globalisation of competition might appear to make the nation less important, instead it seems to make it more so. With fewer impediments to trade to shelter uncompetitive domestic firms and industries, the home nation takes on growing significance because it is the source of the skills and the technology that underpin competitive advantage. (1990:19)

So nations are important, yet only because they exert different impacts on competitive advantage.

> Competitive advantage is created and sustained through a highly localised process. Differences in national economic structures, values, cultures, institutions, and histories contribute profoundly to competitive success. (1990:19)

Thus it is policies of the nation state, rather than attributes of the nation space, which make the difference; policies that can create structures, values, cultures which are compatible with competitive advantage.

Herein lies the agenda for potentially far-reaching nation state intervention, in securing internationally competitive industries, but without reliance on trade restrictions or a low exchange rate. And herein lies the constitution of the nation as an aggregated, economic entity. For a nation to move up the productivity ladder requires its companies to move into higher productivity industries. The corollary is that lower productivity industries must be relinquished, and this requires state mediation of the conflicting interests of different parts of (total) capital. Moreover, industries must not only have high productivity by domestic standards; they must achieve international standards if they are to survive. Competitiveness, therefore, is not itself an attribute of nations, but of specific industries and industry segments, and the role of state policy is to facilitate the development of that attribute.

So how does 'competitive advantage' resolve the contradiction between the internationality of accumulation and the nationality of state policy? The answer lies in terms of the capacity of the theory of competitive advantage to meet the two criteria of 'successful' domestic policy identified at the outset.

First, 'competitive advantage' provides the state with a rationale for structural adjustment policies which, while not meeting the contradictory needs of all parts of capital, can be seen to be securing the transformation of that part of capital which is conspicuously losing in the face of deregulated trade and investment.

Second, and more significantly, while comparative advantage poses the gains from free trade at the level of exchange (because it requires state policy to do no more than free-up the exchange process), competitive advantage poses the gains from free trade at the level of production. Firms are most profitable internationally when they have the best productivity, the best technology, the best service, etc.. Framed in this way, the state has a role in addressing the balance of payments constraint, for the nation state can nurture a culture of productivity, technological development and service. In the process, it encourages domestic production by companies producing internationally-traded goods, so reducing import demand, and increasing exports.[19]

The balance of payments is, therefore, the direct object of policy within a free trade setting; something not possible within the perspective of comparative advantage. But in achieving this policy agenda, the nation is being defined in terms of a shared agenda of increasing the rate of surplus value, under the auspices of the nation state.

Conclusion

Keynesianism and monetarism, as the two premier post-war doctrines of macroeconomic management, each played out historically their incompatibility with comprehensive international capital mobility. Despite their important differences, they both start conceptually with the assumed ontological primacy of national units. The global economy therefore appears as something exogenous, to be reacted to. For countries facing a current account deficit, this meant not purchasing from the 'rest of the world' more than the nation could afford — or otherwise borrowing, or selling assets to foreigners. Residents of countries facing a surplus have the good fortune of being able to afford more imports, or the longer-term strategy of acquiring overseas assets.

Under the aegis of comparative advantage theory, with international specialisation based on factor costs, the response to a balance of payments crisis had two edges: cut domestic demand, to reduce imports, and reduce factor costs. In popular parlance, this has been posed as the nation 'living beyond its means'; 'needing to tighten its belt'. This is a politicised rationale, imposing a collective onus on national labor, derived from the image of collectivity constituted in the theory of comparative advantage.

During the 1980s, this agenda has changed to an individualised, economic (market based) rationale for wage cuts; or at least increases less than productivity to ensure that individual industries, or even companies, are able to compete in internationally-exposed markets. As an economic constraint rather than a politically nominated policy agenda, it now applies to workers in balance of payments surplus as well as deficit countries.

Within a 'free trade' setting, the pursuit of internationally competitive industries developed a new accepted wisdom, in recognition of the reality of international capital mobility. Whether this is attributable explicitly to the theory of 'competitive advantage' as the catalyst for policy is not the critical issue. Policy never unfolds according to the dictates of theory, but competitive advantage theory has certainly depicted the general thrust of many national policy agendas. Porter's theory does, however, illustrate clearly the logic which underlies policy development.

In this framework, the international economy is no longer constituted as exogenous, but as the arena in which all capital competes. State policy is no longer evaluated by the criterion of laissez faire, but in terms of securing the development of an industrial structure and social culture which will ensure that 'national' companies adapt to participate in the productive initiatives occurring in the international system.

Yet while this construct serves to empower domestic policy makers, it does so at the cost of renouncing an established explanation of national collective will and collective economic interest. For comparative advantage, the domestic distribution of the gains from trade comes via an 'objective', market allocation of resources. There are standard (albeit hypothetical, trivial and deceptive) arguments to support this market-driven system. But for competitive advantage, even this rationale is absent.

For competitive advantage, national unity is constituted not by a formula for the nationally-shared benefits of success (or burdens of failure) but by the capacity of state policy to deliver high productivity growth. But, and this is critical, the gains from trade are individually defined, so that collective national gains require widespread success in productivity growth, and this in turn is contingent upon the subordination of social order to the productivity objective. Behind the idealised notion of a flexible, educated and adaptive economy is a primary emphasis on increasing productivity. Porter is emphatic on this point —"productivity is the prime determinant in the long run of a nation's standard of living . . . The only meaningful concept of competitiveness at the national level is national productivity" (Porter 1990: 6).

There are some significant implications of this agenda. First, with national policies to facilitate the development of competitive success as the defining characteristic of the national economy, the national economy is itself defined in terms of productivity. Indeed, the social, cultural, managerial and institutional dimensions of productivity, emphasised by

Porter, are about transforming the totality of social relations to those most compatible with profitable production. The whole of social organisation must be ordered to facilitate productivity increases, and the possibility of subsidising 'uncompetitive' sectors, in 'the national interest' is disappearing.

Second, while national policies can potentially (and must) advance productivity, this, in itself, is not sufficient to secure competitive industries. Productivity must not only increase; it must increase more rapidly than in other countries. The most productivity-centred form of national social, political and economic organisation therefore sets the standard which all other nations must follow.

While Porter's own vision of competitive advantage emphasises the shared virtues of a high productivity society, and the potential for rising wages, the reality of pragmatic policy formation is that international competition in the rate of growth of relative surplus value inevitably (at least in all but the fastest growing countries) has recourse to wage increases less than the rate of growth of production; perhaps even real wage cuts. While reducing the benefits to labor is not the model's ideal path to competitiveness, it can nonetheless be (and widely is being) constructed as an unavoidable (permanent) short term aid to national competitiveness in a fiercely competitive world.

International competition is, of course, not new; but it now manifests with a new fervour. While, in the past, this has been an agenda constructed by the need for national responses to a balance of payments crisis (and hence only a direct threat to workers in balance of payments deficit countries), the new agenda is universal. To avoid being a deficit country, productivity of industries within the nation must keep increasing, and more rapidly than before. Put another way, while wage cuts in the framework of comparative advantage are politicised — as in the implications of the nation living beyond its means — in competitive advantage, the momentum for wage cuts is directly economic — the need for individual capitals to lower their costs of production; and this latter logic applies to all capitals, everywhere.

In Chapter 3, this issue was posed within a formal value-theoretic framework. There it was contended that the law of value on an international scale is consistent with the value of labor power being formulated on a national scale, but national 'determination' has to be consistent with global criteria of surplus value production. Thus cross-national differences in the value of labor power will increasingly reflect the rate of surplus value which can be appropriated within countries. High value of labor power countries are those in which capital can appropriate high (relative) surplus value; low value of labor power countries are those in which capital can only appropriate low rates of surplus value, with reliance on absolute surplus value.

In the context of national strategies for competitive industries, the theory of competitive advantage correctly focuses on the role of the nation state in securing internationally-competitive rates of surplus value. There is the hope, but not the guarantee, that the rate of surplus value can be increased sufficiently to support an increasing value of labor power. But international competition means that increases in surplus value within one country are being compared with increases in other countries and only in those countries with a relative increase in relative surplus value will the value of labor power increase over time, while remaining compatable with international profitability.

So the value of labor power is still nationally formulated, with the nation state instrumental in that process. But international competition is inserted into domestic formulation as a primary determinant. The nation state's role is increasingly to facilitate the internationalisation of the value of labour power, constructed as national competitive necessity. This situation amounts to a global contest between national working classes, to deliver the highest rate of productivity increase for the lowest value of labor power. Stripped of its nationalist presentation, policies for international competitiveness only 'solve' the contradiction between the internationality of accumulation and the nationality of nation state regulation by projecting the national form of class conflict to an international scale.

Notes

1. Those loyal to Keynes, and particularly the emphasis on public control of investment, argue that post-war 'Keynesianism' was a bastardised version of Keynes. This is undoubtedly true, but the issue under consideration is the history of policy, not the theoretical origins of that policy. Moreover, there is no reason to believe that 'legitimate' Keynesianism is any more immune than the 'bastard' version from the following critique of nationalist policy. In particular, Keynes' emphasis on the need to keep domestic interest rates immune from international 'hot money', and to retain control of all capital movements (1980:31) has been historically superseded in a way that no individual nation state could resist.

2. There is debate over whether any policy package can be held responsible for the long boom ('bastard' Keynesian or otherwise), or whether the the long boom was due to particular post-war circumstances which were relatively policy immune. These debates are important, but not central to the current analysis.

3. Tsiang (1950-51:270, n.10) was perspicatious in challenging Machlup's specification of the division of flows into autonomous and accommodating. Machlup's characterisation of accommodating capital movements included foreign exchange speculation (insofar as it is induced by movements in other parts of the balance of payments). Tsiang points out that these capital movements, while induced, are not 'accommodating', in the sense that they do not automatically compensate imbalances in the current account. Indeed, these induced speculative movements would themselves require accomodating adjustments. This turned out to be a critical point some thirty years later.

4. By the same logic, capital flows were incompatible with the Bretton Woods system of international finance because national United States policy could not sustain the value of the United States dollar.

5. See Chapter 6 for a description of purchasing power parity.

6. The termination of money supply targeting is discussed in Chapter 6.

7. Notice that the question as posed is predicated on a non-recognition that a 'boom' had finished; that is, the poor performance of the UK economy is to be explained endogenously.

8. It should be noted that this framework poses constraints in terms of existing propensities to import. There is no real sustained consideration of, for example, state-sponsored strategies of import replacement. Social democratic industry policies which might aspire to lift the constraint by developing import replacement are not addressed in this literature.

9. In the United States, gross savings as a proportion of GDP fell from almost 20% in 1980 to 14% in 1987. Capital inflow, it is argued, was therefore required to compensate for declining savings; not even to fund increasing investment. In Japan, conversely, gross savings increased from 30% in 1980 to 34% in 1989. This was enough to fund both domestic investment, which grew rapidly from 1986, and international investment also.

10. It should not pass without noting, however, how perverse is an economic logic which privileges the pursuit of national accounting balances over production to meet material needs. This is all the more so when constituted as a national response to recession.

11. It may be argued for some countries that the current account deficit derives not from a trade imbalance, but from a deficit on the balance of income payable, reflecting a high foreign debt. The argument then is that the debt has been historically generated, and the nation needs to run a trade surplus to pay off the debt.

12. The problem for the older social democracies is that supervision is predicated upon national autonomy, permitting redistribution to achieve national social and economic goals. Recent internationalisation is making some parts of capital unwilling to participate in the immediate costs of national

redistribution, for their profitability is not directly contingent upon long-run national growth.

13. Except, of course, that a subsidy to circulation may be paid at the point of production.

14. Put another way, the pursuit of efficiency is determined by different processes domestically and internationally. Domestically, efficiency (equalisation of the rate of profit) follows from free mobility of capital. Internationally, efficiency follows from changes in the value of money (classical version) or changes in the exchange rate (modern version). This directly constitutes the nation as a discrete economic unit.

15. Strictly, the notion is purely an aggregate description. It has no implications for individual capitals.

16. Note here the importance of sporting metaphores in the need of individual team members (companies or industries) to 'lift their individual performances' for the good of the 'team' (nation). The coach (state) then has the job of 'motivating' each team member to achieve this goal.

17. Krugman nonetheless retains a belief in comparative advantage as the key to trade theory, and that "international trade is not about competition, it is about mutually beneficial exchange" (1993). And this from one of the most innovative trade theorists!

18. Porter was a member of Reagan's President's Commission on Industrial Competitiveness, referred to in Chapter 8.

19. This need not be a purely mercantilist agenda — the belief that wealth comes from a trade surplus. It is entirely compatible with the theory of competitive advantage that successful development of such industries will lead to exchange rate appreciation, causing the competitiveness of local production to decline. But this is why the state must continue to nurture even higher productivity industries : the increase in national wealth reflected in the exchange rate appreciation is only temporary.

10

What Needs to Be Reclaimed?

International accumulation pre-dates capitalism, and it pre-dates nations. Capitalism and nations were conceived in a world in which capital was mobile. Yet this book has addressed the internationalisation of capital as a 'recent' process — not a fundamental transformation of the nature of capitalism, but a change which is of some significance in determining a broad spectrum of contemporary social relations. How can internationalisation be a change in a system which is inherently international?

The Dictates of Global Competition

The change, though it should not be overstated, is in the form of competition between capitals, and of the role of nation states in mediating the competitive process. Prior to World War One international trade, finance and investment were every bit as prevalent as they are today. But this was trade and investment within the imperial system. Finance and investment was protected by the colonialism, and predominantly under the aegis of the colonial state.

The international mobility of capital is different today because capital is breaking free of national ties, and the nation state no longer secures directly for capital an extra-national space in which to expand. There is, even in the restricted neoclassical sense, much greater international competition, brought about by technological developments in traversing space, and national deregulation of international commodity and money flows. Capital flows not just within the structure of the colonial system, but according to international conditions of profitability. There is, in short, the development of global integration.

This is the novel dimension of the current period. What has surprised most economists is that it has been played out as a period of volatility and uncertainty. The 'free-market' theories which dominate economics have long advocated free mobility in the name of efficiency and stability. The expectation was that the world would form a single, barrier-free market, moving closer and closer to the outcomes of the perfect market. Much recent international economics has focused on fashioning behavioural assumptions about market participants in an attempt to model *ex poste* rationalisations for these unexpected outcomes. There is little consideration of recent history involving qualitative changes in international accumulation.

The orthodox theories have but a limited set of concepts and categories with which to understand these recent changes, for they have pre-determined ways of understanding the relation between the national and the international. Most of the language of economics remains tied to national units. The international economy is still posed in terms of inflows to and outflows from the national economy; or simply as the external sector. The study of international relations is the study of relations between national units. These conceptions retain, generally uncritically, the notion that there is some national economic process which is discrete from global processes, with the global dimension an intrusion.

The orthodox analysis is somewhat less circumscribed than its language would suggest, but this in itself creates limitations of analytical clarity and consistency. Neo-classical economists can analyse globally integrated markets, yet in posing the impact of these markets within any particular nation, the analysis, following the language, converts to the identification of 'foreign impacts'. When the volatility and uncertainty is interpreted at the national level, there is even more confusion, for the predictability and management of most national aggregates has become increasingly difficult. There is an analytical bind: resources flow freely on a global scale with scant regard for national boundaries, yet resource flows are to be *understood* as relations between national units. It is little wonder that this discipline is losing relevance to national policy formation.

But the answer is by no means simple. The temptation is to simply revert to the other extreme of a global perspective, on the premise that all economic processes are globalised, and national space has been transcended. Yet this too is a basic misconception. Nations *are* important. The experience of the global economy is not the same everywhere, and while that experience is not simply a national phenomenon, it has important national dimensions. The nation is, therefore, a part of global accumulation, which exerts an impact in global accumulation, but without sectioning off its own, discrete process of accumulation.

Yet the gulf between the extremes of nation as a discrete economic space, and nation as an arbitrary part of an international space, lacks a language of investigation. It has proved very difficult to develop a language or analysis in which global accumulation is part of the domestic economy, and the local (national) is understood as a specific representation of global processes. Similarly, it has been difficult for economics to develop a conception of the role of the state which is not predicated upon a nationalist conception of accumulation, and the belief that the state's role is to secure 'national' benefit. So international economics and political economy continues to baulk at the ambiguous constitution of boundaries, reverting to the apparent conceptual clarity that is nationalism. Notions of national autonomy being secured or subverted, and gains and losses to the national economy from international interaction, are the terms which continue to dominate debate.

This book has attempted to avoid the limitations of a nationalist starting point, so that the relation of 'the national' to international accumulation could be posed as an open agenda for analysis. The style of this analysis was developed in Chapter 5, in terms of different circuits of capital, with different forms of insertion into international accumulation. The national, market-constrained, investment-constrained and global circuits are defined in terms of the spatial horizons of individual capitals' circulation and reproduction. As it stands, this classification may be somewhat mechanistic. Classification is invariably mechanistic. But the framework does provide a means to conceptualise the multiple ways in which individual capitals are linked into international accumulation, and so identify the opposed interests of capital which national policy must mediate.

A number of important dimensions can be established which are central to a conception of the nation state in the current era.

- International capital is not a single, undifferentiated process, or set of interests. There are contradictions within international accumulation as different parts of capital seek to increase their share of total (global) surplus value.

- This competition for surplus value creates different interests with respect to policy formation in individual nation states, for most state policies, but particularly those pertaining directly to international capital mobility, affect capitals differently.

- The nation state plays central functions in securing the conditions of accumulation on a global scale. There is nothing inherently inconsistent between the international movement of capital and the economic functions of the nation state, nor even between the international movement of capital and nationalism.

- The constitution of a national interest as the guiding vision of policy formation disguises the multiple and conflicting interests within a nation with respect to international accumulation. 'National interest' is invariably the label attached to those policies which reflect the interests of the dominant part of capital, sometimes with, sometimes without the support of organised labor. Hence the 'national interest' changes over time — from protectionism to free trade; from floating to regulated exchange rates, etc., broadly reflecting the shifting balance of capitals.

- It follows that the notion of international mobility of capital obstructing national policy agendas is fundamentally misconceived. It remains based on a conception of international capital as a unified, exogenous force, rather than a contradictory expression of (inherently international) accumulation within national spaces; and on the nation as a set of interests conceptually separable from the global economy.

When, from Chapter 6 on, issues of domestic policy formation are addressed, it is to be hoped that the mechanical aspects of classification in Chapter 5 were seen to be somewhat freed up. But the essential insight remains. The need to understand international accumulation as a domestic, rather than just an exogenous, global force leads to the recognition that national policy is being formulated with respect to international accumulation.

Nation States and National Processes

An analysis of the international/national nexus pivots directly on the role of the nation state with respect to international accumulation. It is states which, at least from an economic perspective, embody national differences. The state can be characterised as playing two types of roles in the construction of national difference. One is the requirement to manage accumulation because capital cannot secure its own conditions of existence. This requirement expresses as a national, and therefore partial, intervention in what is an inherently global process. That process acquires a national 'twist', although not creating an identifiable national economy in the sense of isolating a distinct sphere of national accumulation. The other, related role of the state is to reproduce the nation as lived political reality, by giving national interpretation to global processes. The nation state 'downloads' global processes for local identification and manipulation, and in the process, a distinct national experience is constructed.

The two roles of the state are entirely complementary. The new agenda of competitiveness as the rationale for national economic policy has, in key respects, been the recognition in economic policy that the 'national economy' cannot be regulated in terms of active management of national aggregates — be they the Keynesian aggregates such as investment, consumption and employment, or the monetarist aggregate of national money supply. National policy instead focuses on individual capitals, and their requirement to perform in an international setting. This emerging focus reveals an important change in accumulation and the way in which the contradiction between the internationality of accumulation and the nationality of state regulation is being transformed.

The requirement of the nation state to manage accumulation was broken down in Chapter 4 to the primary functions of securing the money system and securing the labor system, particularly the supply of labor power, and a secondary function of mediating the opposed interests of capitals. These are all national functions, but with recent internationalisation, there has been increasing adherence to global agendas.

The issue of securing the money system in an international context was analysed in Chapter 6. The shift from national monetarism, and domestically-oriented monetary policy to internationally-oriented monetary policy is clear. When monetarism was embraced in the 1970s, the agenda for monetary policy was the control of national inflation as the pre-condition for national growth. The international reorientation of monetary policy first involved abandoning money supply targeting and instead targeting the exchange rate and the balance of payments to secure national 'external balance' in a volatile global economy. That phase of monetary policy has given way to a return to a focus on domestic inflation, but now cast in terms of making national production internationally competitive; not in terms of national growth *per se*.

The issue of securing the labor system in an international context was analysed in Chapter 9. The national policy agenda of creating 'internationally competitive' industries to meet the national requirements of the balance of payments has seen productivity identified as the key to national wealth. Within the vision of a high productivity high wealth society, formal recognition may be given to the contribution of management and technology. But as management practices and technology show increasing global uniformity, the key to productivity as a national characteristic is labor. For local industry to be 'competitive', labor must be more productive than its foreign counterparts, or must 'compensate' for its lower productivity by commanding lower incomes. The effect is that the labor market becomes internationalised by the assertion of global productivity norms ('world's best practice'). Productivity above or below the norm means a standard of living (value of labor power) above or below the norm. So the value of labor power may be nationally constructed, by a process of social and cultural national practices in which the nation state is central, but increasingly, state policy is securing that national value of labor power which conforms to an international determination of the value of labor power.

In general, the nation state secures the labor system and secures the money system on a national scale, but with an international orientation. In the process, the state must mediate the conflicts between different parts of capital which arise in meeting the two primary functions.

Yet in applying national policy to international accumulation, there is not an abandonment of national agendas. The contradiction between the internationality of accumulation and the nationality of state regulation is not solved by the subordination of the latter to the former, but by the role of the state policy being recast so that the dominance of global calculation is presented as beneficial for all nationals. In particular, the working class in each nation must be convinced that the pursuit of international competitiveness is an agenda of labor as well as capital.

In part, this concurrence of labor occurs through the individualism of the agenda of international competitiveness: workers know that their own well-being is directly contingent upon the profitability of their employer in an internationally-exposed market, and much less on the capacity of the nation state to generate national economic growth. The conservatism of workers and the decline of unionism internationally is surely attributable in large part to this reality.

Nonetheless, the spirit of a national collectivity remains critical. Apart from the obvious aspects of political stability, the policies which go under the label of competitiveness require popular adherence for their successful implementation as economic programs. This is why patriotism has become the critical adjunct of 'competitiveness', for the individualism and internationalism implicit in the latter cannot reproduce its own collective adherence. It requires a patriotic commitment, and here the state is pivotal, for it is the nation state which gives essentially global processes a national interpretation and national substance.

Holloway (1994:32) calls this 'the constantly repeated process of decomposing global social relations', and he identifies it with the construction of patriotism — anthems, flag ceremonies, etc.. Yet the construction of national experience is more pervasive than the ceremonial show-cases identified by Holloway. The whole construction of national accounting, and national policy formation, particularly national identification with balance of payments figures and exchange rates, involves the nation state 'decomposing' global economic processes into national economic processes, creating distinctly national meanings. Whether nationals define themselves through anthems and flags, or through balance of payments figures and currency values, the effect is equivalent. Both are being used to develop a national identity, usually with the underlying agenda of extracting more sacrifice for the so-called 'common good'.

Nationalist ideology as a form of macroeconomic policy is not recognised in the economics textbooks, and not found in official government policy documents. But it should not be under-rated as a form of policy. The state, particularly political leaders, have long engaged in national motivation of economic performance, but with 'recent internationalisation', this has developed a different character. Rather than reliance simply on exhortation to work harder, more recent nationalist ideology has been very much about constructing national economic difference.

While the 'conventional' tools of policy have been directed at 'freeing up' markets, and removing restrictions on international capital mobility, all in the name of the gains of efficiency, patriotism as economic policy involves a populist construction of economic autonomy. It draws on sentiment derived from cultural and sometimes ethnic difference to promote a *perception* that commodities and money are not international: that local is preferred to foreign. Tariff barriers are removed, in the name of competitiveness and efficiency; but states sponsor 'buy local' advertising campaigns, in the name of creating local jobs and investment! Patriotic policy thereby promotes a *perception* of national difference (and through that, national economic coherence) and the perception of collective benefits coming from individuals acting as if there is national economic difference. The national objective is to 'get behind' national companies to secure their international success, and to make the national economy an attractive place for internationally-mobile capital to reside. Labor's role is to facilitate capital, with the promise that all will share in the success of local accumulation, and even in the international accumulation of 'national' companies. The metaphor of sport, as the archetypal competitive process, is never far away. Notions of individual commitment to collective success, the collective gains from individual endeavour, and also sacrifice for the common good (team loyalty) provide a more insightful guide to current policy formation than any economic theory.

Patriotism as economic policy goes further than the construction of national difference as a sort of non-tariff barrier. A distinctive characteristic of the new nationalism is that it is outward looking and globally oriented, attempting to nurture international expansion of 'national' capital, probably in a way which more conventional policy tools could never achieve (for example, politically-negotiated access to foreign markets). The state is developing an 'internationalist nationalism', consistent with the mobility of capital. While older patriotism was more often more isolationist and xenophobic (within smaller countries, anyway), establishing the nation as a 'safe haven' for accumulation, the new patriotism is more involved in creating the confidence for capital to expand, although without the political protection which characterised imperialism.

The new patriotism is also capital-centred, for securing national conditions compatible with international competition is the first condition of national policy. This is what makes the creation of national difference directly consistent with the internationality of accumulation: the creation of national difference involves each nation 'discovering' the primacy of productivity as a shared national agenda, and achieving productivity increases in its 'own' way.

Yet the effect of these national experiences has been to internationalise the value of labor power by making national wages a direct reflection of national productivity which itself is validated in international markets. The chase of capital across the globe manifests also as the chase of labor norms across the globe. The contradiction between the internationality of accumulation and the nationality of state regulation of accumulation appears as the expression of the contradiction between classes. Patriotism, the pursuit of national competitiveness and the reproduction of national difference are the means by which the national and international are reconciled. Competitiveness provides the rationale and patriotism provides the means by which national processes are made to adhere to international norms. Patriotism provides the rationale and the reproduction of national difference provides the means by which a global class process can be presented as national processes with cross-class national complicity.

Political Responses

The effect of the combination of economic internationalism and political nationalism has been powerful, for it has set the terms in which most all economic and political debate takes place.

One effect of the combination of competitiveness and patriotism has been to create a new assertiveness from within the national social democratic 'left'. The national-competitive solution has proved seductive.

Class conflict has given way to national conflict, with patriotism the new ideological orthodoxy. Wage cuts and even fiscal austerity are being sold as the short-run costs of becoming 'competitive'. The long run is said to offer efficient, high wage, high employment outcomes. The problem, of course, is that the costs are certain; the benefits doubtful. It is surely an expression of the dominance of capital that this social democratic stand must sacrifice all critique of capitalism in order to achieve a sense of 'political empowerment'!

Another effect has been the emergence of a politics which seeks to realign the space of political regulation with the space of accumulation, requiring some form of a supra-national state. It is now 50 years since the Bretton Woods Agreement was signed. Despite the failure of the Bretton Woods arrangements to offer an administrative solution to international finance, there is a widespread sentimentality about the confidence and sense of direction that financial institutions and national policy makers felt as they faced the post-war period. There is now re-emerging support by some liberals and social democrats for international policy making, to regulate accumulation on its own (international) space. The formation of trading blocs, or stable international currency systems such as the European Currency Union (even a single European currency) are being proffered as solutions to current national uncertainties and instabilities. Some Keynesians are even canvassing the notion of a global monetary system, with an institution such as the International Monetary Fund administering global monetary policy.

In terms of the contradiction between the internationality of capital and the nationality of the state, these proposals might, indeed, be seen as developing a 'solution'. But in this solution the nation state is being imputed with an adaptability it does not have. The nation state is not an institution whose spatial power can simply be re-defined to meet global administrative objectives. The state is not outside society, and its functions are not tools of rational management which can be re-sited as a global forum so as to ensure that all economic variables 'once again' come under the rubric of a single policy authority. There is a Keynesian fantasy that the 'collective interest' can once again be achieved if we can only pull all the economic variables back under the aegis of a single state. The voluntarist nationalism which is patriotism is replaced with a voluntarist internationalism.

If this aspect of state policy is instead posed in terms of mediating the presence of the international within the national, 'progressive reforms' towards supra-nationalism must be judged quite differently. Tendencies towards policy supra-nationalism involve particular interests, and, as has been seen so clearly in the European Union, supra-nationalism is also opposed by particular interests. Where adherence to supra-nationalism

190

appears as national policy, this is to be understood as a particular
outcome in the mediation of opposed domestic interests. Moreover, it is
by no means irreversible. Support for such supra-national administration
must be reproduced at the national level, and this requirement
constrains its capacity to transcend national policy. In Europe, for
example, the resistance to supra-nationalist policy is not just from ultra-
nationalist fascists, but also from capital (and probably the workers they
employ) which loses a form of mediation in their insertion into
international competition.

So some further developments towards supra-nationality can be
expected, though it can also be expected to be a highly conflictual
process. Trading blocs and various arrangements for international
currency management will certainly develop further. Co-operative
currency re-alignments of the G7 countries may also become something
more than *ad hoc*. But relinquishement of state power to institutions
above the nation state is not a one-way path. It is wishful thinking if it is
believed a solution to the contradictions of international accumulation
will involve economic policy slowly, but inexorably, passing over to
supra-national authorities. Indeed, the most likely consequence of this
agenda is the politics of ultra-nationalism.

Is there an alternative to despair? In the realm of national policy
solutions, probably not. Suggestions that nation states can and will
regulate national economic aggregates for shared national benefit is
doubly deceptive: these aggregates are beyond national determination;
and the manipulation of these aggregates which states do undertake is
formulated within an international process of accumulation, not
according to some conception of shared national benefit.

The impossibility for labor of national policy solutions goes to the
heart of the nature of capitalism as a relation between capital and labor.
'Recent internationalisation' has made the global nature of class relations
an explicit and systematic process: the chase of capital across the globe
has been the chase of the social relation of capital as well as of money,
production and commodities. National policy, therefore, unfolds not just
as a national issue, but as an international class issue, securing on a
national scale the dominance of capital globally.

The ideology of international competitiveness presents international
class dominance as national economic necessity, and an alternative class
politics requires that this necessity be exposed as ideology. Competition
as the rationale for policy involves the assertion of capitalist calculation
over the construction of social relations. If the pre-eminence of
'competition' as a form of social relations can be re-politicised — for
individuals as well as for communities — the chase of capital can be
challenged, and production for use rather than for profit re-asserted as

the appropriate agenda for economics. Developments in the last twenty years require that this be a global challenge. The first task in that process is to confront the nationalism which dignifies competition as an expression and experience of social commitment to a collective good.

References

Aglietta, M. 1979. *A Theory of Capitalist Regulation*. London: New Left Books.

_____ 1982. 'World capitalism in the 1980s', *New Left Review* no.136.

Anderson, B. 1983. *Imagined Communities*. London: Verso.

Andreff, V. 1984. 'The international centralization of capital and the re-ordering of world capitalism', *Capital & Class* no.22.

Armstrong, P., A. Glyn and J. Harrison 1991. *Capitalism Since World War II*. Oxford: Basil Blackwell.

Balibar, E. 1991. 'The national form: history and ideology', in E. Balibar and I. Wallerstein, *Race, Nation, Class*. London: Verso.

Bank for International Settlements (BIS) various. *Annual Reports*. Basile: BIS.

Baran, P. and P. Sweezy 1966. *Monopoly Capitalism*. Harmondsworth: Penguin.

Batchelor, R., R. Major and A. Morgan 1980. *Industrialisation and the Basis for Trade*. Cambridge: Cambridge University Press.

Batten, D., M.P. Blackwell, I.-S. Kim, S.E. Nocera and J. Yuzurin 1990. 'The conduct of monetary policy in major industrial countries', *IMF Occasional Paper* no.70.

Becker, J. 1977. *Marxian Political Economy*. Cambridge: Cambridge University Press.

Benzie, R. 1992. 'The development of the international bond market', *BIS Economic Papers* no.32, Basle: Bank for International Settlements.

Bina, C. and B. Yaghmaian 1991. 'Post-war global accumulation and the transnationalisation of capital', *Capital & Class* no.43.

Blair, M. and R. Litan 1990. 'Corporate leverage and leveraged buyouts in the eighties', in J. Shoven and J. Waldfogel, eds., *Debt, Taxes and Corporate Restructuring*. Washington D.C.: The Brookings Institution.

Bluestone, B. and B. Harrison 1982. *The Deindustrialization of America*. New York: Basic Books.

Blundell-Wignal, A. and F. Browne 1991. 'Increasing financial market integration, real exchange rates and macroeconomic adjustment', *OECD Working Papers* no.96. Paris: OECD.

Blundell-Wignal, A. and R. Gregory 1989. 'Exchange rate policy in advanced commodity-exporting countries: The case of Australia and New Zealand', *OECD Department of Economics and Statistics, Working Papers* no.83. Paris: OECD.

Bonturi, M. and Fukasaku, K. 1993. 'Globalisation and intra-firm trade: An empirical note', *OECD Economic Studies* no.20.

Borio, C. 1990. 'Leverage and financing of non-financial companies', *BIS Economic Papers* no.27. Basle: Bank for International Settlements.

Borjas, G., R. Freeman and L. Katz 1992. 'On the labor market effects of immigration and trade', in G. Borjas and R. Freeman, eds., *Immigration and the Workforce*. Chicago: University of Chicago Press.

Borrego, J. 1982. 'Metanational capitalist accumulation and the reintegration of socialist states', in C. Chase-Dunn, ed., *Socialist States in the World-System*. Beverly Hills: Sage.

Bound, J. and G. Johnson 1992. 'Changes in the structure of wages in the 1980s: An evaluation', *American Economic Review* vol.82 no.3.

Bowles, S., D. Gordon and T. Weisskopf 1984. *Beyond the Wasteland: A Democratic Alternative to Economic Decline*. London: Verso.

Boyer, R. 1990. *The Regulation School: A Critical Introduction*. New York: Colombia University Press.

Branson, W. 1980. 'Trends in United States international trade and investment since World War II', in M. Feldstein ed., *The American Economy in Transition*. Chicago: University of Chicago Press.

Brenner, R. 1977. 'The origins of capitalist development: A critique of neo-Smithian Marxism', *New Left Review* no.104.

Bressand, A. 1990. 'Beyond independence: 1992 as a global challenge', *International Affairs* vol.66 no.1.

Brewener, C. 1989. 'Socialist politics and theories of money and credit', *Review of Radical Political Economics* vol.21 no.3.

Bryan, D. 1985. 'Monopoly in Marxist method', *Capital & Class* no.26.

_____ 1991. 'Australian economic nationalism: Old and new', *Australian Economic Papers* vol.30 no.57.

Bryant, R. 1980. *Money and Monetary Policy in Interdependent Nations*. Washington,D.C.: Brookings Institution.

Bukharin N. 1915. *Imperialism and World Economy*. London: The Merlin Press, 1972.

Carchedi, G. 1991. 'Technological innovation, international production prices and exchange rates', *Cambridge Journal of Economics* vol.15 no.1.

Chase-Dunn, C. 1981. 'Interstate system and capitalist world-economy: One logic or two?', *International Studies Quarterly* vol.25 no.1.

_____ 1989. *Global Formation: Structures of the World-Economy*. Oxford: Basil Blackwell.

Christian, D. 1990. 'Accumulation and accumulators: The metaphor Marx muffed', *Science & Society* vol.54 no.2.

Clarke, S. 1978. 'Capital, fractions of capital and the state: "Neo-Marxist" analyses of the South African state', *Capital & Class* no.5.

       1988. 'Overaccumulation, class struggle and the regulation approach', *Capital & Class* no.56.

       1990-91. 'The Marxist theory of overaccumulation and crisis', *Science & Society* vol.54 no.4.

Clawson, P. 1977. 'The internationalisation of capital and Capital accumulation in Iran and Iraq', *The Insurgent Sociologist* vol.7 no.2.

Clifton, J.A. 1977. 'Competition and the evolution of the capitalist mode of production, *Cambridge Journal of Economics* vol.1.

Cooper, R. 1985. 'Comments', Symposium on exchange rates, *Brookings Papers on Economic Activity* no.1.

Cornwall, J. 1977. *Modern Capitalism: Its Growth and Transformation*. Oxford: Martin Robertson.

Cowan, M. 1986. 'Change in state power, international conditions and peasant producers: The case of Kenya', *Journal of Development Studies* vol.22 no.2.

Crotty, J. 1985. 'The centrality of money, credit and financial intermediation in Marx's crisis theory: An interpretation of Marx's methodology', in S. Resnick and R. Wolfe, eds., *Rethinking Marxism: Struggles in Marxist Theory*. New York Autonomedia.

Dealtry M. and J. Van't dack, 1989. 'The US external deficit and associated shifts in international portfolios', *BIS Economic Papers* no.25. Basle: Bank for International Settlements.

DeCecco, M. 1989. 'The European Monetary System and national interest', in P. Guerrieri and P. Padoan, eds., *The Political Economy of European Integration*. London: Harvester Wheatsheaf.

DeBrunhoff, S. 1973. *Marx on Money*. New York: Urizen.

       1976. *The State, Capital and Economic Policy*. London: Pluto.

Devine, J. 1989. 'What is simple labour? A re-examination of the value-creating capacity of skilled labour', *Capital & Class* no.39.

Dobb, M. 1946. *Studies in the Development of Capitalism*. London: George Routledge & Sons.

Dore, E. and J. Weeks 1979. 'International exchange and the causes of backwardness', *Latin American Perspectives*, vol.6 no.21.

Dornbusch, R. 1976. 'Expectations and exchange rate dynamics', *Journal of Political Economy* vol.84 no.6.

       1980. *Open Economy Macroeconomics*. New York: Basic Books.

       1983. 'Exchange rate economics: Where do we stand?', in J. Bhandari and B. Putnam, eds., *Economic Interdependence and Flexible Exchange Rates*. Cambridge, Mass.: MIT Press.

       1989. 'Purchasing power parity', in J. Eatwell, M. Milgate and P. Newman, eds., *The New Palgrave: a Dictionary of Economics*. London: Macmillan.

—— and A. Giovannini 1990. 'Monetary policy in an open economy', in B. Friedman and F. Hahn *Handbook of Monetary Economics*. Amsterdam: North Holland.

Feldstein, M. 1988. 'Distinguished lecture on economics in government: Thinking about international economic coordination', *Journal of Economic Perspectives* vol.2 no.2.

—— and C. Horioka 1980. 'Domestic savings and international capital flows', *Economic Journal* vol.90.

Fine, B. 1985-86. 'Banking capital and the theory of interest', *Science & Society* vol.49 no.1.

Fleming, J. 1962. 'Domestic financial policies under fixed and under floating exchange rates', *International Monetary Fund Staff Papers* vol.9 no.3.

Foley, D.K. 1986. *Money, Accumulation and Crisis*. London: Harwood Academic Publishers.

Frank, A.G. 1969. *Capitalism and Underdevelopment in Latin America*. New York: Monthly Review Press.

—— *Crisis: In the World Economy*. London: Heinemann.

Frankel, J. 1992. 'Measuring international capital mobility: a review', *American Economic Review* vol.80 no.2.

—— and K. Froot 1990. 'Chartists, fundamentalists and the demand for dollars', in A. Courakis and M. Taylor, eds., *Private Behaviour and Government Policy in Interdependent Economies*. Oxford: Clarendon.

Frenkel J. and Johnson, H. 1975. eds., *The Monetary Approach to the Balance of Payments*. London: George Allen & Unwin.

Friedman, B. 1980. 'Postwar changes in the American financial markets', in M. Feldstein ed., *The American Economy in Transition*. Chicago: Chicago University Press.

—— 1988. 'Lessons on monetary policy in the 1980s', *Journal of Economic Perspectives* vol.2 no.3.

—— 1990. 'Targets and instruments of monetary policy', in B. Friedman and F. Hahn, eds., *Handbook of Monetary Economics*. Amsterdam: North Holland.

Friedman, M. 1953. 'The case for flexible exchange rates', in *Essays in Positive Economics*. Chicago: University of Chicago Press.

—— 1968. 'The role of monetary policy', *American Economic Review* vol.58 no.1.

Fröbel, F., J. Heinrichs and O. Kreye 1980. *The New International Division of Labour*. Cambridge: Cambridge University Press.

George, S. 1992. *Debt Boomerang: How the Third World Debt Harms Us All*. London: Pluto.

Gibson, K. and R. Horvath 1983. 'Aspects of a theory of transition within the capitalist mode of production', *Environment and planning D: Society and Space* vol.1 no.2.

Goldstein, M., D. Mathieson, and T. Lare 1991. 'Determinants and systematic consequences of international capital flows', *IMF Occasional Paper* no.77.

Goodhart, C 1989. 'The conduct of monetary policy', *The Economic Journal* vol.99 no.396.

Gordon, D. 1988. 'The global economy: New edifice of crumbling foundations?', *New Left Review* no.168.

_____ R. Edward and M. Reich 1982. *Segmented Work, Divided Workers: the Historical Transformation of Labour in the United States*. New York: Cambridge University Press.

Gourevitch, P. 1986. *Politics in Hard Times: Comparative Responses to International Crisis*. Ithaca: Cornell University Press.

Harman, C. 1991. 'The state and capitalism today', *International Socialism* no.51.

Harris, L. 1977. 'The balance of payments and the international economic system', in F. Green and P. Nore, eds., *Economics: An Anti-Text*. London: Macmillan.

Harris, N. 1983. *Of Bread and Guns: The World Economy in Crisis*. Harmondsworth: Penguin.

Harrison, B. 1987. 'Cold bath or restructuring? An expansion of the Weisskopf-Bowles-Gordon framework', *Science & Society* vol.51 no.1.

Hilferding, R. 1910. *Finance Capital: A Study of the Latest Phase of Capitalist Development*. London: Routledge and Keegan Paul, 1981.

Hirst, P. and G. Thompson 1992. 'The problem of "globalisation": International economic relations, national economic management and the formation of trading blocs', *Economy and Society* vol.21 no.4.

Hobsbawm, E. 1977. 'Some reflections on the break-up of Britain', *New Left Review* no.105.

Hogan, L. 1986. 'A comparison of alternative exchange rate forecasting models', *Economic Record* vol.62 no.177.

Holloway, J. 1994. 'Global capital and the nation state', *Capital & Class* no.52.

_____ and Picciotto, S. 1978. eds., *State and Capital: A Marxist Debate*. London: Edward Arnold.

International Monetary Fund (IMF) various. *Annual Reports*. Washington D.C.: IMF.

_____ various. *Balance of Payments Statistics Yearbook*. Washington D.C.: IMF.

_____ various. *International Financial Statistics*. Washington D.C.: IMF.

_____ 1950. *Balance of Payments Manual*. First Edition. Washington D.C.: IMF.

_____ 1977. *Balance of Payments Manual*. Fourth Edition. Washington D.C.: IMF.

_____ 1985. *World Economic Outlook, May 1985*. Washington DC: IMF.

_____ 1991. *World Economic Outlook, May 1991*. Washington DC: IMF.

Isard, P and L. Stekler 1985. 'US international capital flows and the dollar'. *Brookings Papers on Economic Activity* no.1.

Jenkins, R. 1984. 'Divisions over the international division of labour', *Capital & Class* no.22.

_____ 1987. *Transnational Corporations and Uneven Development: the Internationalisation of Capital and the Third World.* London: Methuen.

Jessop, B. 1988. 'Regulation theory, post-Fordism and the state: More than a reply to Werner Bonefield', *Capital & Class* no.34.

Julius, D. 1990. *Global Companies and Public Policy.* London: Royal Institute of International Affairs/ Pinter.

Kay, G. 1975. *Development and Underdevelopment: A Marxist Analysis.* London: Macmillan.

Kenen, P.B. 1989. *Exchange Rates and Policy Co-ordination.* Manchester: Manchester University Press.

Keynes, J.M. 1980. *The Collected Writings of John Maynard Keynes.* vol.25: *Activities 1940-44: Shaping the Post-War World: the Clearing Union.* New York and Cambridge: Macmillan and Cambridge University Press for the Royal Economics Society.

Kindleberger, C. 1978. 'The aging economy'. *Weltwirtsch. Archiv* vol.114 no.3.

Kravis, I. and R. Lipsey 1992. 'Sources of competitiveness of the United States and of its multinational firms', *Review of Economics and Statistics* vol.74 no.2.

Krugman, P. 1991. *Geography and Trade.* Cambridge, Mass.: MIT Press.

_____ 1993. 'What do undergraduates need to know about trade', *American Economic Review* vol.83 no.2.

_____ 1994. 'Competitiveness: A dangerous obsession', *Foreign Affairs* vol.73 no.2.

Lamfalussy, A. 1985. 'The changing environment of central banking policy', *American Economic Review* vol.75 no.2.

Lash S. and J. Urry 1987. *The End of Organised Capitalism.* London: Polity.

Lawrence, R. 1984. *Can America Compete?.* Washington D.C.: Brookings Institution.

_____ 1994. 'Trade, multinationals and labour', in P. Lowe and J. Dwyer ed., *International Integration of the Australian Economy.* Sydney: Reserve Bank of Australia.

_____ and M. Slaughter 1993. 'International trade and American wages in the 1980s: Giant sucking sound or small hiccup', *Brookings Papers on Economic Activity* no.2.

Lenin, V. 1917. *Imperialism, the Highest Stage of Capitalism.* Moscow: Foreign Languages Publishing House 1950.

Lipietz A. 1982. 'Towards global Fordism?', *New Left Review* no.136.

_____ 1984. 'Imperialism and the beast of the apocalypse', *Capital & Class* no.22.

_____ 1985. *The Enchanted World: Inflation, Credit and the World Crisis.* London: Verso.

198

_____ 1986. 'New tendencies in the international division of labor: Regimes of accumulation and modes of regulation', in A. Scott and M. Storper, eds., *Production, Work, Territory: The Geographical Anatomy of Industrial Capitalism.* Boston: Allen & Unwin.

_____ 1987a. 'An alternative design for the twenty first century', *CEPREMAP Paper* no.8738.

_____ 1987b. *Mirages and Miracles: The Crisis in Global Fordism.* London: Verso.

Lipsey, R. and I. Kravis 1985. 'The competitive position of U.S. manufacturing firms', *Banca Nazionale del Lavoro Quarterly Review* no.153.

_____ and _____ 1987. 'The competitiveness and cpomparative advantage of U.S. multinationals', *Banca Nazionale del Lavoro Quarterly Review* no.161.

Llewellyn, J. and S. Potter 1982. 'Competitiveness and the current account', in A. Boltho ed., *The European Economy: Growth and Crisis.* Oxford: Oxford University Press.

Lowy, M. 1976. 'Marxists and the national question', *New Left Review* no.96.

Luxemburg, R. 1951. *The Accumulation of Capital.* London: Routledge & Kegan Paul.

Machlup, F. 1943. *International Trade and the National Income Multiplier.* Philadelphia.

_____ 1950. 'Three concepts of balance of payments and the so-called dollar shortage', *The Economic Journal* vol.60 no.237.

Maddison, A. 1982. *Phases of Capitalist Development.* Oxford: Oxford University Press.

Magaziner, I. and R. Reich 1983. *Minding America's Business: The Decline and Rise of the American Economy.* New York: Vintage Books.

Mandel, E. 1978. *The Second Slump.* London: Verso.

Marquand, D. 1994. 'Reinventing federalism: Europe and the left', *New Left Review* no.203.

Marx, K. 1852. *The Eighteenth Brumaire of Louis Bonaparte,* reprinted in K. Marx and F. Engels, *Selected Works.* Moscow: Progress, 1969.

_____ 1859. *A Contribution to the Critique of Political Economy.* Moscow: Progress, 1970.

_____ 1867. *Capital.* vol.1. Harmondsworth: Penguin, 1976.

_____ 1885. *Capital.* vol.2. Harmondsworth: Penguin, 1978.

_____ 1894. *Capital.* vol.3. Harmondsworth: Penguin, 1981.

_____ 1939. *Grundrisse: Introduction to the Critique of Political Economy.* Harmondsworth: Penguin, 1973.

_____ 1959. *Theories of Surplus Value.* part 2. Moscow: Progress Publishers, 1971.

_____ and F. Engels 1848. *The Manifesto of the Communist Party,* reprinted in *Collected Works.* vol.6. New York: International Publishers, 1971.

_____ and _____ 1975. *Selected Correspondence*. Third edition. Moscow: Progress Publishers.

Massey, D. 1992. 'Politics and time/space', *New Left Review* no.196.

Mazier, J. 1982. 'Growth and crisis - a Marxist interpretation', in A. Boltho ed., *The European Economy: Growth and Crisis*. Oxford: Oxford University Press.

McDonald, R. and M. Taylor 1990. 'International parity conditions', in A. Courakis and M. Taylor, eds., *Private Behaviour and Government Policy in Interdependent Economics*. Oxford: Clarendon.

McKinnon, R. 1988. 'Monetary and exchange rate policies for international financial stability: a proposal', *Journal of Economic Perspectives* vol.2 no.1.

Meade, J. 1948-49. 'National income, national expenditure and the balance of payments', parts 1 and 2, *The Economic Journal* vol.58 no.232 and vol.59 no.233.

_____ 1951. *The Theory of International Economic Policy*, vol.1, *The Balance of Payments*, Oxford: Oxford University Press,

Meese, R. 1990. 'Currency fluctuations in the post-Bretton Woods era', *Journal of Economic Perspectives* vol.4 no.1.

Mundell, R. 1961. 'A theory of optimum currency areas', *American Economic Review* vol.51 no.4.

_____ 1968. *International Economics*. New York: Macmillan.

_____ 1971. *Monetary Theory*. Pacific Palisades: Goodyear.

Murray, R. 1971. 'The internationalisation of capital and the nation state', *New Left Review* no.67.

Mussa 1990. 'Exchange rates in theory and in reality', *Essays in International Finance* no.179. Princeton: Department of Economics, Princeton University.

Nairn, T. 1981. *The Break-Up of Britain*. London: Verso.

Norton, R. 1986. 'Industrial policy and American renewal', *Journal of Economic Literature* vol.24.

O'Brien, R. 1992. *Global Financial Integration: The End of Geography*. London: Pinder.

Olle, W. and W. Schoeller 1982. 'Direct investment and modern theories of imperialism', *Capital & Class* no.16.

Olson, M. 1982. *The Rise and Decline of Nations: Economic Growth, Stagflation and Social Rigidities*. New Haven: Yale University Press.

Organisation for Economic Co-operation and Development (OECD) various. *Financial Statistics Monthly*, Section 1, *International Markets*. Paris: OECD.

_____ 1993. *National Accounts*, volume II, *Detailed Tables, 1978-1990* Paris: OECD.

Palloix, C. 1975. 'The internationalisation of capital and the circuit of social capital', in H. Radice ed., *International Firms and Modern Imperialism*. Harmondsworth: Penguin.

_____ 1977. 'The self-expansion of capital on a world scale', *Review of Radical Political Economics* vol.9 no.2.

Peet, R. 1987. 'The geography of class struggle and the relocation of United States manufacturing industry', in R. Peet ed., *International Capitalism and Industrial Restructuring*. London: Allen & Unwin.

Phillips, K. 1984. *Staying on Top: The Business Case for a National Industrial Policy*. New York: Random House.

Polanyi K. 1957. *The Great Transformation*. Boston: Beacon.

Porter, M. 1985. *Competitive Advantage: Creating and Sustaining Superior Performance*. New York: The Free Press.

_____ ed., 1986. *Competition in Global Industries*. Boston: Harvard Business School Press.

_____ 1990. *The Competitive Advantage of Nations*. London: Macmillan.

Poulantzas, N. 1975. *Classes in Contemporary Capitalism*. London: New Left Books.

Radice, H. 1984. 'The national economy: A Keynesian myth?', *Capital & Class* no.22.

Ravenga, A. 1992. 'Exporting Jobs? The impact of import competition on employment and wages in U.S. manufacturing', *Quarterly Journal of Economics* vol.107 no.1.

Reich, R. 1982. 'Why the US needs an industrial policy', *Harvard Business Review* January-February.

_____ 1991. *The Work of Nations*. New York: Vintage.

Rosewarne, S. 1990. 'European economic integration: Contradictory accumulations', mimeo, Department of Economics, University of Sydney.

Ross, R. and K. Trachte 1992. *Global Capitalism: The New Leviathan*. Albany: State University of New York Press.

Rowthorn, B. 1980. *Capitalism, Conflict and Inflation*. London: Lawrence and Wishart.

Ruccio, D., S. Resnick and R. Wolff 1991. 'Class beyond the nation-state', *Capital & Class* no.43.

Scott, A. and M. Storper 1986. 'Industrial change and territorial organisation: A summing up', in A. Scott and M. Storper, eds., *Production, Work, Territory: The Geographical Anatomy of Industrial Capitalism*. Boston: Allen & Unwin.

Shaikh, A. 1979-80. Foreign Trade and the Law of Value, parts 1 and 2, *Science and Society* vol.43 no.3 and vol.44 no.1.

Shoven, J. and J. Waldfogel 1990. 'Introduction', in J. Shoven J. Waldfogel, eds., *Debt, Taxes and Corporate Restructuring*. Washington, D.C.: Brookings Institution.

Smith, R.C. and I. Walter 1991. 'Reconfiguration of global financial markets in the 1990s', in R. O'Brien and S. Hewin, eds., *Finance and the International Economy: 4*. Oxford: Oxford University Press for the AMEX Bank Review.

Strange, S. 1986. *Casino Capitalism*. Oxford: Basil Blackwell.

Sweezy, P. and H. Magdoff 1983. 'Production and finance', *Monthly Review* vol.35 no.1.

Szymanski, A. 1981. *The Logic of Imperialism.* New York: Praeger.

Teague, P. 1990. 'The political economy of the Regulation School and the flexible specialisation scenario', *Journal of Economic Studies* vol.17 no.5.

Thompson, G. 1989. 'The American industrial policy debate: any lessons for the UK', in G. Thompson ed., *Industrial Policy US and UK Debates.* London: Routledge.

Thirlwall, A. 1979. 'The balance of payments constraint as an explanation of international growth rate differences', *Banca Nazionale del Lavoro Quarterly Review* vol.32 no.128.

_____ 1992. 'The balance of payments and economic performance', *National Westminster Bank Quarterly Review* May.

Thurow, L. 1992. *Head the Head: The Coming Economic Battle Among Japan, Europe, and America.* New York: Morrow.

Tiffin, R. 1961. *Gold and the Dollar Crisis.* New Haven: Yale University Press.

Tsoukalis, L. 1993. *The New European Economy.* Second Edition. Oxford: Oxford University Press.

Tsiang, S.C. 1951. 'Balance of payments and domestic flow of income and expenditures', *IMF Staff Papers* vol.1.

Turner, P. 1991. 'Capital flows in the 1980s: A survey of major trends', *BIS Economic Ppaers* no.30. Basle: Bank for International Settlements.

United Nations 1989. Centre on Transnational Corporations. *Foreign Direct Investment and Transnational Corporations in Services.* New York: United Nations.

_____ 1991. Conference on Trade and Development. *Handbook of International Trade and Development Statistics, 1990.* New York: United Nations.

_____ 1992. *World Investment Report 1992: Transnational Corporations as Engines of Growth.* New York: United Nations.

_____ 1993a. *World Investment Directory.* vol.3. *Developed Countries.* New York: United Nations.

_____ 1993b. *World Investment Report 1993: Transnational Corporations and Integrated Global Production.* New York: United Nations.

United States. President's Commission on Industrial Competitiveness 1985. *Global Competition: the New Reality.* The report of the President's Commission on Industrial Competitiveness. Washington D.C.: US Government Printing Office.

Vernon, R. 1971. *Sovereignty at Bay.* New York: Longman.

Warren, B. 1971. 'The internationalisation of capital and the nation state: a comment', *New Left Review* no.68.

Wasserman, M. and R. Ware 1965. *The Balance of Payments: History, Methodology, Theory.* New York: Simmons-Boardman.

Wachtel, H. 1986. *The Money Mandarins: The Making of a Supranational Economic Order*. New York: Pantheon.

Webb, M. 1991. 'International economic structures, government interests, and international co-ordination of macroeconomic adjustment policies', *International Organisation* vol.45 no.3.

Weeks, John 1981. *Capital and Exploitation*. Princeton: Princeton University Press.

Zysman, J. and L. Tyson, eds., 1983. *American Industry in International Competition: Governmetn Policies and Corporate Strategies*. Ithaca: Cornell University Press.

Index

About the Book and Author

Over the last 20 years — and especially over the last decade — the international expansion of money and commodities and the international relocation of production have grown tremendously. As a result, there now exists a real contradiction in accumulation: Although global in orientation, it remains structured by the nation state.

Conventional economic literature generally explains the international economy as exogenous to the national economy. Though the former does influence the latter, national economy and policy remain discrete. Conversely, there is a developing literature on globalism that explores the tendency for international capital to eradicate national differences, even to overpower nation states. However, neither interpretation adequately considers the contradictions for national policy that have accompanied the internationalization of capital.

In this volume, Dick Bryan examines the influence of the international economy upon domestic accumulation, describing the process as the expression of the contradiction between the international scope of accumulation and the national scope of its regulation. Developing a theoretical framework for understanding the contradiction within Marxist political economy, he addresses the theory of value on an international scale, as well as theories of global restructuring and crisis. These issues are then applied to those domestic policies — such as monetary policy and balance of payments — that interrelate with the international economy. The author argues that the conventional theories informing these approaches have consistently failed to recognize the contradictions in international accumulation. National economic management has, as a result, reverted to explicit class politics, attempting to solve domestic economic problems by targeting the living standards of labor.

Dick Bryan is a Senior Lecturer in Economics at the University of Sydney.